A Book
of
Poetry - 1

PERSPECTIVES IN LITERATURE

PERSPECTIVES IN LITERATURE

A Book of Poetry -1

JAMES O. ENRIGHT
CLARA M. MARTHALER

HARCOURT BRACE JOVANOVICH

New York   Chicago   San Francisco   Atlanta   Dallas   *and*   London

Cover Photo by Jay Maisel. Photo shows manhole covers and a street on a rainy night.

ISBN 0-15-336810-1

Contents

Dramatic Poetry

Humorous and Satirical Poetry

The Epic

INTRODUCTION

NEAR the Old North Bridge in Concord, Massachusetts, is a statue of a man dressed in militia coat, leggings, and a tricornered hat. In one hand he holds a musket. Beside him is his plow. This statue, called "The Minute Man," is a memorial to the farmers who began the Revolutionary War when they gathered at the bridge on April 19, 1775, and turned back British soldiers marching from Lexington. On the base of the monument is the following inscription:

> By the rude bridge that arched the flood,
> Their flag to April's breeze unfurled,
> Here once the embattled farmers stood,
> And fired the shot heard round the world.

These words, the opening stanza of a sixteen-line poem, "Concord Hymn," were read by their author, the American poet-philosopher Ralph Waldo Emerson, on Independence Day in 1837 at the dedication of the monument.

If a prose statement instead of a poem had been written to commemorate the Minute Men, the following lines might have appeared on the monument:

> This statue is a tribute to the brave, freedom-
> loving farmers, who, on April 19, 1775, fought the
> first battle of the American Revolution and affected
> the lives of men everywhere.

The sentence contains more information than the poem does, but it appears flat by comparison. Why? One reason is that the poem presents a description of the event: the rough-hewn ("rude") arched bridge over the rushing river ("the flood"), the flag unfurling in the spring breeze, and the farmers firing the first shots. The scene comes alive because of the poet's use of *images*, words or phrases which sug-

1

gest things that we can know through our senses of sight, hearing, touch, taste, or smell.
The poet might have picked many images to describe the scene. Or he might have arranged his images in different ways. Why then did Emerson begin the poem by describing the "rude bridge that arched the flood"? Why did he use the word *rude*?

Denotation and Connotation

If we look in the dictionary, we find that the word *rude*, like many other words, has several meanings, or *denotations*. When applied to a person, *rude* denotes an offensive bluntness or impoliteness. Less commonly, an essentially polite person may be called rude if he is not refined, if he is a rustic person who would not know how to behave at a fashionable gathering. (*Rude peasant* was once a common expression denoting the lack of refinement of peasants.) When applied to a thing, the word means, according to Webster's *Third International Dictionary*, "being marked by a rough, plain, or unfinished condition." If we were to define *rude bridge* denotatively, therefore, we would say "a bridge made of unfinished lumber."

The word *rude*, however, was probably chosen by Emerson because of its *connotations*—that is, the impressions a word suggests or calls to mind—as well as the denotation applicable here. The word suggests a rural area where people were in some ways unrefined, or untrained in the genteel arts. The "rude bridge" was built solely for practical reasons; there was no time or energy wasted on finishing it off or trying to make it beautiful. "Rude bridge" prepares us for "embattled farmers," men who worked with their hands and were not trained to fight. These men were essentially builders and cultivators, not destroyers.

Another word in the stanza which has important connotations is *flag*. Literally or denotatively, a flag is a piece of cloth bearing an emblem to indicate a nation, party, or group. Yet the word *flag* suggests many other things: home, country, loyalty, patriotism, honor. These suggestions make *flag* a special type of connotative word. A flag is a *symbol*, an object chosen to stand for or represent something else. In Emerson's lines, "their flag" represents what the farmers are fighting for—their right to rule themselves.

Of course, when Emerson first read this poem to the people of Concord, his listeners did not stop him at each word and ask, "What does this word suggest to me?" A person may respond to the connotations of words without being aware that he is doing so. He also may miss much of what the poet is telling him by *not* thinking about the connotations of words.

All words have denotative meanings, and many have connotative meanings. Both the prose writer and the poet use words that bring to mind no more than the dictionary definition, as well as words that are rich in connotations. The poet, however, generally uses more connotative words than the prose writer. He uses fewer words than the prose writer, but he tries to say more with each word. To most poets, a completely denotative word is like a stone: it may be useful, but it has no life. Connotative words, however, are like stones thrown into water: the first stone creates ripples, movement; the second creates ripples that interact with the first; and so on. Words come alive, and the objects that the poet is describing, the ideas and emotions with which he is concerned, come alive too.

Figures of Speech

Connotative words are often arranged in phrases which we call *figures of speech*. A figure of speech generally suggests a meaning by comparison. "His voice sounds like a foghorn" is a figure of speech in which the sound of a man's voice is compared to the sound of a foghorn. A figure of speech in which there is an indirect comparison by means of the words *like* or *as* is called a *simile*. A figure of speech in which there is a direct comparison without *like* or *as* is called a *metaphor*. "She sees the world through rose-colored glasses" is a metaphor in which an optimistic outlook is compared to the use of glasses which give everything a rosy glow. "The snow blanketed the town" is a metaphor in which a verb is used to compare the effect of the snow to that of a blanket.

There are other figures of speech such as *personification*, in which the writer attributes human qualities to animals, inanimate objects, or ideas. However, simile and metaphor are the most frequently used figures of speech.

Other Elements of Poetry

Poems, however, are more than collections of highly connotative words and figures of speech. The words of a poem are generally contained within a form, usually distinguished from prose passages by the presence of *rhyme* and *rhythm* patterns.

Rhyme

Rhyme occurs when the same sound is repeated in two words placed close to each other. For example, the following lines from the poem "Aladdin" by James Russell Lowell contain two rhymes:

> When I was a beggarly boy
> And lived in a cellar damp,
> I had not a friend nor a toy,
> But I had Aladdin's lamp.

. In these lines, *boy* rhymes with *toy*, and *damp* with *lamp*. That is, the sounds /oy/ and /amp/ each appear twice. (In discussing rhyme, we often refer to the rhyming sounds by italicized letters. The first rhyme is denoted by *a*, the second by *b*, and so on. The rhyme pattern or scheme of the four lines is therefore *abab*.)

Why did the poet want his lines to rhyme? Why did he reverse the normal order of *damp cellar* (line 2) to make a rhyme? One reason is that rhyme, like most of the techniques the poet uses, has a special sound effect: it is pleasing to the ear. Songwriters have known this for centuries. If you repeat the words of most songs, old or new, you will see that the lyrics generally make up a rhymed poem.

Rhythm and Meter

Poetry is close to music in many ways. Some poems were originally meant to be sung. Poets, like composers of music, usually pay a great deal of attention to rhythm, the underlying beat of a poem or a musical composition. In poetry as well as music, the rhythm is sometimes so strong that you can tap your foot to it.

Rhythm is the result of a contrast between accented or stressed and unaccented or unstressed syllables. A stressed syllable is one which the speaker emphasizes. For example, in the word *beggarly*, the syllable *beg* is stressed and the syllables *gar* and *ly* are unstressed. (The word is therefore pronounced BEG·gar·ly.) Poets do not always use the same rhythm throughout a poem, but usually there is a fairly regular, organized rhythmic pattern. This rhythmic pattern is called *meter*. Meter is a second quality which often distinguishes poetry from prose.

The meter of a poem is found by counting, or *scanning*, the number and placement of stressed and unstressed syllables in a line of poetry. The syllables are scanned in groups called *feet*. Each *foot* has at least one stressed syllable; it usually has one or two unstressed syllables. The line, Their FLAG/to A/pril's BREEZE/unFURLED, contains four feet, or four groups, each of which contains one unstressed and one stressed syllable, in that order. Each foot of this type is called an *iamb*, and the meter of the line is called *iambic*. Iambic meter is the most common meter in poetry written in English.

Another common meter is *trochaic* (trō·kā'ik), which is the reverse of the iambic. In trochaic meter, a stressed syllable is followed by an unstressed syllable, as in the following line from Henry Wadsworth Longfellow's "Hiawatha": DARK be/HIND it/ROSE the/FORest. Each foot in trochaic meter is called a *trochee*.

Sometimes the poet chooses a particular meter and uses it more or less strictly to appeal to our sense of rhythm. (However, he usually varies the meter somewhat to avoid a boring singsong effect.) Often he tries to communicate some of his meaning through the choice of meter or through changes in meter within the poem.

Rhythm or meter may be used to communicate a mood, an idea, or an effect. The poet may change the normal order of words so that certain words are stressed by the metric pattern. By means of rhythm, he may appeal to the same instincts within us that respond to music. Rhythm, like imagery, appeals to the senses.

The Types of Poetry

Poetry may be divided into three major types: (1) narrative, (2) lyric, and (3) dramatic. Although there are similar characteristics in all three types, each category has distinctive features.

Narrative poems narrate; that is, they tell a story. The story may be long and complicated, with many characters involved in numerous events; or it may be brief, with one character in conflict with another or with a situation. Narrative poems are similar to short stories in that they have a setting, plot, and characters, and usually have dialogue.

Lyric poems are generally short poems which communicate the emotional response of a speaker to a person, place, object, or idea. Among the common subjects of lyric poems are love and scenes in nature.

Dramatic poems usually reveal more about the speaker's personality than do lyrics or narratives. In a dramatic poem, the speaker talks to someone, revealing conflicts or problems that disturb him. As in narrative poetry, he may tell a story, but the main emphasis is on his reaction to the events rather than on the events themselves.

Narrative Poetry

IN THE DAYS BEFORE writing and printing became common, narrative poems were often composed and sung by ordinary, uneducated persons. Many of these brief story-songs, or *folk ballads*, composed centuries ago by unknown people, are still sung today.

Professional poet-singers also existed before writing became common. Minstrels and ballad singers sang ballads and other types of short songs. Bards composed and sang extremely long story-poems, or *folk epics*. (Because the epic is a complex literary type, it is treated separately in another section of this book.)

Both folk epics and folk ballads have had great literary influence. In the centuries since printing developed, many *literary epics* and *literary ballads* have appeared. In these literary forms, techniques and characteristics of the original folk type were adapted by men of letters. Their works, however, were meant to be printed and not sung.

Folk ballads, or popular ballads, survive by being passed down for generations by word of mouth. In the process, different singers usually change the original song. Because many ballads were sung for a long period before being written down, a number of versions of the same ballad may exist.

Folk ballads were a way of passing on news in the days before newspapers. News of crimes and of sad, tragic, or shocking events particularly interested ballad audiences. Some events, such as important battles or wars, continued to be sung about long after these events had become history. Other current events developed into legends which gave rise to ballads, as in the case of Robin Hood.

"News" of supernatural events was also passed on through ballads. Most people centuries ago believed in ghosts, and many ballads recount the visits supernatural creatures paid to the living.

Ballad audiences also wanted to hear love stories, especially when the lovers came from powerful families and died tragically. Domestic incidents in the lives of ordinary married couples were subjects for humorous ballads.

The oldest existing folk ballads in the English language were composed five or six centuries ago in England and Scotland. We are familiar with many of them because old English and Scottish ballads were brought to America by colonial settlers. Many of these ballads were adapted to fit the conditions of American life.

Native Americans wrote many more ballads about the same general subjects—crime, tragic loves, and the supernatural—found in English and Scottish ballads. Often in these American ballads, the story is basically the same as in their British counterparts, with only superficial differences. For example, American outlaws carried guns and English outlaws carried bows and arrows.

Some differences, however, reflect the deep changes in society which were produced by distinctively American situations, such as the westward movement or the frontier. Instead of the lords and wealthy people who are prominent in English and Scottish ballads, in American ballads we find people who earn their own livings by fair means or foul—cowboys, lumberjacks, miners, gamblers. However, although English lords generally act like real people, the heroes of American ballads often do superhuman feats.

Another major difference between English or Scottish ballads and American ballads is one of approach or attitude. American ballads often tell sad love stories, but rarely are the stories deeply tragic. In general, American ballads, particularly those composed in the West, tend to be more lighthearted than English or Scottish ballads. One reason for this is that many American ballads were composed for dances; even a story of unhappy love sounds gay in a dance rhythm. Another reason is that American ballads reflect the spirit of a pioneer people who refused to let their troubles defeat them.

In the 1960's, a widespread folk ballad revival occurred in the United States. Professional singers introduced to city audiences their own versions of ballads which had been sung for generations in rural areas of England and the United States. Many professional folk singers, both in the 1960's and previously, also wrote ballads about the modern world. These ballads are not folk ballads in the old sense because they are not passed down orally, and they do not undergo change. However, many of them are truly popular ballads. Modern life may modify the conditions in which ballads are created and preserved, but people are still deeply interested in hearing story-songs.

The Douglas Tragedy

There are many versions of this ballad, but they all concern a certain family in Selkirkshire, in the Border Country of Scotland. The lovers in the poem, Lord William and Lady Margaret, were probably members of feuding clans, groups of families, each of which claimed a common ancestor.

"Rise up, rise up now, Lord Douglas," she says,
    "And put on your armor so bright;
Let it never be said that a daughter of thine
    Was married to a lord under night.°

"Rise up, rise up, my seven bold sons,   5
    And put on your armor so bright,
And take better care o' your youngest sister,
    For your eldest's away the last night."

He's° mounted her on a milk-white steed,
    And himself on a dapple gray,   10
With a bugelet° horn hung down by his side,
    And lightly they rode away.

Lord William lookit o'er his left shoulder,
    To see what he could see,
And there he spied her seven brethren bold,   15
    Come riding o'er the lee.°

"Light down,° light down, Lady Margaret," he said,
    "And hold my steed in your hand,
Until that against your seven brethren bold,
    And your father, I make a stand."   20

She held his steed in her milk-white hand,
    And never shed one tear,
Until that she saw her seven brethren fall,
    And her father hard-fighting, who loved her so dear.

4. married . . . under night: eloped under cover of night. **9. He's:** refers to Lord William, the lover who eloped with Lord Douglas's daughter. **11. bugelet:** small bugle. **16. lee:** a place protected from the wind; probably a hillside. **17. light down:** alight, get down.

"O hold your hand, Lord William!" she said,   25
   "For your strokes they are wondrous sore;°
True lovers I can get many a one,
   But a father I can never get more."

O she's ta'en out her handkerchief,
   It was o' the Holland° so fine,   30
And aye° she dighted° her father's bloody wounds,
   That were redder than the wine.

"O choose, O choose, Lady Margaret," he said,
   "O whether will ye gang or bide?"°
"I'll gang, I'll gang, Lord William," she said,   35
   "For ye have left me no other guide."

He's lifted her on a milk-white steed.
   And himself on a dapple gray,
With a bugelet horn hung down by his side,
   And slowly they both rode away.   40

O they rode on, and on they rode,
   And all by the light o' the moon,
Until they came to yon wan water,°
   And there they lighted down.

They lighted down to take a drink   45
   O' the spring that ran so clear
And down the stream ran his good heart's blood,
   And sore° she 'gan to fear.

"Hold up, hold up, Lord William," she says,
   "For I fear that you are slain."   50
" 'Tis nothing but the shadow o' my scarlet cloak,
   That shines in the water so plain."

O they rode on, and on they rode,
   And all by the light o' the moon

---

26. **sore:** painful, severe. **30. Holland:** a fine fabric originally made in the Netherlands. **31. aye** (ī): continually; **dighted:** wiped. **34. gang or bide:** go or stay. **43. yon wan water:** yonder pale water. The original singer was describing a place his listeners knew. **48. sore:** greatly.

Until they came to his mother's hall° door,   55
    And there they lighted down.

"Get up, get up, lady mother," he says,
    "Get up and let me in!
Get up, get up, lady mother," he says,
    "For this night my fair lady I've win.   60

"O make my bed,° lady mother," he says,
    "O make it broad and deep,
And lay Lady Margaret close at my back,
    And the sounder I will sleep."

Lord William was dead long ere° midnight,   65
    Lady Margaret long ere day,
And all true lovers that go together,
    May they have more luck than they!

Lord William was buried in St. Mary's kirk,°
    Lady Margaret in Mary's quire;°   70
Out o' the lady's grave grew a bonny red rose,
    And out o' the knight's a briar.

And they two met, and they two plat,°
    And fain° they would be near;
And all the world might ken° right well°   75
    They were two lovers dear.

[But bye and rode the Black Douglas,
    And wow, but he was rough!
For he pulled up the bonny briar,
    And flung 't in St. Mary's Loch.°]   80

---

55. hall: castle. **61. make my bed:** In folk ballads, this request is usually a preparation for death. **65. ere:** before. **69. kirk:** church. **70. quire:** choir. In old English churches, the choir was near the altar. **71–73. red rose . . . plat:** Plat means intertwined. The image of a rose and a briar growing out of the lovers' graves and forming a lover's knot is a standard ballad image. **74. fain:** willingly. **75. ken:** know; **right well:** without doubt. **80. Loch:** lake.

Meaning

1. Who is the speaker in the first two stanzas? How do you know? Why is the speaker disturbed?
2. What is Lady Margaret's attitude toward the fight at the beginning? Why and when does her attitude change? Does the fight affect her feeling for Lord William? Explain your answers.
3. Why do the lovers ride "lightly" in line 12 and "slowly" in line 40?
4. Why, in your opinion, does Lord William lie to Lady Margaret about his blood in the water? What does this show about him?
5. Why do you think Lady Margaret dies? Is the reason evident in the ballad?
6. Why does Black Douglas pull up the briar in the bracketed stanza (lines 77–80), which in some versions is added to the ballad? What characteristics does Black Douglas have in common with the other Douglases in the ballad?

Method

1. The ballad begins with a call to action. There is no time allowed for setting the scene and describing characters. What might have been gained by descriptions of characters and places at the beginning and throughout the ballad? What would have been lost?
2. The few details given have meaningful connotations. What are the connotations of (a) the colors of the lovers' horses, (b) the color of Lord William's cloak, and (c) the name Black Douglas? Why are they significant? What is the significance of the fact that the action takes place at night?
3. From dialogue and action, how would you characterize Lord William? Lady Margaret? Lord Douglas? Lady Douglas? Do you need to know anything about these characters that is *not* told in the ballad? Why or why not?
4. How does the addition of the bracketed stanza change the effect of the ballad? Which ending emphasizes the romantic qualities of the love? the violence produced by the love?

Language: Origins of Names

Last names usually have origins that can be traced to an occupation or place of birth. The name "Douglas," for example, which comes from the Gaelic *dubh glas* (dark water) indicates that the first Douglases probably lived near a muddy or dark river or lake.

The name "Black Douglas," however, though it might seem related to *dark water*, actually is not. It was given to a fourteenth-century Lord Douglas who terrified residents in the North Country of England with his raids from across the border in Scotland. For centuries afterward, his branch of the family was known as the "Black Douglases." They were a very powerful family and appear often in accounts of British and Scottish history.

Besides Douglas, other names which refer to features of a landscape are Brooks, Hill, Marsh, and Woods. Many other names, such as Baker, Butler, or Miller, originally reflected occupations. Still other names were derived from colors—for example, Brown, Rossi ("red" in Italian), Schwartz ("black" in German)—and from physical characteristics—for example, Small and Klein ("little" in German). How many other names can you think of which reflect places of birth, occupation, colors, or physical characteristics?

First names also have meanings. In a dictionary, find the origin and meaning of your first name, and be prepared to explain it in class.

Barbara Allen

Many ballads originating in England and Scotland were brought to America by the early settlers. "Barbara Allen," one of the most popular, exists in more than a hundred versions. Here are two of them, the first from Scotland and the second from West Virginia.

It was in and about the Martinmas° time,
  When the green leaves were a-fallin',
That Sir John Graeme in the West Country
  Fell in love with Barbara Allen.°

He sent his man down through the town   5
  To the place where she was dwellin':
"O haste and come to my master dear,
  Gin° ye be Barbara Allen."

O slowly, slowly rase° she up,
  To the place where he was lyin',   10
And when she drew the curtain by:
  "Young man, I think you're dyin'."

"O it's I'm sick, and very, very sick,
  And 'tis a' for Barbara Allen."
"O the better for me ye sal° never be,   15
  Though your heart's blood were a-spillin'.

"O dinna ye mind,° young man," said she,
  "When ye the cups were fillin',
That ye made the healths° gae round and round,
  And slighted Barbara Allen?"   20

He turned his face unto the wall,
  And death with him was dealin':

---

1. **Martinmas:** also spelled Martinmass; November 11th, the feast of St. Martin of Tours, a day of harvest and thanksgiving celebration. 4. **Barbara Allen:** also spelled Barbra Allen, or Barbara Allan. 8. **Gin:** if. 9. **rase:** rose. 15. **sal:** shall. 17. **dinna ye mind:** don't you remember. 19. **healths:** toasts to prosperity or health.

"Adieu,° adieu, my dear friends all,
And be kind to Barbara Allen."

And slowly, slowly, rase she up,   25
And slowly, slowly left him;
And sighing said she could not stay,
Since death of life had reft° him.

She had not gane a mile but twa,°
When she heard the dead-bell knellin',   30
And every jow° that the dead-bell ga'ed°
It cried, "Woe to Barbara Allen!"

"O mother, mother, make my bed,
O make it soft and narrow:
Since my love died for me today,   35
I'll die for him tomorrow."

23. adieu (ə·doo′): goodbye. 28. reft: deprived. 29. not . . . twa: gone only
two miles. 31. jow: stroke; ga'ed: gave.

Barbara Allen

In Scarlet town, where I was born,
There was a fair maid dwelling,
Made every youth cry "Well away!"
Her name was Barbara Allen.

All in the merry month of May,   5
When green buds they were swelling,
Young Jimmy Green on his death bed lay
For the love of Barbara Allen.

He sent his man unto her there,
To the town where she was dwelling: 10
"O you must come to my master dear,
If your name is Barbara Allen.

"For death is printed on his face
And o'er his heart is stealing;

O haste away to comfort him,   15
O lovely Barbara Allen!"

"If death is printed on his face   *Dialogue*
And o'er his heart is stealing,
Yet little better shall he be
For the love of Barbara Allen."   20

So, slowly, slowly, she came up,
And slowly she came nigh him;
And all she said when there she came,
"Young man, I think you're dying."

He turned his face unto her straight,   25
With deadly sorrow sighing:
"O lovely maid, come pity me!
I'm on my death bed lying."

"If on your death bed you do lie,
What need the tale your telling?   30
I cannot keep you from your death:
Farewell," said Barbara Allen.

He turned his face unto the wall,
And deadly pains he fell in:
"Adieu, adieu, adieu to all,   35
Adieu to Barbara Allen."

As she was walking o'er the fields,
She heard the bell a-knelling:
And every stroke it seemed to say,
"Unworthy Barbara Allen."   40

She turned herself around about
And spied the corpse a-coming:
"Lay down, lay down the corpse," said she,
"That I may look upon him."

With scornful eyes she did look down,   45
Her cheeks with laughter swelling;

While all her friends cried out amen,°
"Unworthy Barbara Allen!"

When he was dead and laid in grave,
Her heart was struck with sorrow: 50
"O mother, mother, make my bed,
For I shall die tomorrow.

"Hard-hearted creature him to slight,
He who loved me so dearly!
O had I been more kind to him,   55
When he was alive and near me!"

On her death bed as she did lay,
She begged to be buried by him,
And sorely repented of that day
That she e'er did deny him.   .   ´   60

"Farewell, ye virgins all," she said,
"And shun the fault I've fell in;
Henceforward take warning by the fall   } *Theme*
Of cruel Barbara Allen."

[One was buried in the high churchyard,   65
The other in the choir;
On one there grew a red rose bush,
On the other there grew a briar.

They grew and they grew to the high steeple top, } *Symbolism*
Till they could grow no higher;   70
And there they locked in a true-lover's knot,
For true lovers to admire.]

47. amen: a form of *amain*, which means vehemently or without delay.

Meaning

1. In the Scottish version of the ballad, why did Barbara scorn her love? What was her reason in the American version? In which version is she more cruel? more sympathetic?
2. In the American version, why does Barbara undergo a change of heart

after Jimmy dies? How is her first reaction to the death different from that of Barbara in the Scottish version? Did either Barbara love the dead man? In your answer, discuss the final speech of each Barbara.

3. In the Scottish version, the bell cries, "Woe to Barbara Allen." In the American version, the phrase is "Unworthy Barbara Allen." How does the change in what the bell says illustrate an important difference between the two versions?

4. A theme is the main idea or one of the ideas developed in a poem, story, or essay. What are the main themes of the two versions of "Barbara Allen"? Are they the same?

5. Is the rose-and-briar ending which appears in some of the American versions a natural development of the story in lines 1–64? Why might it have been added?

Method

1. From dialogue and action, attempt to characterize each of the two Barbaras. Which are more striking or noticeable—their differences or their similiarities?

2. The American version is more explicit than the Scottish version. For example, in the American version Barbara is told that Jimmy is dying, whereas the Scottish Barbara is simply told to "haste and come to my master dear." Are the reactions of the two Barbaras after the young man's death another example of this difference? Use details from the text to support your answer.

3. Most ballads are composed in *ballad stanzas*—that is, four-line stanzas with the last words of the second and fourth lines rhyming. The *rhyme scheme*, or pattern of rhymed lines, is therefore *abcb* (*b* represents the two rhymed sounds; *a* and *c*, the nonrhymed sounds). The meter of ballad stanzas consists of an alternation of four stressed syllables in one line with three stressed syllables in the next.

Are both ballads written in ballad stanzas? Explain.

Language: Dialects

When Barbara Allen says, "Dinna ye mind," she is speaking in the Scottish *dialect*, a variation of standard English in which pronunciations and expressions peculiar to the Scots are used. Dialects most often develop when one part of a country is relatively isolated. However, even when the original cause of isolation—for example, the difficulty of traveling long distances—has been overcome, dialects continue to be spoken. One generation passes on its way of speaking to the next.

Some examples of dialect used in poetry are:

1. "I got wings, you got wings,
   All God's chillun got wings;
   When I git to Heb'n goin' to put on my wings. . . ."
   American Negro spiritual, "All God's Chillun" (Southern Negro dialect)
2. "How can ye chant, ye little birds,
   And I sae fu' o' care. . . ."
   Robert Burns, "The Banks o' Doon" (Scottish dialect)
3. "He mowed all day. At last he feels
   A pisen sarpent bite his heels."
   Traditional ballad, "Springfield Mountain" (Appalachian mountain dialect)

Rewrite these verses in standard English.

Composition

Take a story from a newspaper that you think might make a good ballad. Rewrite the story in your own words in one paragraph. In a second paragraph, explain why you have chosen it. In a concluding paragraph, tell what parts of the story you would emphasize if you were writing a ballad, and give reasons for your choices.

Lord Randal

In this ballad, the dialogue between a nobleman and his mother slowly reveals a tragedy.

"O where hae° ye been, Lord Randal my son?
O where hae ye been, my handsome young man?"
  "I hae been to the wild wood; mother, make my bed soon,
  For I'm weary wi' hunting, and fain wald° lie down."

"Where got ye your dinner, Lord Randal my son?   5
Where got ye your dinner, my handsome young man?"
  "I dined wi' my true-love; mother, make my bed soon,
  For I'm weary wi' hunting, and fain wald lie down."

"What got ye to your dinner, Lord Randal my son?
What got ye to your dinner, my handsome young man?"   10
  "I got eels boiled in broo;° mother, make my bed soon,
  For I'm weary wi' hunting, and fain wald lie down."

"What became of your bloodhounds, Lord Randal my son?
What became of your bloodhounds, my handsome young man?"
  "O they swelled and they died; mother, make my bed soon,   15
  For I'm weary wi' hunting, and fain wald lie down."

"O I fear ye are poisoned, Lord Randal my son!
O I fear ye are poisoned, my handsome young man!"
  "O yes, I am poisoned; mother, make my bed soon,
  For I'm sick at the heart, and I fain wald lie down."   20

1. hae: have. 4. fain wald: gladly would. 11. broo: broth.

Meaning

1. What facts does the mother know about Lord Randal before she begins questioning him? What does she suspect? Give reasons for your answers.
2. Which question indicates that the mother realized what had happened? Explain.
3. Why, in your opinion, does Lord Randal not immediately tell his mother that he has been poisoned? Why does he call the girl who poisoned him his "true-love"? In what ways is he "sick at the heart"?

4. Attempt to characterize Lord Randal and his mother. For example, is she protective? possessive? a shrewd judge of character? Is he suspicious? trusting? fierce? gentlemanly? How would you describe their attitudes toward each other?

Method

1. Repetition, a common ballad technique, is used to characterize the mother. What characteristic is shown by her repetition of questions? Is repetition used to characterize Lord Randal? to emphasize the meaning of his words? for some other reason?
2. A *refrain* is a frequent repetition of the same line or lines, usually at the end of each stanza. Is the change in the refrain in the last line shocking? surprising? unimportant? Why?
3. The story is told entirely by means of questions and answers. Why does this method arouse the curiosity of the reader? Is there anything you need to know that has not been told?
4. The long lines in which the speakers talk help create a mood of weariness. How does the repetition of the last word in the four lines of each stanza add to this effect?

Language: Origins of the English Language

A language, like a person or a nation, does not develop overnight. The English language took many centuries to reach its present state and, like all living languages, it is constantly changing.

The first major stage through which the English language passed is now known as Old English or Anglo-Saxon, since the language was derived from the dialects spoken by the Angles, Saxons, and other Germanic tribes who migrated to England in the fifth and sixth centuries A.D. Though Old English now seems like a foreign language to us, many of our basic words, such as *child, life, house, speak, old, bone, boat,* and *meat,* are derived from it. Words derived from Anglo-Saxon or Old English are usually short, concrete words.

The second major stage in the development of the English language began after William the Conqueror's successful invasion of England in 1066. William came from a part of France known as Normandy and spoke in a language we now refer to as Old French.

For almost two centuries after the conquest, Old French was the primary language of the government, clergy, and nobles in England. It was not until the end of the thirteenth century that English had strongly reestablished itself. However, thirteenth-century English, or Middle English, was a new language, one greatly enriched by the addition of Old French words.

Dined and *dinner,* which Lord Randal and his mother use in the second stanza of the ballad, are among the words derived from Old French. Some other words are *court, joy, beauty, dance, servant, heir, taste, story, government,* and *poet.*

Look up each of these words in a dictionary and tell whether the meaning of the Old French word was exactly the same as that of the English word. If not, try to explain how the English word developed from the French. Words derived from French (one of the two major foreign sources of modern English; the other is Latin) are marked OF, MF, or F. Note that many of the words which entered the language from French came originally from Latin (L. or Lat.) or Greek (Gk.).

Composition and Discussion

The following four stanzas appeared in later versions of "Lord Randal":

"What d' ye leave to your mother, Lord Randal my son?
What d' ye leave to your mother, my handsome young man?"
"Four and twenty milk kye,° mother, make my bed soon,
For I'm sick at the heart, and I fain wald lie down."

"What d' ye leave to your sister, Lord Randal my son?   5
What d' ye leave to your sister, my handsome young man?"
"My gold and my silver, mother, make my bed soon,
For I'm sick at the heart, and I fain wald lie down."

"What d' ye leave to your brother, Lord Randal, my son?
What d' ye leave to your brother, my handsome young man?"   10
"My houses and my lands, mother, make my bed soon,
For I'm sick at the heart, and I fain wald lie down."

"What d' ye leave to your true-love, Lord Randal, my son?
What d' ye leave to your true-love, my handsome young man?"
"I leave her hell and fire, mother, make my bed soon,   15
For I'm sick at the heart, and I fain wald lie down."

3. kye: cows.

Discuss whether these four stanzas add to or detract from the effect of the ballad. Why? Which version is more appealing? more dramatic? Why?

Get Up and Bar the Door

Although tragic events were the most frequent subjects of folk ballads, humorous domestic situations, such as an argument between a husband and wife, were also used.

It fell about the Martinmas time,
   And a gay time it was then,
When our goodwife° got puddings to make,
   And she's boiled them in the pan.

The wind so cold blew south and north,   5
   And blew into the floor;
Quoth our goodman° to our goodwife,
   "Go out and bar the door."

"My hand is in my hussyfskap,°
   Goodman, as ye may see;   10
It should not be barred this hundred year,
   If it's to be barred by me!"

They made a paction° tween them two,
   They made it firm and sure,
That the first word whoe'er should speak,   15
   Should rise and bar the door.

Then by there came two gentlemen,
   At twelve o'clock at night,
And they could neither see house nor hall,
   Nor coal nor candlelight.   20

"Now whether is this a rich man's house,
   Or whether is it a poor?"
But ne'er a word would one of them° speak
   For barring of the door.

And first they° ate the white puddings,   25
   And then they ate the black;

3. **goodwife:** equivalent to Mrs. 7. **goodman:** equivalent to Mr. 9. **hussyfskap:** housework. 13. **paction:** agreement, pact. 23. **them:** the husband and wife. 25. **they:** the strangers.

Though muckle° thought the goodwife to herself,
Yet ne'er a word she spake.

Then said the one unto the other,
"Here, man, take ye my knife;   30
Do ye take off the old man's beard,
And I'll kiss the goodwife."

"But there's no water° in the house,
And what shall we do than?"
"What ails ye at the pudding broo,°   35
That boils into° the pan?"

O up then started our goodman,
An angry man was he:
"Will ye kiss my wife before my een,°
And scald me with pudding bree?"°   40

Then up and started our good wife,
Gied° three skips on the floor:
"Goodman, you've spoken the foremost word,
Get up and bar the door!"

27. **muckle:** much. 33. **water:** probably to scald the beard and make it easier to scrape off. 35. **"What . . . broo":** Why not use the pudding broth? 36. **into:** in. 39. **een:** eyes. 40. **bree:** broth, liquid. 42. **Gied:** gave.

Meaning and Method

1. What details in lines 1–4 indicate that puddings were not usually part of the couple's meals?
2. What was the cause of the disagreement between husband and wife? What "paction" did they agree to? What does their behavior reveal about their characters? their relationship?
3. Why did the gentlemen not know whether they had come to a rich or poor man's house? Do you think that it would have made any difference in their behavior? Why or why not?
4. Why did the wife not speak when her puddings were being eaten? In your opinion, did the husband finally speak because he was less stubborn than the wife, or because he was threatened more directly?
5. What does the wife's reaction to the husband's speech show about her character?

6. A *Pyrrhic* (pir'ik) *victory* is one in which the victor's losses are greater than the advantages of having won. Would you call the wife's victory Pyrrhic?
7. Why would this ballad *not* have been humorous if the men had stolen money or suggested that they would strangle the wife and cut the man's throat? What do eating puddings, kissing an old man's wife, and shaving a beard have in common? For example, are they events of great importance? Are they blown up out of proportion?
8. Exaggeration is a technique of humorists. What exaggeration has been used to achieve humor in lines 11–12?

Language: Pronunciation and Spelling

Spelling does not always reflect present pronunciation, but it may reflect the original pronunciation of the word. For example, the word *knife* (spelled cnīf in Old English or Anglo-Saxon) was originally pronounced cə·nīf. The now silent first letter of such words as *gnaw, write,* and *knee* were also pronounced at one time. In these cases, spelling did not change to reflect changing pronunciation.

A contrasting peculiarity occurs with such words as *where, when,* and *what.* These were originally spelled hwær, hwæn, and hwat, respectively, and most English-speaking people still pronounce the /hw/ sounds of their original spelling.

In a dictionary, look up the words *why, whether, whole, who,* and *white.* Which are pronounced with /hw/ sounds? Which are not? Why?

Composition

"Translate" this poem into modern English. For example, in line 30, you would write: "Here, man, you take my knife." Wherever possible, try to keep the original rhyme scheme and meter.

Sweet Betsy from Pike

*This humorous American ballad recounts the adventures of a
pioneer couple. Pike County, their original home, is in Missouri.*

Oh, do you remember Sweet Betsy from Pike,
Who crossed the wide prairie with her lover Ike,
With two yoke of cattle° and one spotted hog,
A tall Shanghai rooster, an old yaller dog?

Refrain
Sing too ra li oo ra li oo ra li ay,   5
Sing too ra li oo ra li oo ra li ay.

One evening quite early they camped on the Platte,°
'Twas near by the road on a green shady flat;
Where Betsy, sore-footed, lay down to repose—
With wonder Ike gazed on his Pike County rose.   10

They swam the wide rivers and crossed the tall peaks,
And camped on the prairies for weeks upon weeks,
Starvation and cholera and hard work and slaughter,
They reached California spite of hell and high water.

Out on the prairie one bright starry night   15
They broke out the whiskey and Betsy got tight;
She sang and she shouted and danced o'er the plain,
And she put on a show for the whole wagon train.

The Injuns came down with a wild yelling horde,
And Betsy was skeered they would scalp her adored;   20
Behind the front wagon wheel Betsy did crawl,
And there fought the Injuns with musket and ball.

The alkali° desert was burning and bare,
And Isaac's° soul shrank from the death that lurked there:

3. two yoke of cattle: a yoke is a wooden device used to hold two animals together. Two yoke of cattle is therefore four animals. **7. Platte:** a river in Nebraska.
23. alkali: a type of salt. **24. Isaac's:** Ike is a nickname of Isaac.

"Oh, Dear Old Pike County, I'll go back to you."   25
Says Betsy, "You'll go by yourself if you do."

The Shanghai ran off and the cattle all died,
The last piece of bacon that morning was fried;
Poor Ike got discouraged, and Betsy got mad,
The dog wagged his tail and looked wonderfully sad.   30

One morning they stopped on a very high hill,
And with wonder looked down upon old Placerville;°
Ike shouted and said, as he cast his eyes down,
"Sweet Betsy, my darling, we'll go to Hangtown."

Long Ike and Sweet Betsy attended a dance,   35
Where Ike wore a pair of his Pike County pants;
Sweet Betsy was covered with ribbons and rings;
Says Ike, "You're an angel but where are your wings?"

A miner said, "Betsy, will you dance with me?"
"I will that, old hoss, if you don't make too free;   40
But don't dance me hard. Do you want to know why?
Dog on ye! I'm chock full of strong alkali!"

Long Ike and Sweet Betsy got married of course,
And Ike became jealous—obtained a divorce;
Sweet Betsy, well satisfied, said with a shout,   45
"Good-by, you big lummox, I'm glad you backed out!"

32. **Placerville:** in California.

Meaning and Method

1. *Mood* is a state of mind or feeling. For example, your mood, or the
   mood of a literary work, may be happy, gay, sad, serious, etc. What
   is the mood of the ballad? How do the refrain and rhythm of the
   ballad emphasize the mood?
2. How would you characterize Betsy? Ike? Does the name "Sweet Betsy"
   accurately describe the character, or is it humorous? Considering the
   way she is dressed, are Betsy's words in lines 40–42 surprising? humorous?
3. In line 42, is the word *alkali* being used in the same sense as in line
   23? Explain.

4. In what ways are Ike and Betsy similar to the English couple in "Get Up and Bar the Door?" Why, nevertheless, is this ballad unmistakably American? In your answer, comment on the language of the ballad as well as on the situation. Give examples of American dialect (see page 18) and slang expressions in the ballad.

5. Two successive lines which form a single unit of verse are called a *couplet*. Couplets are usually rhymed, and are often used for humorous effects. Find several rhymed couplets in this poem which seem to you to be humorous.

6. Ballads are more often sung than read. What musical characteristics does this ballad have?

Composition

Using the same rhythm and rhyme scheme (with different rhymes), write several stanzas of a ballad in which you humorously describe a real or imagined adventure. Start with, "Oh who could forget bald Gus from Green Bay," or any other names or descriptions which seem humorous.

John Henry

This American Negro ballad tells the story of a heroic man who was both more and less powerful than the machine which was encroaching on his world.

When John Henry was a little fellow,
You could hold him in the palm of your hand,
He said to his pa, "When I grow up
I'm gonna be a steel-driving° man.
Gonna be a steel-driving man."   5

When John Henry was a little baby,
Setting on his mammy's knee,
He said, "The Big Bend Tunnel on the C. & O. Road°
Is gonna be the death of me,
Gonna be the death of me."   10

One day his captain told him,
How he had bet a man
That John Henry would beat his steam drill down,
Cause John Henry was the best in the land,
John Henry was the best in the land.   15

John Henry kissed his hammer,
White man turned on steam,
Shaker° held John Henry's trusty steel,
Was the biggest race the world had ever seen,
Lord, biggest race the world ever seen.   20

John Henry on the right side,
The steam drill on the left,
"Before I'll let your steam drill beat me down,
I'll hammer my fool self to death,
Hammer my fool self to death."   25

4. steel-driving man: a man who hammered on the steel drill which, before the steam drill, was used to cut into rock. **8. C & O Road:** Chesapeake and Ohio railroad. **18. Shaker:** the man who held the steel drill.

"John Henry" from *John Henry: Tracking Down a Negro Legend* by Guy B. Johnson. Reprinted by permission of The University of North Carolina Press.

Captain heard a mighty rumbling,
Said, "The mountain must be caving in,"
John Henry said to the Captain,
"It's my hammer swinging in de wind,
My hammer swinging in de wind."   30

John Henry said to his shaker,
"Shaker, you'd better pray;
For if ever I miss this piece of steel,
Tomorrow'll be your burial day,
Tomorrow'll be your burial day."   35

John Henry said to his captain,
"Before I ever leave town,
Gimme a twelve-pound hammer wid a whale-bone handle,
And I'll hammer dat steam drill on down,
I'll hammer dat steam drill on down."   40

John Henry said to his captain,
"A man ain't nothin' but a man,
But before I'll let dat steam drill beat me down
I'll die wid my hammer in my hand,
Die wid my hammer in my hand."   45

The man that invented the steam drill
He thought he was mighty fine,
John Henry drove down fourteen feet,
While the steam drill only made nine,
Steam drill only made nine.   50

"Oh, lookaway over yonder, captain,
You can't see like me,"
He gave a long and loud and lonesome cry,
"Lawd, a hammer be the death of me,
A hammer be the death of me!"   55

John Henry hammering on the mountain
As the whistle blew for half-past two,
The last words his captain heard him say,
"I've done hammered my insides in two,
Lawd, I've hammered my insides in two."   60

The hammer that John Henry swung
It weighed over twelve pound,
He broke a rib in his left hand side
And his intrels° fell on the ground,
And his intrels fell on the ground.   65

John Henry, O, John Henry, *deletion*
His blood is running red,
Fell right down with his hammer to the ground
Said, "I beat him to the bottom but I'm dead,
Lawd, beat him to the bottom but I'm dead."   70

When John Henry was laying there dying,
The people all by his side,
The very last words they heard him say,
"Give me a cool drink of water 'fore I die,
Cool drink of water 'fore I die."   75

John Henry had a little woman,
The dress she wore was red,
She went down the track, and she never looked back,
Going where her man fell dead,
Going where her man fell dead.   80

They carried him down by the river,
And buried him in the sand,
And everybody that passed that way,
Said, "There lies that steel-driving man,
There lies a steel-driving man."   85

They carried him down by the river,
And buried him in the sand,
And every locomotive come a-roaring by,
Says, "There lies that steel-drivin' man,
Lawd, there lies a steel-drivin' man."   90

Some say he came from Georgia,
And some from Alabam,
But its wrote on the rock at the Big Bend Tunnel,

64. **intrels:** a dialectal pronunciation of entrails.

That he was an East Virginia man,
Lord, Lord, an East Virginia man.   95

Meaning and Method

1. What characteristics of John Henry indicate that he was unlike ordinary men? Why is he, nevertheless, believable? What specific details contribute to the impression that John Henry is a real human being?
2. John Henry's comment, "A man ain't nothin' but a man" (line 42) is a theme of the ballad. What does it mean? Are there other themes in the ballad? If so, state them in your own words.
3. What was John Henry fighting for? In your opinion, did he win or lose? Do you admire, pity, or sympathize with him? Why?
4. What are John Henry's conflicts in the ballad? That is, is he in conflict with (a) the captain, (b) society, (c) progress and modernity, (d) his own stubborn pride, (e) all of these, or (f) something else? Explain.
5. What physical action does the rhythm of this ballad imitate? Why is the rhythm appropriate for a work song—a song sung by workers at their jobs?
6. *Alliteration* is the repetition of the same sound (usually a consonant) at the beginning of two or more words in close proximity. Like rhyme, alliteration is used for its sound effects. For example, in line 39, "And I'll hammer dat steam drill on down," the alliterative repetition of the /d/ sound suggests hammering. (The /d/ and the /r/ in the word *drill* are a blend sound.) What examples of alliteration can you find in lines 67 and 69?

Composition

One of the reasons that "John Henry" is meaningful to the modern world, although it was written approximately a century ago, is that it is about the problem of automation—the use of machines to replace human labor. In a three- or four-paragraph composition, explain the benefits and disadvantages which result from automation. Use specific examples, real or imagined, to support your points.

Leigh * Hunt
[1784–1859]

The life of Leigh Hunt was changed in 1812 by the phrase "a fat Adonis † of fifty." The "Adonis," who was identified as the Prince Regent ‡ in *The Examiner*, a liberal newspaper Hunt edited, sued for libel. As a result, Hunt and his elder brother, John, the publisher of the paper, were imprisoned for two years.

During those years, Hunt was allowed to write and to receive his friends and family. The prison, in fact, must sometimes have seemed like a literary meeting place, for important writers came to visit Hunt and express their sympathy and support for him. By the time he was released, Hunt was in contact with most of the notable literary figures in England.

Hunt was a popular poet and essayist in his own time, but today he is remembered chiefly for a few short poems, particularly "Jenny Kissed Me" and "Abou ben Adhem." He used words and rhythm with ease and precision, but he did not have the great poet's gift of creating deeply meaningful images. His verse bears the mark of the journalist and essayist he was, rather than the serious poet he aspired to be.

The Glove and the Lions

King Francis was a hearty king, and loved a royal sport,
And one day, as his lions fought, sat looking on the court;
The nobles filled the benches, with the ladies in their pride,
And 'mongst them sat the Count de Lorge, with one for whom he
    sighed.
And truly 'twas a gallant thing to see that crowning show,   5
Valor and love, and a king above, and the royal beasts below.

---

* **Leigh** (lē).
† **Adonis:** in Greek mythology, a beautiful youth beloved by Aphrodite, goddess of love. As used here, the reference implies behavior that is not suitable for someone of his age and appearance.
‡ **Prince Regent:** the future George IV, who ruled Great Britain as Regent from 1811 to 1820, after his father, George III, was declared legally insane.

Ramped° and roared the lions, with horrid laughing jaws;
They bit, they glared, gave blows like beams, a wind went with their
    paws;
With wallowing might and stifled roar they rolled on one another,
Till all the pit with sand and mane was in a thunderous smother;   10
The bloody foam above the bars came whizzing through the air;
Said Francis then, "Faith,° gentlemen, we're better here than there."

De Lorge's love o'erheard the King, a beauteous lively dame.
With smiling lips and sharp bright eyes, which always seemed the
    same;
She thought, "The Count, my lover, is brave as brave can be;   15
He surely would do wondrous things to show his love of me;
King, ladies, lovers, all look on; the occasion is divine;
I'll drop my glove, to prove his love; great glory will be mine."

She dropped her glove, to prove his love, then looked at him and
    smiled;
He bowed, and in a moment leaped among the lions wild.   20
The leap was quick, return was quick, he has regained his place,
Then threw the glove, but not with love, right in the lady's face.
"By heaven!" said Francis. "Rightly done!" and he rose from where
    he sat;
"No love," quoth he, "but vanity, sets love a task like that."

7. **ramped:** reared up menacingly. 12. **faith:** *here,* short for "in faith," an old expression meaning "really."

Meaning

1. Explain the phrases *wallowing might* (line 9) and *a thunderous smother* (line 10) within the context of the poem.
2. What descriptive words give us a hint of the true character of De Lorge's lady?
3. Why, in your opinion, did the Count leap into the arena to pick up the glove?
4. Why did the King commend the Count for throwing the glove in the lady's face? In your answer, explain the last line of the poem.

Method

1. What images appealing to our senses of sight, sound, and touch does the poet use in describing the lions' fight?

2. One of the techniques used by Hunt is that of *contrast*, in which the differences between two people, objects, actions, etc., are shown. In what ways does the lions' fight in the second stanza contrast with the scene in the first stanza?

3. Line 22 comes as a surprise to most readers. Why? Does it have a comic or serious effect?

4. Most of this poem is written in *iambic meter* (see page 5), with seven stressed syllables to each line. Show how the first two lines illustrate this meter. Read the poem aloud. Does the meter produce a singsong effect?

5. Part of line 7 is written in *trochaic meter*, which is defined on page 5. How does the change of meter here emphasize the strength and noise of the lions?

6. In medieval times, a lady gave her glove to a knight to symbolize her attachment to him. Reread the definition of symbol on page 2. Is de Lorge's lady's glove a symbol of her attachment? Explain.

7. This poem is a simple narrative. Retell the story in your own words. Do you think the story is as effective in prose as in verse? Why or why not?

Sir Walter Scott
[1771–1832]

Like many of the writers of folk ballads, Sir Walter Scott lived for some time in the Border Country of Scotland. There he listened to the ballads of the Scottish past which he later collected in the three volumes of his *Minstrelsy of the Scottish Border*. The Border tales and ballads inspired him to write long narrative poems, one of which, *The Lay of the Last Minstrel*, made him famous when it was published in 1805. By 1810, Scott was considered one of Scotland's greatest poets.

Throughout his career, the land, people, and past of Scotland were Scott's primary interests. His best-known poem, *The Lady of the Lake*, illustrates his love for the Scottish countryside. The novels he wrote after his interest in poetry declined are, like his narrative poems, usually set in the heroic past of Scotland and are filled with action. For example, Rob Roy, Quentin Durward, and Ivanhoe, the title characters of three of the Waverley novels, are all heroic Scots.

In his later years, Scott, like his fictional heroes, was forced to fight for his honor. His "adversary," however, was not a single person but the immense debts he had accumulated through unwise borrowing and the mismanagement of a publishing firm in which he had invested. He literally fought this battle with his pen, for he forced himself to turn out novel after novel in an effort to pay back his creditors. The creditors were finally repaid—but only after his death, when the copyrights to his novels were sold.

Proud Maisie *

Proud Maisie is in the wood,
  Walking so early;
Sweet Robin sits on the bush,
  Singing so rarely.

"Tell me, thou bonny bird,   5
  When shall I marry me?"—

* **Proud Maisie:** a song sung by Madge Wildfire, a character in Scott's novel, *The Heart of Midlothian*, as she lay dying.

"When six braw° gentlemen
Kirkward° shall carry ye."

"Who makes the bridal bed,
Birdie, say truly?"— 10
"The gray-headed sexton
That delves° the grave duly.°

"The glowworm o'er grave and stone
Shall light thee steady.
The owl from the steeple sing, 15
'Welcome, proud lady.'"

7. **braw:** fine. 8. **Kirkward:** churchward; toward the church. 12. **delves:** digs; **duly:** properly.

Meaning

1. Does Maisie's first question reveal confidence? pride? a lighthearted attitude?
2. Express in your own words the prophecy of the bird.
3. The word *carry* in line 8 can also mean "escort." Is this Maisie's interpretation of the word? How do you know? What does her interpretation of the prophecy emphasize about her character?
4. Do you think that the robin is teaching Maisie a lesson for being proud? Why or why not?
5. What is the main theme of "Proud Maisie?" How does the fact that this song is sung by a dying girl in Scott's novel emphasize the theme?

Method

1. At the beginning of the poem, a girl is walking in the woods, and a robin is singing: the reader expects to hear a pleasant tale. At the end of the poem, however, the mood is somber. What words in the poem help create first the light mood and then the somber mood?
2. Read the first stanza aloud, noticing the repetition of the soft /s/ sound. Then read lines 11–13 aloud. What sounds are repeated? Are these pleasant or harsh? How do the sounds emphasize the meanings of the words?
3. Scott chose to use the robin and the owl because of their connotations. When we think of the robin, we think of a songbird that is brightly colored. The robin, which is considered a day bird, therefore suggests

light and music. What does the owl, which is a night bird, suggest? Would the poem have been as effective if the owl had made the prophecy and the robin had sung from the steeple?
4. Why, in your opinion, did Scott choose a *glowworm* rather than a *candle* to light Maisie's funeral? In your answer, consider the connotations of each word.

Composition

Write a composition in which you describe an imaginary encounter with a talking bird or animal, or a talking mechanical object such as a refrigerator, car, or computer. Include a detailed description of the setting as well as dialogue and action.

Roy Helton

Roy Helton would seem to have his roots in city culture, since he was born in 1886 in Washington, D.C., and studied at the University of Pennsylvania in Philadelphia. However, his ancestors lived in the Appalachian hill country, and he has, as he says of himself, "wandered alone for the most part, over the Appalachians from Maine to Carolina, studying the people of the highlands from whom I came." His experiences in the Appalachians are reflected in many of his poems, which show the influence of the simple, direct manner of the mountain folk and the balladlike stories they still tell.

Old Christmas

This literary ballad is based on an old folk legend of the Kentucky hill people.

"Where you coming from, Lomey Carter,
   So airly° over the snow?
And what's them pretties° you got in your hand,
   And where you aiming to go?

"Step in, honey! Old Christmas° morning   5
   I ain't got nothing much;
Maybe a bite of sweetness and corn bread,
   A little ham meat and such.

"But come in, honey! Sally Anne Barton's
   Hungering after your face.   10
Wait till I light my candle up:
   Set down! There's your old place.

2. airly: early. **3. pretties:** usually means toys or decorations. Here the word probably means cuttings from the elder bushes which are supposed to bloom in honor of the birth of Christ. **5. Old Christmas:** January 6th, the twelfth day of Christmas, is also known as Epiphany, Little Christmas, and Old Christmas. According to tradition, it was on this date that the Magi visited the infant Jesus. In some places, the birth of Jesus is also celebrated on this day, and gifts are exchanged.

"Now where you been so airly this morning?"
"Graveyard, Sally Anne.
Up by the trace° in the salt-lick° meadows   15
Where Taulbe kilt my man."

"Taulbe ain't to home this morning. . . .
    I can't scratch up a light:
Dampness gets on the heads of the matches;
    But I'll blow up the embers bright."   20

"Needn't trouble. I won't be stopping:
    Going a long ways still."
"You didn't see nothing, Lomey Carter,
    Up on the graveyard hill?"

"What should I see there, Sally Anne Barton?"   25
"Well, sperits do walk last night."
"There were an elderbush° a-blooming
    While the moon still give some light."

"Yes, elderbushes, they bloom, Old Christmas,
    And critters kneel down in their straw   30
Anything else up in the graveyard?"

    "One thing more I saw:
I saw my man with his head all bleeding
    Where Taulbe's shot went through."

"What did he say?"   35
            "He stooped and kissed me."
    "What did he say to you?"

"Said, Lord Jesus forguv your Taulbe;
    But he told me another word;
He said it soft when he stooped and kissed me.   40
    That were the last I heard."

---

15. **trace**: path; **salt-lick**: a place in which there is a deposit of mineral salt which animals lick; therefore, good hunting ground. 27. **elderbush**: a shrub which usually blooms in the summer.

"Taulbe ain't to home this morning."
"I know that, Sally Anne,
For I kilt him coming down through the meadow
    Where Taulbe kilt my man.   45

"I met him upon the meadow trace
    When the moon were fainting fast,
And I had my dead man's rifle gun
    And kilt him as he came past."

"But I heard two shots."   50
            " 'Twas his was second:
    He shot me 'fore he died:
You'll find us at daybreak, Sally Anne Barton:
    I'm laying there dead at his side."

Meaning

1. What details in the first two stanzas make you think that Lomey and Sally Anne are good friends? Why does the third stanza change your impression? What fact revealed later in the poem has affected their friendship?
2. How does Sally Anne know that "Taulbe ain't to home" (line 17)? Why does she repeat this statement in line 42?
3. Do you think the word Lomey's husband whispered to her in the graveyard contrasted with the sentence she quotes in line 38? Why or why not? Why, in your opinion, does Lomey repeat one thing her husband says and not the other?
4. In line 50, Sally Anne reveals that she had "heard two shots." Does this statement indicate that she might have been suspicious of Lomey at the beginning? If so, why did she act so friendly?

Method

1. How has the poet created suspense in this ballad? What passages in particular contribute to the overall suspense?
2. How does the fact that the murder takes place on Old Christmas emphasize the tragedy?
3. At the beginning of the poem, there are many homey touches. One occurs when Sally Anne invites Lomey in for cornbread and ham. What other homey details can you find? Why were they included?
4. Lomey and Sally Anne speak in the dialect of Kentucky hill people. Find some examples of dialectal expressions or regional pronunciation and explain how this type of speech contributes to the effect.

Composition

The folk ballads you have read have the following characteristics:

1. *Story told dramatically.* The listener may be plunged directly into the main action of the story, or suspense may be built up and the listener may not find out what has happened until the end of the ballad. Throughout the ballad, the listener or reader is shown things happening, rather than being told about them.

2. *Concentration on one major episode.* The events leading up to the crucial dramatic situation are not described in detail. All unnecessary information is omitted so that the listeners can concentrate on the narrator's, or storyteller's, account of the main action.

3. *Character types.* The characters are generally mothers and sons, husbands and wives, or lovers who do not have individual and unusual personalities. Character is sketched dramatically either through action or dialogue.

4. *Commonplace words and images.* Primarily denotative rather than connotative words are used because the listening audience does not have a chance to ponder each word. In the rare instances when a place or character is described, standard images, such as "milk-white hands," tend to be used.

5. *Repetition.* Important statements are repeated for emphasis. Often there is a refrain—a frequent repetition of the same line or lines.

6. *Impersonal narrator.* The narrator is primarily interested in telling a story. Although he often chooses to tell tales of people who are punished for something they have done, he rarely introduces his own judgments.

7. *Ballad stanzas.* Four-line stanzas, usually rhymed *abcb*, with four stressed syllables in the first and third lines and three stressed syllables in the second and fourth lines, are most commonly used (see page 18).

8. *Similar subject matter.* Current events, history, legends, love, and the supernatural are the most common subjects.

"Old Christmas" was written by a modern poet in imitation of folk ballads. Select one way in which "Old Christmas" is like a folk ballad, and, in a paragraph, give reasons to support your choice. In a second paragraph, give reasons why one characteristic in the list could *not* be applied to "Old Christmas."

Rudyard Kipling
[1865–1936]

Kipling was a child of both East and West. He was born of British parents in Bombay, India, when India was part of the British Empire. As a young boy, he spoke both English and Hindustani (the most widely used of the many languages spoken in India), and was taken by servants to Hindu as well as Christian religious services. From the ages of six to sixteen, he went to school in England, but returned to India to become a sub-editor of a small military newspaper.

His bicultural upbringing played a large part in Kipling's literary career. The fact that he had writing talent was apparent early (the poems of sixteen-year-old Rudyard so impressed his father that he had them privately printed as *Schoolboy Lyrics*), but even writers of great talent often remain unknown. Kipling, however, had a unique subject matter. He introduced the exotic world of India to British readers, and moreover, he generally did this from the point of view of a British foot soldier or a low-ranking government employee with whom most people in England could identify. The identification was immediate; by the time he returned to England at the age of twenty-four, he was famous.

Besides his subject matter, a major reason for Kipling's popularity was that he was a master storyteller. Both in prose and verse, he created vigorous, sympathetic characters and fast-paced narratives. Kipling had an excellent ear for speech patterns and could convey, with equal ease, the cockney dialect of a British soldier or the stilted English of an Indian. Even more remarkable, the dialogue in his strongly rhythmic verse usually seems to flow naturally.

In 1907, these characteristics of his work were recognized and honored when he became the first Englishman to receive the Nobel Prize for Literature. The peak of his popularity, however, had passed. The empire Kipling deeply admired was being reevaluated, and Kipling's imperialistic views, his feeling that it was the "white man's burden" to "civilize" the natives of non-Western countries, had become increasingly distasteful to many people.

Kipling lived until 1936, long enough to see the beginning of the slow process by which the British Empire became a Commonwealth, a collection of self-governing states. He disapproved of the change, and he would have felt satisfied to know that much of his work has such vitality that the reader almost believes that British India still exists.

The Ballad of East and West

Oh, East is East, and West is West and never the twain shall meet,
Till Earth and Sky stand presently at God's great Judgment Seat;
But there is neither East nor West, Border, nor Breed, nor Birth,
When two strong men stand face to face, though they come from the
  ends of the earth!

Kamal° is out with twenty men to raise° the Border side,   5
And he has lifted° the Colonel's mare that is the Colonel's pride.
He has lifted her out of the stable-door between the dawn and the day,
And turned the calkins° upon her feet, and ridden her far away.
Then up and spoke the Colonel's son that led a troop of the Guides:°
"Is there never a man of all my men can say where Kamal hides?"   10
Then up and spoke Mohammed Khan, the son of the Ressaldar:°
"If ye know the track of the morning mist, ye know where his pickets°
  are.
At dusk he harries° the Abazai°—at dawn he is into Bonair,°
But he must go by Fort Bukloh to his own place to fare.
So if ye gallop to Fort Bukloh as fast as a bird can fly,   15
By the favor of God ye may cut him off ere he win° to the Tongue of
  Jagai.°
But if he be past the Tongue of Jagai, right swiftly turn ye then,
For the length and the breadth of that grisly plain is sown with
  Kamal's men.
There is rock to the left, and rock to the right, and low lean thorn
  between,
And ye may hear a breech-bolt snick° where never a man is seen."   20
The Colonel's son has taken horse, and a raw rough dun° was he,
With the mouth of a bell and the heart of Hell and the head of a
  gallows-tree.°

5. Kamal (kä·mal'): an Afghan chief who led raiding parties across the border
into northwest India; raise: stir up. 6. lifted: stolen. 8. calkins (kôk'·inz): sharp-
pointed metal pieces on horseshoes which prevent slipping. 9. Guides: native
troops who served with the English. 11. Ressaldar: native commander of a troop
of Indian cavalry. 12. pickets: guards. 13. harries: raids; Abazai (ə·bä·sē'),
Bonair (bun·âr'): settlements about forty miles apart on the northern frontier of
India. 16. win: succeed in reaching; Tongue of Jagai: a pass between the hills.
20. breech-bolt snick: the sound of a rifle being loaded and cocked. 21. dun: a
horse of a grayish-brown color. 22. gallows-tree: a wooden construction used for
hanging a man; it has two upright beams and a crossbeam.

"The Ballad of East and West" from *Rudyard Kipling's Verse: Definitive Edition.* Reprinted
by permission of Doubleday & Company, Inc., Mrs. George Bambridge, and The Macmillan
Company of Canada Limited.

The Colonel's son to the Fort has won, they bid him stay to eat—
Who rides at the tail of a Border thief, he sits not long at his meat.
He's up and away from Fort Bukloh as fast as he can fly,   25
Till he was aware of his father's mare in the gut° of the Tongue of
     Jagai,
Till he was aware of his father's mare with Kamal upon her back,
And when he could spy the white of her eye, he made the pistol crack.
He has fired once, he has fired twice, but the whistling ball went wide.
"Ye shoot like a soldier," Kamal said. "Show now if ye can ride!"   30
It's up and over the Tongue of Jagai, as blown dust-devils° go;
The dun he fled like a stag of ten, but the mare like a barren doe.
The dun he leaned against the bit and slugged his head above,
But the red mare played with the snaffle-bars,° as a maiden plays with
     a glove.
There was rock to the left and rock to the right, and low, lean thorn
     between;   35
And thrice he heard a breech-bolt snick tho' never a man was seen.
They had ridden the low moon out of the sky, their hoofs drum up
     the dawn.
The dun he went like a wounded bull, but the mare like a new-roused
     fawn.
The dun he fell at a watercourse°—in a woeful heap fell he;
And Kamal has turned the red mare back, and pulled the rider
     free.   40
He has knocked the pistol out of his hand—small room was there to
     strive.
" 'Twas only by favor of mine," quoth he, "ye rode so long alive:
There was not a rock for twenty mile, there was not a clump of tree,
But covered a man of my own men with his rifle cocked on his knee.
If I had raised my bridle-hand, as I have held it low,   45
The little jackals° that flee so fast were feasting all in a row:
If I had bowed my head on my breast, as I have held it high,
The kite° that whistles above us now were gorged till she could not
     fly."
Lightly answered the Colonel's son: "Do good to bird and beast,
But count who come for the broken meats before thou makest a
     feast.   50

26. **gut:** a narrow passageway. 31. **dust-devils:** small whirlwinds of dust or sand
which seem to change shape as they move along. 34. **snaffle-bars:** bridle bit.
39. **watercourse:** a stream, river, or brook. 46. **jackals:** doglike animals that feed
on small animals and dead flesh. 48. **kite:** a bird that feeds on dead flesh; a member of the hawk family.

If there should follow a thousand swords to carry my bones away,
Belike° the price of a jackal's meal were more than a thief could pay.
They° will feed their horse on the standing crop, their men on the
  garnered° grain,
The thatch of the byres° will serve their fires when all the cattle are
  slain.
But if thou thinkest the price be fair,—thy brethren wait to sup,   55
The hound is kin to the jackal-spawn,°—howl, dog, and call them up!
And if thou thinkest the price be high, in steer° and gear and stack,°
Give me my father's mare again, and I'll fight my own way back!"
Kamal has gripped him by the hand and set him upon his feet.
"No talk shall be of dogs," said he, "when wolf and gray wolf meet. 60
May I eat dirt if thou hast hurt of° me in deed or breath;
What dam° of lances brought thee forth to jest at the dawn with
  Death?"
Lightly answered the Colonel's son: "I hold by the blood of my clan:
Take up the mare for my father's gift—by God, she has carried a man!"
The red mare ran to the Colonel's son and nuzzled against his
  breast;   65
"We be two strong men," said Kamal then, "but she loveth the
  younger best.
So she shall go with a lifter's dower,° my turquoise-studded rein,
My 'broidered saddle and saddlecloth, and silver stirrups twain."
The Colonel's son a pistol drew, and held it muzzle end,
"Ye have taken the one from a foe," said he, "Will ye take the mate
  from a friend?"   70
"A gift for a gift," said Kamal straight; "a limb for the risk of a limb.
Thy father has sent his son to me, I'll send my son to him!"
With that he whistled his only son, that dropped from a mountain
  crest—
He trod the ling° like a buck in spring, and he looked like a lance in
  rest.
"Now here is thy master," Kamal said, "who leads a troop of the
  Guides,   75
And thou must ride at his left side as shield on shoulder rides.
Till Death or I cut loose the tie, at camp and board and bed,
Thy life is his—thy fate it is to guard him with thy head.

---

52. belike: perhaps. 53. they: the British soldiers; garnered: gathered. 54. byres:
barns. 56. spawn: offspring. 57. steer: steers; stack: grain. 61. hurt of: been hurt
by. 62. dam: mother. 67. lifter's dower: dowry, or gift, given by a thief. 74. ling:
heather, a shrub.

So, thou must eat the White Queen's° meat, and all her foes are thine,
And thou must harry thy father's hold° for the peace of the Border-
line.   80
And thou must make a trooper tough and hack thy way to power—
Belike they will raise thee to Ressaldar when I am hanged in Pesh-
awur!°"

They have looked each other between the eyes, and there have found
no fault.
They have taken the Oath of the Brother-in-Blood on leavened bread°
and salt;°
They have taken the Oath of the Brother-in-Blood on fire and fresh-
cut sod,°   85
On the hilt and the haft of the Khyber knife,° and the Wondrous
Names of God.°
The Colonel's son he rides the mare and Kamal's boy the dun,
And two have come back to Fort Bukloh where there went forth but
one.
And when they drew to the Quarter-Guard,° full twenty swords flew
clear—
There was not a man but carried his feud with the blood of the moun-
taineer.   90
"Ha' done! ha' done!" said the Colonel's son. "Put up the steel at
your sides!
Last night ye had struck at a Border thief—tonight 'tis a man of the
Guides!"

Oh, East is East, and West is West, and never the twain shall meet,
Till Earth and Sky stand presently at God's great Judgment Seat;
But there is neither East nor West, Border, nor Breed, nor Birth,   95
When two strong men stand face to face, though they come from the
ends of the earth!

79. **White Queen:** Queen Victoria of England, who was also Empress of India.
80. **hold:** stronghold. 82. **Peshawur** (pə·shä′wər): the center of the British government in Northwest Frontier Province. 84. **leavened bread:** When yeast is
added to dough, the dough rises. The risen dough when baked is called leavened
bread; **salt:** In the Bible, "a covenant of salt" (Numbers, 18:19) is a promise of
friendship. 85. **sod:** soil which is held together by matted grass roots; sometimes
used to make fires. 86. **Khyber** (kī′bər) **knife:** named for the Khyber Pass, a
narrow pass between India and Afghanistan; **Wondrous Names of God:** one
hundred Moslem names given to God. 89. **Quarter-Guard:** sentries.

Meaning

1. Why was Kamal being pursued? What does Mohammed Khan tell the Colonel's son about Kamal? Is Mohammed's statement that "the length and breadth of that grisly plain is sown with Kamal's men" (line 18) meant literally or figuratively? Why?
2. Why did Kamal challenge the Colonel's son to a race? Why did he pull the rider free after the dun had fallen down? Why did he not kill the Colonel's son? Explain what you learn about Kamal's character from the answers to these questions. Do you think that Kamal is an ordinary thief? Why does he steal?
3. Explain in your own words the speech of the Colonel's son in lines 49–58. What does this speech show about his character? Does he frighten Kamal with his threats?
4. Explain in your own words Kamal's reply in lines 60–62. Why does Kamal admire the Colonel's son?
5. Why does the Colonel's son want to give the mare to Kamal (line 64)? Why does Kamal give it back? Do you think that the reasons for their actions are similar or different?
6. Why, in your opinion, does Kamal send his only son away with the Colonel's son? What orders does Kamal give his son? What do these orders show about Kamal's attitude toward the British? toward his son?
7. Why did twenty swords fly when the Colonel's son rode back to Fort Bukloh? Why did the British not kill Kamal's son?
8. The first and last stanzas state the main theme of the poem. What is it? How does the story of Kamal and the Colonel's son illustrate this theme?

Method

1. What physical action does the rhythm of the poem suggest? Why is the rhythmic effect appropriate?
2. Find the five similes (see definition on page 3) in lines 32–38 and explain what each suggests about the horses being described. Which is the better horse?
3. How does Kipling's description of the Tongue of Jagai in line 35 add to the effect of the race?
4. In line 62, Kamal asks the Colonel's son: "What dam of lances brought thee forth to jest at the dawn with Death?" In this question, he is obviously considering Death as a person, someone with whom the Colonel's son could jest. He is therefore using *personification*, a figure of speech in which human qualities are attributed to an animal, object, or idea. Kamal's "Death" is a personified idea.

   In line 77, Kamal makes another reference to Death. Is this reference also an example of personification? Explain.

Stephen Vincent Benét*
[1898–1943]

All of America was home to Stephen Vincent Benét. He was born in Bethlehem, Pennsylvania, but because his father was an army officer, he lived in California, Kentucky, and Georgia. He attended Yale University in Connecticut, and was later married in Chicago. After brief European travels, he lived in Rhode Island and finally settled in New York City.

Benét's love for his country and its various regions is evident in his poetry, much of which is about America. His imaginative portraits of the American present and past, particularly that of *John Brown's Body*, a verse narrative which won the Pulitzer Prize for poetry in 1929, gained him enormous popularity.

Benét's choice of the fanatic abolitionist John Brown was characteristic, for in both his fiction and poetry, he showed a strong interest in extraordinary historical characters. His short story, "The Devil and Daniel Webster," which was made into a play, an opera, and a movie, presents the famous American orator as being so clever that he beats the devil in a verbal duel. His narrative poem "The Ballad of Marco Polo" tells a true but almost unbelievable adventure story about three Venetian traders who visited the fabulous land of Cathay (China) two centuries before Columbus discovered America. In both of these works, and in others, he shows that he is a master of dramatic technique, as he draws the reader along with him to the border between fantasy and reality.

* **Benét** (bə·nā′).

The Ballad of Marco Polo

Marco Polo, curious man,
What drove you to seek for Kublai Khan?°

Perhaps it was youth, for I was young,
Perhaps it was my father's tongue

2. **Kublai Khan** (koo′blī kän′): thirteenth-century ruler of China and great-grandson of Genghis Khan. The Khans, who came from Mongolia, north of China proper, conquered China. The word *khan* means lord or prince.

49

The desert hawk I had never seen   5
Till the years of my age were turned fifteen,
For I was not born when he went away
To trade beyond the rim of the day,°
And, when he returned, we were strange and shy,
Meeting each other, he and I,   10
For a lost bride's eyes looked out at him,
My mother's, who died in bearing me,
And the lines in his visage° were great and grim
And I knew he had been in Tartary.°

Marco Polo, how did it fall   15
That at last you followed him, after all?

When the world shut in with candlelight,
They° would talk to each other, night on night,
While the water lapped at the landing stair°
And they hardly knew that I was there   20
Except as a shadow the candle threw
When the wind before the morning blew
And the great house creaked like a ship of stone,
Maffeo and Nicolo,
Talking of marvels past renown,   25
Talking of wonders still to do—
Their talk was honey and wine and snow,
How could I help but drink it down?
How could I help but thirst and burn,
When they opened the bag of camel's hair   30
And looked at the marvel hidden there
And said, "It is time and we must return"?

Marco Polo, what did you see,
When at length you came to Tartary?

I know I have been where I have been,   35
But how can I tell you what I have seen?

7–8. he went . . . day: His father Nicolo and his uncle Maffeo Polo left in
1260, two years after the trade routes to China had been opened for the first
time. 13. visage (viz'ij): face or facial expression. 14. Tartary: a region of Asia
under Mongol leadership in the thirteenth and fourteenth centuries. The people
of Tartary were called Tartars. 18. They: Marco's father and uncle. 19. While
. . . stair: Venetian houses have landings with stairs where boats dock.

I know the desert of the dry tree
Whose branches bear eternity,
And the hot sickness of the noon.
I drank the mare's milk of the tents,   40
I saw the musk ox gape at me,
I have had gold and frankincense°
And silks that glitter like the moon,
But what can I tell that will make you see?

Marco Polo, wandering sword,   45
What manner of man did you call lord?

I have been the pope's and the doge's° man,
But I never knew master like Kublai Khan.
The sons of his body sit ten by ten
At buffets of precious napery,°   50
When he hunts, he hunts with ten thousand men
And his Tartar falcons darken the sky,
He has jewels uncounted and golden plate
Whence even his meanest slaves may eat,
And he sits and numbers the hairs of fate   55
With a great, tame lion crouched at his feet,
And his mercy as fair as a white ram's fleece,
Mighty in battle and just in peace,
Star of the city of Kanbalu,°
Khan of Khans° and Great of the Great   60
Whose bounty falls like the morning dew—
Since Adam delved° and Eve span°
Who ever saw prince like Kublai Khan?

Marco Polo, tell me how
Your Venice° talks of your travels now.   65

They call me braggart, they call me liar,
They gawk at me like an eater of fire,

42. **frankincense:** a fragrant substance made from Arabian or East African herbs.
47. **doge** (dōzh): the chief magistrate of the city of Venice when it was an independent republic. 50. **buffets** (bŏō·fāz′) . . . **napery** (nā′pər·ē): *here,* tables set with precious table linen. 59. **Kanbalu:** the capital of China; now Peking. 60. **Khan of Khans:** Prince of Princes. 62. **delved:** dug; **span:** old past tense of spin. 65. **Venice** (ven′əs): At this time, Venice was the greatest European trading city. However, her ships did not venture past the bounds of Europe and Africa.

"Millions" Polo, the fable-monger,
Who dines on a lizard to stay his hunger,
Such being his custom in Cathay.   70
But they laughed with their beards another way,
When we came back in '95°
Like ghosts returned to a world alive,
With our gear still smelling of musk and civet°
And my father's beard grown whiter than privet,°   75
Two old men and a younger one
Who had looked in the eye of the Eastern sun
And lived—and lived to tell the tale
Which I tell to the shadows in this, my jail.
Why, my very cousins did not own° us   80
And the jeering crowd was ready to stone us
Till we ripped the riches out of our rags
And proved we were Polos—by moneybags!

Let them laugh as long as they like today!
I have seen Cathay, I have seen Cathay!   85
Their little Europe—their dwarfish West—
Their doge with his ring and his marriage fee!°
I have stolen the eggs from the phoenix° nest
And walked by the shores of the Ocean-Sea,°
The earth-encircler, the Asian main,   90

And, if Kublai lived, I would go again,
For what is their quarrel of gimcrack° lords,
Their toy fleets sailing a herring pond,
By the might that mastered the Tartar hordes?
There are worlds beyond, there are worlds beyond, 95
Worlds to be conquered, worlds to be found
By the river and desert and burning ground,
Even, perchance, by the Ocean-Sea
If a man has courage enough to dare,

---

72. '95: 1295. Marco Polo stayed in Cathay for nineteen years. 74. musk and
civet: substances used in making perfume. 75. privet: a bushy shrub with white
flowers and black berries. 80. own: *here*, admit they knew. 87. marriage fee: the
doge collected a fee for licensing marriages. 88. phoenix (fē′niks): a legendary
bird; it is supposed to be consumed by its own fire, and then rise young from
the ashes. 89. Ocean-Sea: a great ocean was believed to surround Europe, Asia,
and Africa. No one dreamed of the existence of America on the other side of the
ocean. 92. gimcrack (jim′krak): showy but cheap.

And I know that others will follow me   100
And I mark the roads that will take them there,
The roads of the golden caravan,
The whole great East in its roaring youth,
For—there was a prince named Kublai Khan—
And I, the liar, have told the truth.   105

Meaning

1. Why did Marco Polo go to seek Kublai Khan?
2. Why does Marco feel that he cannot tell his questioner what he has seen (see line 36)?
3. Why do the people of Venice not believe Marco's tales? Why did they believe the Polos in '95? What do these reactions show about the Venetian people? about human nature?
4. Why does Marco not care if the Venetians laugh at him? What does he mean when he says, "I have stolen the eggs from the phoenix nest" (line 88)?
5. In line 79, Marco says that he is talking to "shadows" in jail. Do you think that he is talking to himself? to another person? Or is *shadow* used symbolically? Explain.
6. What, in your opinion, is the main theme of the poem? In your answer, comment particularly on lines 95–105.
7. How would you characterize Marco Polo? Support your answers by citing specific lines.

Method

1. Reread the definitions of simile and metaphor in the Glossary and tell why each of the following quotations is a simile or a metaphor:
   (a) "beyond the rim of the day" (line 8);
   (b) "the great house creaked like a ship of stone" (line 23);
   (c) "their talk was honey and wine and snow" (line 27);
   (d) "silks that glitter like the moon" (line 43);
   (e) "his mercy as fair as a white ram's fleece" (line 57).
   What ideas does each figure of speech visualize or compress into a very few words?
2. Marco compares the land of Kublai Khan to "little Europe." What examples does Marco give to show that Kublai Khan's domain was exotic and full of luxury? What words or phrases make Europe seem small, poor, and confined?
3. What feeling does repetition convey in lines 85 and 95?
4. The narrative, unlike those in the other poems you have read, is told by a speaker talking in the first person, as *I*. How does this *I* point of view add to the effect of the poem?

5. Why do you think Benét called this poem a ballad? What characteristics does it share with "The Ballad of East and West?"

Language: Words Derived from Mythology

Marco Polo in Benét's poem says that Kublai Khan "sits and numbers the hairs of fate" (line 55). In his view, Kublai Khan is so powerful that he controls fate, or the forces which govern our future.

The word *fate* is derived from a story in Greek mythology. (*Mythology* is a collection of the fables or tales of a particular people. Usually these tales describe the exploits of gods and heroes, and attempt to provide explanations for life as it is. Each of these tales is called a *myth*.) The Fates were supposed to have been three sisters. The first one spun the thread of life, the second one measured the thread, and the third one snipped it off. No plans made by men had any effect on the Fates.

Many other words have been derived from the myths of the ancient Greeks. Among these words are the following:

1. fortune
2. atlas
3. titanic
4. sphinx
5. muse
6. martial
7. phosphorus
8. helium

Look up these words in a dictionary. Explain in class the meaning and origin of each of these words.

Composition

1. In Marco Polo's day, not much of the earth was known to Europeans, and the possibilities for exploration were enormous. Today, with most of the earth's surface mapped, written about, and photographed, adventurers turn to the sky.

Write a short composition in which you explain why you would like to explore the moon, another planet, or another galaxy. Either try to communicate your feelings about the trip, or discuss what you expect to find. Your composition may be humorous or serious.

2. Although the great explorations of the earth have been made, every person can explore part of the earth for himself or herself. Write a short composition about a large or small exploration in which you took part or would like to take part. For example, you might have explored a campsite, a river or lake, a beach, an attic or a cellar, a new neighborhood, etc. Describe what you found and tell how you reacted to your "discoveries." Try to tell the story of your "exploration" in such a way that your "discoveries" are presented in chronological order.

John Greenleaf Whittier
[1807–1892]

When Whittier was born on the farm at Haverhill, Massachusetts, which had been settled by his ancestors in the seventeenth century, his parents assumed that he would become a farmer. As he grew up, they considered his farm chores more important than his schooling, which was irregular and rudimentary. Young Whittier, however, had other ideas. As he wrote:

> And must I always swing the flail,
> And help to fill the milking pail?
> I wish to go away to school;
> I do not wish to be a fool.

Although he did not go "away to school," Whittier did manage to educate himself. In between farm chores, he often walked miles to borrow a book, and he began to write verse as a teen-ager. When, in 1826, he submitted some poems to William Lloyd Garrison, the antislavery editor of the *Free Press*, Garrison was so impressed that he drove to the Whittier farm and tried to convince the father to let young Whittier get more education. "Sir," the father told Garrison, "poetry will not give him *bread*."

Whittier's meeting with Garrison marked a turning point in his life, for the two men shared not only literary interests but also a hatred of slavery. In 1829, Garrison helped Whittier get a job as editor of an antislavery Boston weekly. For the next three decades, Whittier, belying his father, earned his bread by working as an editor and by writing scores of poems and articles against slavery. He also gave antislavery speeches. Several times his life was threatened by angry crowds, but he stubbornly continued to fight verbally for his beliefs.

Whittier, a Quaker and a peace-loving man, hoped that the slavery question could be settled without war, but he was wrong. During the Civil War and after, he turned from politics to writing poems primarily about the peaceful New England farm life he had known—a life he had at one time wanted to escape. It is for these often nostalgic poems about New England life that the once controversial Whittier was beloved in his later years and is remembered today.

Telling the Bees

"A remarkable custom, brought from the Old Country, formerly prevailed in the rural districts of New England. On the death of a member of the family, the bees were at once informed of the event, and their hives dressed in mourning. This ceremonial was supposed to be necessary to prevent the swarms from leaving their hives and seeking a new home."—Whittier's *Writings*

Here is the place; right over the hill
    Runs the path I took;
You can see the gap in the old wall still,
    And the stepping-stones in the shallow brook.

There is the house, with the gate red-barred,   5
    And the poplars tall;
And the barn's brown length, and the cattle-yard,
    And the white horns tossing above the wall.

There are the beehives ranged in the sun;
    And down by the brink   10
Of the brook are her poor flowers, weed-o'errun,
    Pansy and daffodil, rose and pink.

A year has gone, as the tortoise° goes,
    Heavy and slow;
And the same rose blows,° and the same sun glows,   15
    And the same brook sings of a year ago.

There's the same sweet clover-smell in the breeze;
    And the June sun warm
Tangles his wings of fire in the trees,
    Setting, as then, over Fernside farm.   20

I mind me° how with a lover's care
    From my Sunday coat
I brushed off the burrs, and smoothed my hair,
    And cooled at the brookside my brow and throat.

---

13. tortoise (tôr′təs): turtle. **15. blows:** blooms. **21. mind me:** remind myself.

Since we parted, a month had passed—
    To love, a year;
Down through the beeches I looked at last
    On the little red gate and the well-sweep° near.

I can see it all now—the slantwise rain
    Of light through the leaves,   30
The sundown's blaze on her window-pane,
    The bloom of her roses under the eaves.°

Just the same as a month before—
    The house and the trees,
The barn's brown gable, the vine by the door—   35
    Nothing changed but the hives of bees.

Before them, under the garden wall,
    Forward and back,
Went drearily singing the chore-girl small,
    Draping each hive with a shred of black.   40

Trembling, I listened: the summer sun
    Had the chill of snow;
For I knew she was telling the bees of one
    Gone on the journey we all must go!

Then I said to myself, "My Mary weeps   45
    For the dead to-day:
Haply° her blind old grandsire sleeps
    The fret and the pain of his age away."

But her dog whined low; on the doorway sill,
    With his cane to his chin,   50
The old man sat; and the chore-girl still
    Sung to the bees stealing out and in.

And the song she was singing ever since
    In my ear sounds on:
"Stay at home, pretty bees, fly not hence!   55
    Mistress Mary is dead and gone!"

---

28. well-sweep: a device used for drawing water from a well. **32. eaves:** the lower edge of a projecting roof. **47. haply:** perhaps.

Meaning and Method

1. The speaker in this poem is going back over the path he took a year ago. Why does he retrace his steps? Why is it important for the story that, on his former visit, he had been absent for a month (see lines 25–26)?

2. Why and how does the speaker emphasize that the scene is essentially the same as on his former visit? What is his attitude toward the lack of change?

3. In line 11, the speaker notices one change that has taken place. In what way does this change *foreshadow*, or present advance indications of, the information given in line 56?

4. Through most of the poem, the speaker creates an idyllic mood. Where is this idyllic mood definitely broken—that is, where is the turning point of the poem? What new mood then appears? What particular words or images indicate this shift?

5. *Irony* is a figure of speech in which the writer or speaker says one thing and means another. It can also be applied to a situation in which the result is the opposite of what is expected. Why was the death of Mary ironic? How does the poet emphasize the irony of the situation?

6. How do you know that the speaker feels a sense of loss about Mary's death? If the speaker had been impersonal, as in most of the other narratives you have read, would the poem have had the same effect? Why or why not?

7. The rhyme scheme (see Glossary, page 253) of this poem is *ababcdcd*, etc. In the fourth stanza, however, the *end rhymes*—or rhymes at the ends of lines—are much more alike than in the other stanzas, because each of the rhymes contains an /o/ sound. In addition, line 15 contains an *internal rhyme*, a rhyme within a line, and so the /o/ sound is again repeated. Considering the subject of the poem and the specific stanza, why do you think the poet chose to repeat this sound so many times?

8. The poet makes the reader see, hear, and feel what it is like to be at Fernside farm on two June days. With what specific images does he do this?

Composition

In "Telling the Bees," Whittier writes:

> A year has gone, as the tortoise goes
> Heavy and slow.

The slowness of the tortoise is the subject of a famous *fable* by a Greek writer named Aesop (ē′sop). A fable is a story made up to illustrate what the writer considers to be a truth. Fables may use people as characters, but more often they use talking animals. At the end of each fable, there is a *moral*, a conclusion which teaches a lesson.

In Aesop's fable about the race between the tortoise and the hare, the hare is so much faster than the tortoise that he decides he has time to take a nap on the racetrack. But the steadily plodding tortoise overtakes the sleeping hare. When the hare finally wakes up, the tortoise is near the finish line. Though the hare puts on a burst of speed, the tortoise crosses the finish line first and wins the race. The moral of the story is: Slow and steady wins the race.

Among the many other expressions that have come from Aesop's fables are the following:

1. That's just sour grapes.
2. Forewarned is forearmed.
3. Look before you leap.
4. Seeing is believing.
5. God helps those who help themselves.

Choose one of these expressions, and in a composition with your own animal characters, create a fable which illustrates it.

Siegfried Sassoon
[1886–1967]

Perhaps the most dramatic moment in the life of the English poet Siegfried Sassoon occurred in 1917, during World War I, when he threw into the sea the Military Cross which he had received for heroism on the battlefield in France and announced publicly that he would no longer serve in the British armed forces. Ironically, his action turned out to be as futile and inglorious as the war he detested.

Instead of being court-martialed, as he had hoped, he was declared "temporarily insane" and confined to a sanitarium. From there, he was shipped to an army unit in Palestine, which at that time was occupied by the British. Finally, he was returned to his own army unit in France. Though he was still bitterly opposed to the war, he fought with valor; by the end of the war, he had been promoted from second lieutenant to captain.

Before the war, Sassoon had lived the life of a young gentleman of wealth and culture whose interests were almost equally divided between hunting, playing tennis, and writing poetry. When he volunteered for duty at the beginning of the war, he, like many others, envisioned war as an opportunity to display heroism and win glory. His contact with war's realities shocked and disillusioned him.

In bitter and angry poems full of detailed, realistic descriptions, he set down the horrors he saw or experienced. Although he later wrote many fine poems on other subjects, it is for these war poems—most of them as vivid and disturbing now as they were more than half a century ago—that he is best known and most admired.

The Rear-Guard

Groping along the tunnel,° step by step,
He winked his prying torch° with patching glare
From side to side, and sniffed the unwholesome air.

1. **tunnel:** In World War I—a war characterized by stalemates for very long periods of time—an intricate system of trenches connected by tunnels was devised to protect the troops. Although the trenches were usually shallow, they were sometimes developed into deep excavations connected by deep tunnels to provide greater protection—in this case for the officers in "headquarters." 2. **torch:** British word for flashlight.

Tins, boxes, bottles, shapes too vague to know,
A mirror smashed, the mattress from a bed;   5
And he, exploring fifty feet below
The rosy gloom of battle overhead.
Tripping, he grabbed the wall; saw someone lie
Humped at his feet, half-hidden by a rug,°
And stopped to give the sleeper's arm a tug.   10
"I'm looking for headquarters." No reply.
"God blast your neck!" (For days he'd had no sleep.)
"Get up and guide me through this stinking place."
Savage, he kicked a soft, unanswering heap,
And flashed his beam across the livid° face   15
Terribly glaring up, whose eyes yet wore
Agony dying hard ten days before;
And fists of fingers clutched a blackening wound.
Alone he staggered on until he found
Dawn's ghost that filtered down a shafted stair°   20
To the dazed, muttering creatures underground
Who hear the boom of shells in muffled sound.
At last, with sweat of horror in his hair,
He climbed through darkness to the twilight air,
Unloading hell behind him step by step.   25

9. **rug**: British word for blanket. **15. livid**: abnormally discolored. **20. shafted stair**: here, a narrow, vertical, or inclined excavation.

Meaning and Method

1. In lines 4–5, the narrator lists some things which might be found in a home. Does the description of these things give you the feeling that the tunnel is "homelike," or does it indicate the contrast between life in this tunnel and life in a normal home? Why?
2. Why do the actions and statements of the rear guard ("he") in lines 8–13 become bitterly ironic as you read lines 14–17? In what ways does this incident show that war dehumanizes man? What words or phrases in line 21 emphasize the dehumanizing aspects of war?
3. What words or phrases in lines 1–8 give an impression of the darkness of the tunnel? Is the world overhead dark too? How do you know?
4. Note that the rear guard is literally lost in this dark underground maze. In what ways is the dark maze a symbol of the war? In your answer, comment on the last line of the poem.
5. The narrator in this poem is not emotionally detached from the incidents he describes. Which of the following emotions does he seem

to feel about the situation: (a) pity; (b) anger; (c) horror? Which seems to you the most dominant? Why?

6. How do the connotations of the following words, phrases, or clauses help create the mood or atmosphere of the poem: (a) *groping* (line 1); (b) *a mirror smashed* (line 5); (c) *Alone he staggered* (line 19); (d) *Dawn's ghost* (line 20)?

7. The poet gives the impression of the "muffled sound" (line 22) in the tunnel by the constant repetition of the /u/ sound in *muffled*. List some of the other words that contain the /u/ sound. (Note that many of these words contain the nasal /m/ and /n/ sounds as well, adding to the muffled effect.)

8. Is there an orderly rhyme scheme in this poem, or are the rhymes irregular? Why is the method of rhyming appropriate for the subject?

9. The dominant meter of this poem is *iambic pentameter*—a meter in which each line consists of five iambs (*pente* is the Greek word for five). Line 2, for example, is a perfect iambic pentameter line: He WINKED/ his PRY/ing TORCH/ with PATCH/ing GLARE. Other lines, however, depart somewhat from the dominant meter. How do lines 1, 4, and 8 differ in meter from line 2? Can you think of any reasons—such as emphasis of certain words or sounds—for these departures?

Robert Frost

[1874–1963]

For Robert Frost, the road to recognition and then to fame was as rocky as the soil of New England which he had tried to farm. His father died when Frost was eleven, and the boy came with his mother from San Francisco, his birthplace, to the East Coast. After graduating as valedictorian of his high school class in Lawrence, Massachusetts, he set out on a stubbornly independent path which for many years led to worldly failure.

He attended Dartmouth and Harvard colleges but never earned a degree. As a husband and father, he barely managed to support his family by farming and teaching in New Hampshire. Nor was he more successful in his early attempts to be a poet than he was as a college student or farmer: most of his poems were rejected by the editors of the American magazines and publishing houses to which he sent them.

Searching for a more responsive environment, he and his family—consisting then of his wife and four children—moved in 1912 to a farm in England. In 1913, when Frost was thirty-nine, his first book of poems was published in England and received favorable reviews; in 1914, his second book won enthusiastic critical acclaim. A good deal of the praise was for being "so American" a poet, for "putting New England rural life into verse," and for daring to write "in the natural speech of New England." In 1915, when he returned to America, these books were published in American editions and Frost was recognized as a major American poet.

For nearly half a century afterward, he continued to write original and significant poems, while honors—including four Pulitzer Prizes for poetry and numerous honorary university degrees—were heaped upon him. Perhaps the greatest tribute to him occurred in 1961, when he became the first poet in American history to speak at the inauguration of a President. John F. Kennedy had asked Frost to read a poem; Frost went one step further and wrote a poem commemorating Kennedy's inaugural. However, the bright glare of the snowy January day on which the inauguration took place prevented the aged poet from seeing what he had written. Instead of reading his new poem, therefore, he recited from memory another poem, "The Gift Outright."

By the time of his death, Frost was in many ways the national poet of America. Millions of Americans admired his outspoken personality and responded to the rural characters in his poems who talked in everyday language and rhythms. But Frost's poems are rarely as simple as they seem. Usually these "easy" poems are full of subtle ironies, connotative images, and words with many levels of meaning. In his complexity, Frost was true to his subject: he wrote about reality, and reality—rural or urban—is not simple.

The Vanishing Red

He is said to have been the last Red Man
In Acton. And the Miller is said to have laughed—
If you like to call such a sound a laugh.
But he gave no one else a laugher's license.
For he turned suddenly grave as if to say,   5
"Whose business—if I take it on myself,
Whose business—but why talk round the barn?—
When it's just that I hold with getting a thing done with."
You can't get back and see it as he saw it.
It's too long a story to go into now.   10
You'd have to have been there and lived it.
Then you wouldn't have looked on it as just a matter
Of who began it between the two races.

Some guttural° exclamation of surprise
The Red Man gave in poking about the mill   15
Over the great big thumping shuffling millstone
Disgusted the Miller physically as coming
From one who had no right to be heard from.
"Come, John," he said, "you want to see the wheel-pit?"

He took him down below a cramping rafter,°   20
And showed him, through a manhole in the floor,
The water in desperate straits like frantic fish,

14. **guttural:** having a harsh, grating quality, as sounds made in the throat. 20. **cramping rafter:** a beam holding up a roof or a ceiling which restrains or hampers movement.

Salmon and sturgeon, lashing with their tails.
Then he shut down the trap door with a ring in it
That jangled even above the general noise,   25

And came up stairs alone—and gave that laugh,
And said something to a man with a meal-sack
That the man with the meal-sack didn't catch—then.
Oh, yes, he showed John the wheel-pit all right.

Meaning

1. The speaker is telling a story that he himself was once told. (He says that the Indian "is said" to have been the last Red Man in town, and that the Miller "is said to have laughed.") What statements in lines 9–13 tell you that this story took place a long time ago? Does the narrator think that people today can understand the reasons for this —or perhaps any—incident in the past? Does his listener agree with him? How do you know?

2. There are three characters in the story: the Miller, the Red Man, and an anonymous "man with a meal sack." From line 3, how can you tell whether the Miller's laugh was pleasant or unpleasant? What is the meaning of line 4, and what does it tell you about the Miller's character? What is the Red Man like, and how does he differ from the Miller?

3. What word or phrase in line 26 tells you definitely that the Miller pushed the Red Man into the water and closed the trap door? What words or phrases in lines 20–25 prepared you for this revelation?

4. The Miller's attitude toward the murder of the Indian is indicated in the beginning of the poem. That is, in lines 26–28, we are told that he "gave that laugh" and said something which his listener did not understand at the time. "That laugh" was described in lines 2–3; his statement is indicated in lines 6–8. After reading lines 6–8, would you say that the Miller felt guilty? self-satisfied? some other emotion?

5. What does the Miller's thought that the Indian "had no right to be heard from" (line 18) indicate about his attitude toward the Indian? Did the Miller consider the Indian a human being? an equal? What did the Indian do to disgust the Miller?

6. Why is line 29 ironic? How is the Miller's idea of *showed* different from what John would have expected?

7. In what ways does the story of the Red Man and the Miller symbolize the white man's treatment of the Indian? For example, how might all Indians be said to have been led under "cramping rafters" and shut under "trap doors"? How were all Indians put into "desperate straits" (line 22) by the actions of the white man?

Method

1. The narrator does not tell the story in a straightforward manner—that is, by starting at one moment and continuing in chronological order to a later moment. How does his method of narration help to give the impression of a man talking? What other elements in the poem add to this impression?
2. Does the narrator characterize the Red Man and the Miller by action? by dialogue? something else? Do you have a strong impression of the personalities of the Red Man and the Miller? of their contrasts? What does the fact that the Indian is named John rather than, for example, Running Deer, tell you about him? Are he and the Miller primarily individuals or *types*, that is, representatives of a group?
3. Frost emphasizes the Miller's disgust by repeating the unpleasant /u/ sound in *disgust* several times in the second stanza. In which words is the sound repeated?

Composition and Discussion

1. What are the problems of American Indians today? To find an answer, write to the Bureau of Indian Affairs in Washington, D.C., or in a library, look under *Indians, American* in a recent *Reader's Guide to Periodical Literature* and read one or two magazine or newspaper articles listed there. Then write a composition explaining in your own words the main problems of a specific tribe, or of all Indians in this country.
2. Like later colonial peoples, those who first settled in America felt that they had to bring the natives under their control. In a composition or discussion, compare and contrast the attitudes of two colonials—the Colonel's son in Kipling's "The Ballad of East and West" (pages 44–47), and the Miller in Frost's "The Vanishing Red."

James Russell Lowell
[1819–1891]

When Lowell was a young man living in Boston, a wit made up the following verse:

> And this is good old Boston,
> The home of the bean and the cod,
> Where the Lowells talk only to Cabots,
> And the Cabots talk only to God.

Harvard-educated James Russell Lowell was one of the poorer members of this socially prominent family. Like many of the others, however, he was in the forefront of the literary and political life of his day.

In the years before the Civil War, Lowell wrote poetry and contributed antislavery articles to newspapers and magazines. His major achievement was the two series of politically oriented poems called *The Biglow Papers*. In the first, his speaker, Hosea Biglow, a natively shrewd but uneducated farmer who uses Yankee dialect, ridiculed war in general and the Mexican War in particular. In the second series, Biglow similarly ridiculed the secession of the South and gave his opinions about the progress of the Civil War. Lowell in these poems proved that American dialect could be used in serious poetry, and also gave poetic voice to the feelings of a great many of his countrymen.

Another facet of Lowell's varied talents showed itself in his poem *A Fable for Critics*, in which he pointedly but humorously criticized many of the leading literary figures of his day. Among these were Ralph Waldo Emerson, William Cullen Bryant, Edgar Allan Poe—and Lowell himself. Lowell criticized himself for not having learned "the distinction 'twixt singing and preaching"—a good point, for his poems usually emphasize moral lessons, sometimes at the expense of other qualities. However, he did have natural gifts for singing in verse and for visualizing in figurative language, and these gifts have made some of his poems memorable.

The Vision of Sir Launfal

The author's own note of explanation is helpful: ". . . the San Greal, or Holy Grail, was the cup out of which Jesus partook of the Last Supper with his disciples. It was brought into England by Joseph of Arimathea, and remained there, an object of pilgrimage and adoration for many years. . . . It was incumbent upon those who had charge of it to be chaste in thought, word, and deed; but one of the keepers having broken this condition, the Holy Grail disappeared. From that time it was a favorite enterprise of the knights of Arthur's court to go in search of it. . . ."

PRELUDE TO PART ONE

Over his keys the musing organist,
    Beginning doubtfully and far away,
First lets his fingers wander as they list,°
    And builds a bridge from Dreamland for his lay:°
Then, as the touch of his loved instrument   5
    Gives hope and fervor, nearer draws his theme,
First guessed by faint auroral° flushes sent
    Along the wavering vista° of his dream.

    Not only around our infancy
    Doth Heaven with all its splendors lie;°   10
    Daily, with souls that cringe and plot,
    We Sinais° climb and know it not.
Over our manhood bend the skies;
    Against our fallen and traitor lives
The great winds utter prophecies;   15
    With our faint hearts the mountain strives;

    Its arms outstretched, the druid° wood
    Waits with its benedicite;°

---

3. list: wish, choose. **4. lay:** song. **7. auroral** (ô·rôr′əl): like the dawn. **8. vista:** prospect; a mental view covering a series of events. **9–10. Not . . . lie:** the English poet William Wordsworth, in his poem *Ode: Intimations of Immortality*, wrote, "Heaven lies about us in our infancy!" **12. Sinais** (sī′nīz): God gave Moses the Ten Commandments on Mount Sinai. **17. druid** (drōō′id): an ancient Celtic priest who worshiped in the woods. *Druid* is said to be derived from an old Celtic word meaning oak. **18. benedicite** (ben′ə·dis′ə·tē): blessing.

And to our age's drowsy blood
    Still shouts the inspiring sea.   20

Earth gets its price for what Earth gives us;
    The beggar is taxed for a corner to die in,
The priest hath his fee who comes and shrives° us,
    We bargain for the graves we lie in;
At the devil's booth are all things sold,   25
Each ounce of dross° costs its ounce of gold;
    For a cap and bells° our lives we pay,
Bubbles we buy with a whole soul's tasking:
    'Tis Heaven alone that is given away,
'Tis only God may be had for the asking;   30
No price is set on the lavish summer;
June may be had by the poorest comer.

And what is so rare as a day in June?
    Then, if ever, come perfect days;
Then Heaven tries earth if it be in tune,   35
    And over it softly her warm ear lays;
Whether we look, or whether we listen,
We hear life murmur, or see it glisten;
Every clod feels a stir of might,
    An instinct within it that reaches and towers,   40
And, groping blindly above it for light,
    Climbs to a soul in grass and flowers;
The flush of life may well be seen
    Thrilling back over hills and valleys;
The cowslip startles in meadows green,   45
    The buttercup catches the sun in its chalice,°
And there's never a leaf nor a blade too mean
    To be some happy creature's palace;
The little bird sits at his door in the sun,
    Atilt like a blossom among the leaves,
And lets his illumined being o'errun   50
    With the deluge of summer it receives;

---

23. shrives (shrīvz): hears confession and gives absolution in the sacrament of penance, which is performed to show that the person is sorry for his sins. 26. dross (drôs): scum. 27. cap and bells: the emblem of a king's jester; symbolically, superficial pleasures. 46. chalice: cup. From Latin *calix*, cup or bowl. Usually connotes a cup used for religious worship.

His mate feels the eggs beneath her wings,
And the heart in her dumb breast flutters and sings;
He sings to the wide world, and she to her nest—   55
In the nice° ear of Nature which song is the best?

Now is the high-tide of the year,
    And whatever of life hath ebbed away
Comes flooding back with a ripply cheer,
    Into every bare inlet and creek and bay;   60
Now the heart is so full that a drop overfills it,
We are happy now because God wills it;
No matter how barren the past may have been,

'Tis enough for us now that the leaves are green;
We sit in the warm shade and feel right well   65
How the sap creeps up and the blossoms swell;
We may shut our eyes, but we cannot help knowing
That skies are clear and grass is growing;
The breeze comes whispering in our ear,
That dandelions are blossoming near,
    That maize has sprouted, that streams are flowing,   70
That the river is bluer than the sky,
That the robin is plastering his house hard by;
And if the breeze kept the good news back,
For other couriers we should not lack;
    We could guess it all by yon heifer's lowing,   75
And hark! how clear bold chanticleer,°
Warmed with the new wine of the year,
    Tells all in his lusty crowing!
Joy comes, grief goes, we know not how;   80
Everything is happy now,
    Everything is upward striving;
'Tis as easy now for the heart to be true
As for grass to be green or skies to be blue—
    'Tis the natural way of living: 85
Who knows whither the clouds have fled?
    In the unscarred heaven they leave no wake;°

---

56. nice: discriminating. **76. chanticleer** (chan'tə·kli[ə]r) : a cock. From French *chanter*, to sing, plus *cler*, clear. **87. no wake:** A wake is the track left by a vessel in the water; in this context, it means no record.

And the eyes forget the tears they have shed,
    The heart forgets its sorrow and ache;
The soul partakes the season's youth,   90
    And the sulfurous rifts° of passion and woe
Lie deep 'neath a silence pure and smooth,
    Like burnt-out craters° healed with snow.
What wonder if Sir Launfal now
Remembered the keeping of his vow?   95

PART ONE

I

"My golden spurs now bring to me,
    And bring to me my richest mail,°
For tomorrow I go over land and sea
    In search of the Holy Grail;
Shall never a bed for me be spread,   100
Nor shall a pillow be under my head,
Till I begin my vow to keep;
Here on the rushes° will I sleep.
And perchance there may come a vision true
Ere day create the world anew."   105
    Slowly Sir Launfal's eyes grew dim
    Slumber fell like a cloud on him,
And into his soul the vision flew.

II

The crows flapped over by twos and threes,
In the pool drowsed the cattle up to their knees,   110
    The little birds sang as if it were
    The one day of summer in all the year,
And the very leaves seemed to sing on the trees:
The castle alone in the landscape lay
Like an outpost of winter, dull and gray: 115
'Twas the proudest hall in the North Countree,

---

91. **sulfurous rifts:** openings through which burning sulfur fumes pass. Notice how this metaphor is carried out in "lie deep 'neath" (line 92), and "burnt-out craters" (line 93). **93. craters:** *here,* volcano craters. **97. mail:** armor made of linked metal rings. **103. rushes:** Inside the castle, the floors were covered with rushes, grasslike herbs.

And never its gates might opened be,
Save to lord or lady of high degree;
Summer besieged° it on every side,
But the churlish° stone her assaults defield;   120
She could not scale° the chilly wall,
Though around it for leagues her pavilions° tall
Stretched left and right,
Over the hills and out of sight;
  Green and broad was every tent,   125
  And out of each a murmur went
Till the breeze fell off at night.

III

The drawbridge dropped with a surly clang,
And through the dark arch a charger° sprang,
Bearing Sir Launfal, the maiden knight,°   130
In his gilded mail, that flamed so bright
It seemed the dark castle had gathered all
Those shafts the fierce sun had shot over its wall
  In his siege of three hundred summers long,
And, binding them all in one blazing sheaf,   135
  Had cast them forth: so, young and strong,
And lightsome as a locust-leaf,
Sir Launfal flashed forth in his unscarred mail,
To seek in all climes° for the Holy Grail.

IV

It was morning on hill and stream and tree,   140
  And morning in the young knight's heart;
Only the castle moodily
Rebuffed the gifts of the sunshine free,
  And gloomed by itself apart;
The season brimmed all other things up   145
Full as the rain fills the pitcher-plant's° cup.

---

119. besieged: surrounded, with the intent of capturing. **120. churlish:** *here,* hard to manipulate, resistant. **121. scale:** climb over. **122. pavilions:** tents; *here,* refers to trees which provided shelter as in a tent or summerhouse. **129. charger:** a horse for making a charge in battle. **130. maiden knight:** a knight who has never been in battle. **139. climes:** climates. **146. pitcher-plant:** any plant having leaves arranged in the form of pitchers.

V

As Sir Launfal made morn through the darksome gate,
    He was 'ware of a leper,° crouched by the same,
Who begged with his hand and moaned as he sate;°
    And a loathing over Sir Launfal came;   150
The sunshine went out of his soul with a thrill,
    The flesh 'neath his armor 'gan shrink and crawl,
And midway its leap his heart stood still
    Like a frozen waterfall;
For this man, so foul and bent of stature,   155
Rasped harshly against his dainty nature,
And seemed the one blot on the summer morn—
So he tossed him a piece of gold in scorn.

VI

The leper raised not the gold from the dust:
    "Better to me the poor man's crust,   160
Better the blessing of the poor,
    Though I turn me empty from his door;
That is no true alms° which the hand can hold;
    He gives nothing but worthless gold
        Who gives from a sense of duty;   165
But he who gives but a slender mite,°
And gives to that which is out of sight,
    That thread of the all-sustaining Beauty
Which runs through all and doth all unite—
The hand cannot clasp the whole of his alms,   170
The heart outstretches its eager palms,
For a god goes with it and makes it store°
To the soul that was starving in darkness before."

PRELUDE TO PART TWO

Down swept the chill wind from the mountain peak,
    From the snow five thousand summers old;   175
On open wold° and hilltop bleak
    It had gathered all the cold,

---

148. leper (lep′ər): one who has leprosy, a skin disease which disfigures the victim. **149. sate:** sat. **163. alms:** charity. **166. mite:** small sum of money. **172. store:** abundance. **176. wold:** a tract of land which rises and falls gradually.

And whirled it like sleet on the wanderer's cheek;
It carried a shiver everywhere
From the unleafed boughs and pastures bare;   180
The little brook heard it and built a roof
'Neath which he could house him, winterproof;
All night by the white stars' frosty gleams
He groined° his arches and matched his beams;
Slender and clear were his crystal spars°   185
As the lashes of light that trim the stars:
He sculptured every summer delight
In his halls and chambers out of sight;
Sometimes his tinkling waters slipped
Down through a frost-leaved forest crypt,°   190
Long, sparkling aisles of steel-stemmed trees
Bending to counterfeit a breeze;
Sometimes the roof no fretwork° knew
But silvery mosses that downward grew;
Sometimes it was carved in sharp relief°   195
With quaint arabesques° of ice-fern leaf;
Sometimes it was simply smooth and clear
For the gladness of heaven to shine through, and here
He had caught the nodding bulrush-tops
And hung them thickly with diamond drops,   200
That crystaled the beams of moon and sun,
And made a star of every one:
No mortal builder's most rare device
Could match this winter-palace of ice;
'Twas as if every image that mirrored lay   205
In his depths serene through the summer day,
Each fleeting shadow of earth and sky,
       Lest the happy model should be lost,
Had been mimicked in fairy masonry
       By the elfin builders of the frost.   210

Within the hall are song and laughter,
       The cheeks of Christmas glow red and jolly,

---

184. **groined:** in architecture, a groin is a curve formed by the intersection of
two arches. 185. **spars:** supports, as for the roof of a house. 190. **crypt** (kript):
here, a pit. Usually a crypt is a vault beneath a church used for burial. 193. **fret-
work:** ornamental openwork. 195. **relief:** a sculpture projecting from a surface.
196. **arabesques** (ar′ə·besks′): *here,* ornaments of intertwined leaves.

And sprouting is every corbel° and rafter
With lightsome green of ivy and holly;
Through the deep gulf of the chimney wide   215
Wallows the Yule-log's roaring tide;
The broad flame pennons° droop and flap
And belly and tug as a flag in the wind;
Like a locust shrills the imprisoned sap,
Hunted to death in its galleries blind;   220
And swift little troops of silent sparks,
Now pausing, now scattering away as in fear,
Go threading the soot-forest's tangled darks
Like herds of startled deer.
But the wind without was eager and sharp,   225
Of Sir Launfal's gray hair it makes a harp,
And rattles and wrings
The icy strings,
Singing, in dreary monotone,
A Christmas carol of its own,   230
Whose burden° still, as he might guess,
Was "Shelterless, shelterless, shelterless!"
The voice of the seneschal° flared like a torch
As he shouted the wanderer away from the porch,
And he sat in the gateway and saw all night   235
The great hall-fire, so cheery and bold,
Through the window-slits of the castle old,
Build out its piers of ruddy light
Against the drift of the cold.

PART TWO

I

There was never a leaf on bush or tree,   240
The bare boughs rattled shudderingly;
The river was dumb and could not speak,
For the weaver Winter its shroud° had spun;
A single crow on the treetop bleak
From his shining feathers shed off the cold sun;   245

---

213. **corbel** (kor'bəl): an architectural projection from the face of a wall; it supports an overhanging weight. 217. **pennons:** banners. 231. **burden:** refrain. 233. **seneschal** (sen'ə·shəl): steward. 243. **shroud:** a garment for the dead.

Again it was morning, but shrunk and cold,
As if her veins were sapless and old,
And she rose up decrepitly
For a last dim look at earth and sea.

II

Sir Launfal turned from his own hard gate,   250
For another heir in his earldom sate;
An old, bent man, worn out and frail,
He came back from seeking the Holy Grail;
Little he recked° of his earldom's loss,
No more on his surcoat was blazoned the cross,°   255
But deep in his soul the sign he wore,
The badge of the suffering and the poor.

III

Sir Launfal's raiment thin and spare
Was idle mail 'gainst the barbèd air
For it was just at the Christmas time;   260
So he mused, as he sat, of a sunnier clime,
And sought for a shelter from cold and snow
In the light and warmth of long-ago;
He sees the snakelike caravan crawl
O'er the edge of the desert, black and small,   265
Then nearer and nearer, till, one by one,
He can count the camels in the sun,
As over the red-hot sands they pass
To where, in its slender necklace of grass,
The little spring laughed and leaped in the shade,   270
And with its own self like an infant played,
And waved its signal of palms.

IV

"For Christ's sweet sake, I beg an alms"—
The happy camels may reach the spring,
But Sir Launfal sees only the gruesome thing,   275
The leper, lank as the rain-blanched bone,°

254. recked: cared. 255. blazoned the cross: The red cross was an emblem of
the Crusaders. 276. lank as the rain-blanched bone: thin as the bone bleached
white by rain.

That cowers beside him, a thing as lone
And white as the ice-isles of Northern seas
In the desolate horror of his disease.

V

And Sir Launfal said, "I behold in thee   280
An image of him who died on the tree;°
Thou also hast had thy crown of thorns,
Thou also hast had the world's buffets and scorns,
And to thy life were not denied
The wounds in the hands and feet and side: 285
Mild Mary's Son, acknowledge me;
Behold, through him, I give to thee!"

VI

Then the soul of the leper stood up in his eyes
        And looked at Sir Launfal, and straightway he
Remembered in what a haughtier guise   290
        He had flung an alms to leprosy,
When he girt his young life up in gilded mail
And set forth in search of the Holy Grail.
The heart within him was ashes and dust;
He parted in twain his single crust,   295
He broke the ice on the streamlet's brink,
And gave the leper to eat and drink,
'Twas a moldy crust of coarse brown bread,
        'Twas water out of a wooden bowl—
Yet with fine wheaten bread was the leper fed,   300
        And 'twas red wine he drank with his thirsty soul.

VII

As Sir Launfal mused with a downcast face,
A light shone round about the place;
The leper no longer crouched at his side,
But stood before him glorified,   305
Shining and tall and fair and straight
As the pillar that stood by the Beautiful Gate°—
Himself the Gate° whereby men can
Enter the temple of God in Man.

281. tree: cross. 307. the Beautiful Gate: a gate leading into the Temple at Jerusalem. 308. Himself the Gate: Jesus said, "I am the door." (John 10:9)

VIII

His words were shed softer than leaves from the pine,   310
And they fell on Sir Launfal as snows on the brine,
That mingle their softness and quiet in one
With the shaggy unrest they float down upon;
And the voice that was calmer than silence said,
"Lo, it is I, be not afraid!   315
In many climes, without avail,
Thou hast spent thy life for the Holy Grail;
Behold, it is here, this cup which thou
Didst fill at the streamlet for me but now;
This crust is my body broken for thee   320
This water his blood that died on the tree;
The Holy Supper° is kept, indeed,
In whatso we share with another's need;
Not what we give, but what we share.
For the gift without the giver is bare;   325
Who gives himself with his alms feeds three,
Himself, his hungering neighbor, and me."

IX

Sir Launfal awoke as from a swound:°
"The Grail in my castle here is found!
Hang my idle armor up on the wall,   330
Let it be the spider's banquet-hall;
He must be fenced with stronger mail
Who would seek and find the Holy Grail."

X

The castle gate stands open now,
    And the wanderer is welcome to the hall   335
As the hangbird° is to the elm-tree bough;
    No longer scowl the turrets tall,
The Summer's long siege at last is o'er;
When the first poor outcast went in at the door
She entered with him in disguise,   340
And mastered the fortress by surprise;
There is no spot she loves so well on ground,
She lingers and smiles there the whole year round;

---

322. **Holy Supper:** the last supper of Jesus and his disciples. **328. swound:** faint.
336. **hangbird:** a bird that builds a hanging nest.

The meanest serf° on Sir Launfal's land
Has hall and bower° at his command;   345
And there's no poor man in the North Countree
But is lord of the earldom as much as he.

344. meanest serf: poorest peasant; a serf owed part of his crops and all of his allegiance to his lord. **345. bower:** a shaded place, an arbor.

Meaning: Prelude to Part One

1. What words or phrases in lines 9–20 indicate that the speaker thinks nature is an active and holy force in life? What is meant by "We Sinais climb and know it not" (line 12)? How does man, in lines 9–20, contrast with nature?
2. What kinds of things can man buy? What can he get free? Which, in the speaker's opinion, is more valuable? Do you agree?
3. Why is it appropriate that Sir Launfal remembers his vow in June (see lines 94–95)?

Meaning: Part One

1. Why does Sir Launfal want his "richest mail" (line 97)? Why does he not sleep in his bed?
2. In what way is Sir Launfal like the season? With what words or phrases is the castle personified, or given human qualities, in lines 142–144? Is Sir Launfal like or unlike the castle?
3. Why does Sir Launfal shrink from the leper? What does this reaction show about his character?
4. Explain the leper's speech in lines 160–173. Should it have any meaning for Sir Launfal? Why or why not?

Meaning: Prelude to Part Two

1. What are the characteristics of the house built by the brook? of the inside of the castle?
2. How does the winter scene reflect what has happened to Sir Launfal between Part One and this prelude? Why is Sir Launfal turned away from the porch?

Meaning: Part Two

1. Does an actual transformation take place in lines 298–301? Give reasons for your answer. Why does the change take place or seem to take place?
2. How does the leper change in lines 304–307? Explain his speech to

Sir Launfal in lines 315–327. Is his message basically similar to that of his first speech in lines 160–173? Why or why not?

3. How does Sir Launfal "find" the Holy Grail? How is his "discovery" related to the main theme of the poem?

4. According to the speaker in line 134, summer has besieged the castle for three hundred years. Considering the main theme, explain why Summer finally enters with "the first poor outcast" (line 339)? Why is it "in disguise?" Approximately how much time has elapsed between lines 107–109 and this moment in line 339?

5. Explain why the opening and shutting of the castle gate (see lines 116–118 and 334–336) are symbolic of the attitudes of the inhabitants. To what other symbolic gate in the poem is the castle gate related?

Method: Preludes and Parts One and Two

1. The poet often presents scenes and images which the reader is meant to contrast with each other. What examples of contrast can you think of? Which contrasting scenes or attitudes correspond to or emphasize the changes in Sir Launfal?

2. What verbs of action does the poet use in lines 39–79 to give the impression of summer's activity? What words in lines 183–210 give the impression of the frozen nature of winter?

3. An *allusion* is a reference to a person, place, or thing found originally in literature, mythology, religion, or art. Allusions are generally used for comparison. They imply or suggest moods, attitudes, or situations which are related to the subjects being discussed.

   How does the allusion to Wordsworth's poem in lines 9–10 indicate that Lowell's attitude toward life differs from that of the English poet? What do the Biblical allusions in lines 306–309 indicate?

4. Some of the metaphors in this poem, such as "the buttercup catches the sun in its chalice" (line 46), are effective because they combine realistic description and connotative words. How do the connotations of "chalice" indicate the poet's attitude toward nature? Why is it a realistic description?

5. Lowell also uses *extended metaphors*—that is, a metaphor sustained and developed at length through related words and images. For example, in line 57, he states "Now is the high-tide of the year." What words in the next four lines extend the water metaphor? What is the basis of the extended metaphors in lines 21–32, 119–125, and 181–210, and what words are particularly significant in these extensions?

6. Explain how the preludes are used to (a) create atmosphere or mood, (b) introduce themes, and (c) aid in the characterization of Sir Launfal.

Language: Roots of Words

Words derived from Latin are often the basis of new words. When they are, the unchanged part of the Latin word is called the *root*. For example, the root *visus*, past participle of the Latin verb *videre*, meaning "to see," has produced *television*, *envision*, *revision*, and *visionary*. How do the meanings of these four words reflect the root?

Other important roots are:

1. *port*– from the Latin word *portare*, meaning "to carry";
2. *val*– from the Latin word *valere*, meaning "strong" or "of worth"; and
3. *scrib*– from the Latin word *scribere*, meaning "to write."

Give examples of several words which have been derived from these roots.

Composition

Write a short composition on one of the following themes:

(1) "He gives nothing but worthless gold/Who gives from a sense of duty" (lines 164–165).
(2) "The gift without the giver is bare" (line 325).

Explain and defend the idea contained in your choice. If possible, illustrate your point with real or imagined incidents and examples.

Robert Frost

A biographical sketch of Robert Frost appears on page 63.

Two Tramps in Mud Time

Out of the mud two strangers came
And caught me splitting wood in the yard,
And one of them put me off my aim
By hailing cheerily "Hit them hard!"
I knew pretty well why he dropped behind   5
And let the other go on a way.
I knew pretty well what he had in mind:
He wanted to take my job for pay.

Good blocks of beech it was I split,
As large around as the chopping block;   10
And every piece I squarely hit
Fell splinterless as a cloven° rock.
The blows that a life of self-control
Spares to strike° for the common good
That day, giving a loose to my soul,   15
I spent on the unimportant wood.

The sun was warm but the wind was chill.
You know how it is with an April day
When the sun is out and the wind is still,
You're one month on in the middle of May.   20
But if you so much as dare to speak,
A cloud comes over the sunlit arch,
A wind comes off a frozen peak,
And you're two months back in the middle of March.

A bluebird comes tenderly up to alight   25
And fronts the wind to unruffle a plume
His song so pitched as not to excite

12. **cloven**: parted; split. 14. **spares to strike**: refrains from striking.

A single flower as yet to bloom.
It is snowing a flake: and he half knew
Winter was only playing possum.   30
Except in color he isn't blue,
But he wouldn't advise a thing to blossom.

The water for which we may have to look
In summertime with a witching wand,°
In every wheelrut's now a brook,   35
In every print of a hoof a pond.
Be glad of water, but don't forget
The lurking frost in the earth beneath
That will steal forth after the sun is set
And show on the water its crystal teeth.   40

The time when most I loved my task
These two must make me love it more
By coming with what they came to ask.
You'd think I never had felt before
The weight of an ax-head poised aloft,   45
The grip on earth of outspread feet.
The life of muscles rocking soft
And smooth and moist in vernal° heat.

Out of the woods two hulking tramps
(From sleeping God knows where last night,   50
But not long since in the lumber camps).
They thought all chopping was theirs of right.
Men of the woods and lumberjacks,
They judged me by their appropriate tool.
Except as a fellow handled an ax,   55
They had no way of knowing a fool.

Nothing on either side was said.
They knew they had but to stay their stay
And all their logic would fill my head:
As that I had no right to play   60
With what was another man's work for gain.

34. **witching wand:** a twig which some believe will lead the holder to water.
48. **vernal:** spring (*ver* is the Latin word for spring).

My right might be love but theirs was need.
And where the two exist in twain
Theirs was the better right—agreed.

But yield who will to their separation,   65
My object in living is to unite
My avocation and my vocation°
As my two eyes make one in sight.
Only where love and need are one,
And the work is play for mortal stakes,   70
Is the deed ever really done
For Heaven and the future's sakes.

67. avocation . . . vocation: A vocation is an occupation, something for which
you are paid; an avocation is a hobby—work for its own sake or reward. (The
prefix a- means "not" or "without.")

Meaning and Method

1. In the first stanza, is the speaker pleased to see the strangers? disturbed
by their sudden appearance? Explain. What do the strangers—one of
whom speaks while the other walks a short distance away—want from
the speaker?
2. In the second stanza, what words or phrases indicate that chopping
wood pleased the speaker? that for him, it was a release of tension
or of a desire to do violent acts? Why is the wood described as "unimportant" (line 16)?
3. The scene takes place on "an April day" (line 18). What words in
line 17 indicate that a delicate balance between opposites was achieved
by the weather? Is this delicate balance permanent, according to the
speaker in lines 19–24? What, if anything, might disturb this balance?
4. In lines 33–36, the speaker contrasts the overflow of water in spring
with the absence of water in summer, indicating that a "balance"
between opposites exists in the seasons too. He warns that beneath
the growth of spring, the contrasting destructiveness of winter is
present. What words or phrases in lines 38–40 begin and extend the
metaphor of the danger and destructiveness present in winter?
5. The speaker says that the men and their unasked question make him
"love" his task "more" (see lines 42–43). What does he particularly
love about chopping wood, according to lines 44–48? What words or
phrases indicate the balance required for the act?
6. Why do the tramps (note that the one who walked away in line 6
has now returned) think that "all chopping" was "theirs of right"

(line 52)? Does the speaker agree with them wholly? partially? not at all? In your answer, comment on lines 58–64.

7. What is the speaker's "object in living" (line 66)? Does he aim at a balance, or a balanced uniting of opposites? Does chopping wood fulfill his objective at the present time? In your answer, comment on lines 69–72.

8. In your own words, retell the story of this poem. What is its conflict? Even though the speaker agrees that the right of the tramps was "the better right" (line 64), do we know definitely how the conflict was resolved? That is, do we know whether the speaker keeps on chopping or lets the tramps take over?

Language: Prefixes

Words are often formed to indicate that they are the opposite of something else. For example, *avocation* is the opposite of *vocation, unfriendly* is the opposite of *friendly, nonsense* is the opposite of *sense, impossible* is the opposite of *possible,* and *dislike* is the opposite of *like.* In these cases, the prefixes, or fixed forms at the beginning of the words (*a–, un–, non–, im–,* and *dis–*) all have negative meanings.

Prefixes, however, are not always negative. For example, the prefix *re–* means "back" or "again." The word *return* therefore means "to turn back"; the word *resell* means "to sell again."

Other common prefixes which do not have negative meanings are (a) *pre–,* (b) *post–,* (c) *en–,* (d) *ex–,* and (e) *com–.*

Look up the meanings of these prefixes in a dictionary. Then find several words starting with each of these prefixes whose meanings reflect that of the prefix.

Edgar Allan Poe

[1809–1849]

Poe lived a life as dark and twisted as the plots of many of his short stories and poems. His father, an actor who drank heavily, deserted his family when Poe was a year and a half old, and his young mother, an actress, died when he was two. Although Poe became the ward of a wealthy, childless couple and was well educated by them in Richmond, Virginia, and in England, he never felt loved by them.

As he grew older, Poe began to quarrel seriously with his foster father, John Allan (from whom he took his middle name). One cause of the quarrels was that Poe, then a student in his first year at the University of Virginia, had got himself deeply in debt. When Allan refused to pay his debts, the eighteen-year-old Poe enlisted in the army. Two years later, Allan secured a West Point appointment for him. After a time, however, Poe deliberately neglected his duties, was dismissed from West Point, and broke off completely with his foster father.

His break with Allan (Mrs. Allan had died) in some ways set him free. The brilliant though erratic young man had always wanted to become a writer, and by 1829 had published two volumes of poems. After leaving West Point, he tried to support himself by writing for magazines. In 1835 he became the editor of *The Southern Literary Messenger*. A year later, the twenty-six-year-old Poe married his thirteen-year-old cousin, Virginia Clemm, and with her mother, the couple set up housekeeping.

Poe's problems, however, did not end. His potentially brilliant career as a writer and editor was interrupted by bouts of drunkenness, and he was constantly in need of money. In addition, his wife's health was extremely delicate. In 1842, Virginia Poe developed tuberculosis, and five years later she was dead. After his adored wife's death, Poe became increasingly unstable. In 1849, he was found dead outside a tavern in Baltimore, and his body was placed in a nameless grave.

Poe's life is reflected in his poems and short stories. The characters he created, like the author, are often haunted literally or figuratively by the dark forces of life. Many of his most famous stories are horror stories or sinister detective stories, a form of which he is considered the inventor. Some of his poems, particularly "The Raven" and "The Haunted Palace," also illustrate this almost grotesque morbidity.

In other poems, however, notably "Annabel Lee," he often imagines an incandescently bright world of love. In general, Poe exalts women, often presenting a gloomy, tortured man worshiping a glorious woman who is out of his reach—usually because she is dead. At his most optimistic, Poe imagines the ecstatic world of his dreams being realized after death.

The moods of ecstasy and horror—the twin poles which so intensely attracted Poe—are communicated to the reader partly through dazzling technical effects, for Poe used all manner of virtuoso sound devices to achieve a single effect. Critical judgment of the results varies. Many agree with James Russell Lowell, who in his *Fable for Critics* wrote:

> There comes Poe with his raven, like Barnaby Rudge,*
> Three-fifths sheer genius, and two-fifths sheer fudge.

Others echo the inscription on the bronze and marble memorial set up for him in the New York Museum of Art in 1855:

> He was great in his genius, unhappy in his life, wretched in his death. But in his fame he is immortal.

* **Barnaby Rudge:** the hero of Dicken's novel of the same name; he was a half-witted youth who was always accompanied by a raven.

The Raven

Once upon a midnight dreary, while I pondered, weak and weary,
Over many a quaint and curious volume of forgotten lore—
While I nodded, nearly napping, suddenly there came a tapping,
As of someone gently rapping, rapping at my chamber door.
" 'Tis some visitor," I muttered, "tapping at my chamber door—   5
        Only this, and nothing more."

Ah, distinctly I remember it was in the bleak December,
And each separate dying ember wrought its ghost upon the floor.
Eagerly I wished the morrow;—vainly I had sought to borrow
From my books surcease° of sorrow—sorrow for the lost Lenore—   10
For the rare and radiant maiden whom the angels named Lenore—
        Nameless *here* for evermore.

10. **surcease:** end.

And the silken, sad, uncertain rustling of each purple curtain
Thrilled me—filled me with fantastic terrors never felt before;
So that now, to still the beating of my heart, I stood repeating,   15
" 'Tis some visitor entreating entrance at my chamber door—
Some late visitor entreating entrance at my chamber door;—
      This it is and nothing more."

Presently my soul grew stronger; hesitating then no longer,
"Sir," said I, "or Madam, truly your forgiveness I implore;   20
But the fact is I was napping, and so gently you came rapping,
And so faintly you came tapping, tapping at my chamber door,
That I scarce was sure I heard you"—here I opened wide the door:
      Darkness there and nothing more.

Deep into that darkness peering, long I stood there wondering,
    fearing,   25
Doubting, dreaming dreams no mortal ever dared to dream before;
But the silence was unbroken, and the stillness gave no token,
And the only word there spoken was the whispered word, "Lenore?"
This I whispered, and an echo murmured back the word, "Lenore!"
      Merely this, and nothing more.   30

Back into the chamber turning, all my soul within me burning,
Soon again I heard a tapping somewhat louder than before.
"Surely," said I, "surely that is something at my window lattice;
Let me see, then, what thereat is, and this mystery explore—
Let my heart be still a moment and this mystery explore;—   35
      'Tis the wind, and nothing more!"

Open here I flung the shutter, when, with many a flirt and flutter,
In there stepped a stately Raven of the saintly days of yore;°
Not the least obeisance° made he; not a minute stopped or stayed he;
But, with mien° of lord or lady, perched above my chamber door—   40
Perched upon a bust of Pallas° just above my chamber door—
      Perched, and sat, and nothing more.

38. yore: long ago. **39. obeisance** (ō·bā′səns): act of expressing respect. **40. mien** (mēn): air or manner. **41. Pallas** (pal′əs): Pallas Athene, Greek goddess of wisdom.

Then this ebony bird beguiling my sad fancy into smiling,
By the grave and stern decorum of the countenance it wore,
"Though thy crest be shorn and shaven, thou," I said, "art sure no
    craven,   45
Ghastly, grim, and ancient Raven, wandering from the Nightly shore—
Tell me what thy lordly name is on the Night's Plutonian° shore!"
        Quoth the Raven, "Nevermore."

Much I marvelled this ungainly fowl to hear discourse so plainly,
Though its answer little meaning—little relevancy bore;   50
For we cannot help agreeing that no living human being
Ever yet was blessed with seeing bird above his chamber door—
Bird or beast upon the sculptured bust above his chamber door,
        With such name as "Nevermore."

But the Raven, sitting lonely on the placid bust, spoke only   55
That one word, as if his soul in that one word he did outpour.
Nothing farther then he uttered—not a feather then he fluttered—
Till I scarcely more than muttered, "Other friends have flown before—
On the morrow *he* will leave me, as my Hopes have flown before."
        Then the bird said, "Nevermore."   60

Startled at the stillness broken by reply so aptly spoken,
"Doubtless," said I, "what it utters is its only stock and store
Caught from some unhappy master whom unmerciful Disaster
Followed fast and followed faster till his songs one burden bore—
Till the dirges° of his Hope that melancholy burden bore   65
        Of "Never—nevermore."

But the Raven still beguiling all my fancy into smiling,
Straight I wheeled a cushioned seat in front of bird and bust and door;
Then, upon the velvet sinking, I betook myself to linking
Fancy unto fancy, thinking what this ominous bird of yore—   70
What this grim, ungainly, ghastly, gaunt, and ominous bird of yore
        Meant in croaking "Nevermore."

---

47. **Plutonian** (plōō·tō′nē·ən): hellish; in Greek and Roman mythology, Pluto
presided over the regions of the dead. 65. **dirges:** funeral songs.

This I sat engaged in guessing, but no syllable expressing
To the fowl whose fiery eyes now burned into my bosom's core;
This and more I sat divining,° with my head at ease reclining   75
On the cushion's velvet lining that the lamplight gloated o'er,
But whose velvet-violet lining with the lamplight gloating o'er,
   She shall press, ah, nevermore!

Then, methought, the air grew denser, perfumed from an unseen
  censer°
Swung by seraphim° whose footfalls tinkled on the tufted floor.   80
"Wretch," I cried, "thy God hath lent thee—by these angels he hath
  sent thee
Respite—respite and nepenthe° from thy memories of Lenore;
Quaff,° oh, quaff this kind nepenthe and forget this lost Lenore!"
   Quoth the Raven, "Nevermore."

"Prophet!" said I, "thing of evil!—prophet still, if bird or devil!   85
Whether Tempter sent, or whether tempest tossed thee here ashore,
Desolate, yet all undaunted, on this desert land enchanted—
On this home by Horror haunted—tell me truly, I implore—
Is there—*is* there balm in Gilead?°—tell me—tell me, I implore!"
   Quoth the Raven, "Nevermore."   90

"Prophet!" said I, "thing of evil!—prophet still, if bird or devil!
By that Heaven that bends above us—by that God we both adore—
Tell this soul with sorrow laden if, within the distant Aidenn,°
It shall clasp a sainted maiden whom the angels name Lenore—
Clasp a rare and radiant maiden whom the angels name Lenore."   95
   Quoth the Raven, "Nevermore."

"Be that word our sign of parting, bird or fiend!" I shrieked, upstarting
"Get thee back into the tempest and the Night's Plutonian shore!
Leave no black plume as a token of that lie thy soul hath spoken!

75. divining: conjecturing or surmising about a future event by insight or instinct.
79. censer: *here,* a vessel which contains burning incense. **80. seraphim** (ser′ə·fim): the highest order of angels. **82. nepenthe** (ni·pen′thē): a drug that brings forgetfulness or makes suffering more bearable. **83. quaff:** drink deeply. **89. balm in Gilead** (gil′ē·ad): Gilead in ancient Palestine produced a healing ointment. The expression, which means "relief from affliction," was used by the prophet Jeremiah. (See Jeremiah 8:22 and 46:11.) **93. Aidenn** (ā′dən): Arabic for Eden.

Leave my loneliness unbroken!—quit the bust above my door!   100
Take thy beak from out my heart, and take thy form from off my door!"
    Quoth the Raven, "Nevermore."

And the Raven, never flitting, still is sitting, *still* is sitting
On the pallid bust of Pallas just above my chamber door;
And his eyes have all the seeming of a demon's that is dreaming,   105
And the lamplight o'er him streaming throws his shadow on the floor;
And my soul from out that shadow that lies floating on the floor
    Shall be lifted—nevermore!

Meaning

1. Why does the speaker not open the door immediately? What do the reactions of the speaker to the sounds of tapping and rustling show about his character and state of mind?
2. Why is Lenore important to the speaker? Does he want to remember or forget her? Does he have any hope that they will be reunited? Can you tell from the poem whether the speaker mourns Lenore's death for her sake or his own?
3. Does the speaker take the Raven seriously at first? What does the Raven come to symbolize to the speaker?
4. Why does the speaker finally tell the Raven to leave? What does he mean when he says that his soul will never be lifted "from out that shadow that lies floating on the floor" (line 107)? What does this statement indicate about his state of mind?
5. How is hope shattered for the speaker in lines 28–30, 79–84, and 92–96?
6. In your own words, characterize the speaker. How and why does his state of mind change during the poem?

Method

1. How does the description of the room and its furnishings contribute to the mood or atmosphere of gloom?
2. Does the repetition of *nevermore* have the same effect on the speaker each time? Why does *nevermore* produce a greater sense of hopelessness than, for example, the word *no*?
3. What are the connotations of the word *raven*? Are these connotations used in the poem? Explain.
4. Considering the subject and mood of the poem, explain why the allusions in line 47 are appropriate and effective.
5. How is the speaker's growing agitation conveyed? Quote specific lines or phrases to support your answer.

6. Poe is famous for his use of complicated rhyme patterns. In this poem, for example, all of the end rhymes (see page 57) end with the sound /or/. The effect is similar to that of a man frequently hitting one note on a piano, emphasizing the obsession of the speaker with Lenore. Is there a pattern in his use of internal rhymes? If so, what is it?

7. Each of the lines in each of the stanzas has the same number of stressed syllables. Count, or scan, the stressed syllables in the first stanza to prove this statement. Is the major effect of this rhythm monotonous? (Read the poem aloud before you answer.) Why does the rhythm contribute to the effect of the poem?

Language: Allusions to Mythology

Myths (see page 54), like ballads and legends, are the products of folk culture, and tell of the supposed deeds of gods and goddesses. The stories are not true, but they may reveal truths if they are understood symbolically.

The most famous myths are those of the Greeks and the Romans. When the Romans conquered Greece, they adopted the Greek deities or gods, but usually changed their names. For example, the Greek goddess Pallas Athene (or Athena), alluded to in line 41, was called Minerva by the Romans. Allusions to Greek and Roman mythology appear frequently in Western literature.

The Greek and Roman deities were personifications of human and natural forces and activities. There were, among others, gods of love, war, the sun, the moon, the sea, earth, and death. Each god or goddess was thought to rule over one or more spheres of activity, and each had a symbol or symbols identified with him or her. The symbol of Jupiter or Jove (Latin) or Zeus (Greek), king of the gods, was a thunderbolt; the symbol of Athene or Minerva, goddess of wisdom, was the owl.

Check a dictionary or a book of mythology and identify the following gods and goddesses as to their functions and, if possible, their symbols.

Greek	Roman
Hera	Juno
Aphrodite	Venus
Ares	Mars
Pluto (Hades)	Pluto (Dis)
Poseidon	Neptune
Apollo	Apollo
Artemis	Diana
Hermes	Mercury
Hephaestus	Vulcan
Demeter	Ceres

Lyric
Poetry

MORE THAN TWO THOUSAND years ago in Greece, short poems called *lyrikos* were sung to the accompaniment of a lyre, a stringed musical instrument. Even when the poems were no longer sung, the name lyric remained.

Lyric poems are still usually short and musical. However, the main characteristic of a lyric poem is that it communicates the emotional attitude of the writer toward a person, scene, object, belief, or idea. Thus, lyric poetry is *subjective or personal* instead of *objective or impersonal*. A poet may tell a story in a lyric poem, but his or her feelings about the story are more important than the events themselves.

Over the centuries, certain types of lyric poems have become particularly well known. Among these are the song, the sonnet, the ode, and the elegy, each of which will be discussed in the following section. However, most lyric poems do not fall under any of these categories. The forms of the lyric are as varied as its infinite subjects and treatments.

William Shakespeare

[1564–1616]

"To be, or not to be—that is the question."

"Romeo, Romeo, wherefore art thou, Romeo?"

"Out, out, brief candle!
Life's but a walking shadow, a poor player
That struts and frets his hour upon the stage
And then is heard no more."

"How sharper than a serpent's tooth it is
To have a thankless child."

These lines have been spoken in theaters for more than three centuries and have been translated into many languages. Curiously, however, playgoers and scholars know more about the characters who speak them—Hamlet, Juliet, Macbeth, and Lear, respectively—than they know about the man who wrote them.

Scholars know the dates of Shakespeare's birth and death, and the place where he was born and died (Stratford-on-Avon, England). They know the name of his wife (Anne Hathaway), and the number of his children (three). However, they know little else beside the facts that he was an actor and poet as well as a playwright.

Shakespeare the actor and poet is very evident in the plays. He had the actor's ability to make characters come alive, and he wrote his plays for the most part in verse. Most of his plays are written in unrhymed verse, but rhymed poems occasionally appear in the plays. All of his comedies, as well as some of his tragedies, contain rhymed songs.

Shakespeare's gifts as a playwright and a poet were recognized in his own time as well as by posterity. Several years after his death, his contemporary, the poet and playwright Ben Jonson, eulogized Shakespeare as the "star of poets." And hundreds of years later, Jonson's judgment still seems correct: "He was not of an age, but for all time."

When Icicles Hang by the Wall

This is one of the two songs at the end of Shakespeare's play Love's Labor's Lost. *The first one describes spring; the second one, winter.*

When icicles hang by the wall,
    And Dick the shepherd blows his nail,°
And Tom bears logs into the hall,
    And milk comes frozen home in pail,
When blood is nipped, and ways° be foul,   5
Then nightly sings the staring owl—
        Tu-whit,
Tu-who—a merry note,
While greasy Joan doth keel° the pot.

When all aloud the wind doth blow,   10
    And coughing drowns the parson's saw,°
And birds sit brooding in the snow,
    And Marian's nose looks red and raw,
When roasted crabs° hiss in the bowl,
Then nightly sings the staring owl,   15
        Tu-whit,
Tu-who—a merry note,
While greasy Joan doth keel the pot.

2. **blows his nail:** warms his fingertips. 5. **ways:** roads. 9. **keel:** cool, or prevent from boiling over, as by skimming. 11. **saw:** familiar moral saying. 14. **crabs:** crab apples.

Meaning and Method

1. What descriptive words or images give an impression of the coldness of winter? Is the picture Shakespeare presents unpleasant? pleasant? both? How does the scene in the inside of the house contrast with the outdoor scenes?
2. Is the owl's song merry in itself, or does it *seem* merry because it is heard from within a warm house after the men's work is done?
3. Identify the sounds in the following words as unpleasant or harsh:

    (a) *foul—owl*   (d) *birds sit brooding*
    (b) *blood is nipped*   (e) *red and raw—saw*
    (c) *greasy—keel*   (f) *roasted crabs hiss*

    Why would Shakespeare have wanted to use unpleasant or harsh sounds in the poem?
4. If you were writing music for this poem, would you write slow-paced or fast-paced music? Why?

Ben Jonson
[1572–1637]

Poet, playwright, actor, and scholar, Ben Jonson was a man of many talents and many contrasts. In his poems, he used the Greek and Latin classics as models and tried to imitate classical balance and harmony. In his life, however, his violent temper created havoc. Once, he was imprisoned for killing a fellow actor in a duel. At another time—when the Scottish James VI had just become James I of England—he was imprisoned for insulting the Scots.

As might be expected from his behavior, Jonson had emphatic literary opinions. He engaged in sharp battles in speech and print with many of his fellow poets and playwrights. Some poets, however, were so strongly influenced by him that they were called "Sons of Ben."

Jonson is best known for a series of bitter comedies—the most famous of which is *Volpone*—in which he attacked the greed, hypocrisy, and gullibility of his fellow men. However, he was also capable of creating lyrics which expressed tender feelings. Some of these lyrics are in his plays where they are often used to show that the language of love may mask sordid intentions.

Jonson's personality antagonized many people, but his talents were widely admired. In 1616, Jonson was named poet laureate by James I. Although his plays are rarely performed today, in his lifetime he was considered second only to Shakespeare as a playwright. He is buried in Westminster Abbey, under a stone bearing the inscription, "O Rare Ben Jonson."

Song: To Celia

> Drink to me only with thine eyes,
>   And I will pledge with mine;
> Or leave a kiss but° in the cup,
>   And I'll not look for wine.
> The thirst that from the soul doth rise,   5
>   Doth ask a drink divine;
> But might I of Jove's nectar° sup,
>   I would not change for thine.

3. **but:** only.

I sent thee late° a rosy wreath,
　Not so much honoring thee,   10
As giving it a hope that there
　It could not withered be;
But thou thereon did'st only breathe,
　And sent'st it back to me;
Since when it grows, and smells, I swear,   15
　Not of itself, but thee.

7. **Jove's nectar:** Jove is one of the Roman names for the king of the gods. (The Greek name is Zeus.) Nectar is the drink of the gods. 9. **late:** lately.

Meaning and Method

1. Explain what the speaker means in line 1. Through what words in the first stanza is the drinking metaphor extended? What compliment is the speaker paying the lady by means of this extended metaphor?
2. What other compliments does the speaker pay the lady in the poem?
3. What evidence in the poem indicates that the lady does not return the speaker's feelings? How might the speaker's exaggerations, and small requests, be related to this knowledge?
4. Does the exaggeration seem ludicrous, or does it seem delicate and tender?
5. If you know the melody which for centuries has been sung with these lyrics, attempt to characterize it. Is it dreamy, melancholy, gay? Does it fit the lyrics?

Robert Burns

[1759–1796]

For centuries, the lyrics of Robert Burns celebrating the beauties of Scotland and Scottish women have been loved throughout the English-speaking world. Burns himself, however, had a life that was far from beautiful.

Burns was born near Ayr, Scotland, in a two-room cottage which his family shared with several of their animals. The family of tenant farmers was desperately poor; the thin soil of the region yielded meager crops, and what little income there was went to landlords. The Burns children had only a few years of formal schooling because they were needed in the fields.

The hard life Burns led as a young man had its compensations, however. His father communicated his own joy in learning to his son; at every meal, young Robert sat "with a book in one hand and a spoon in the other." His mother taught him old Scottish folk stories and songs—some of which later became parts of his best poems—and he read collections of folk ballads and lyrics as he drove a cart or walked to work. Moreover, he was a handsome young man with an arresting personality, who spent many hours "among the lasses."

After his father died, Burns tried farming on his own, but without success. Finally, discouraged by this failure and by the refusal of the father of his sweetheart, Jean Armour, to permit their marriage, he decided to emigrate to Jamaica. His plans, however, were changed by the surprising and immediate success of a volume of verse he had published as his "farewell" to Scotland.

For a short time, life became easier for him. He was treated as a celebrity by the cultured society of Edinburgh. Jean Armour's father relented and permitted their marriage. Burns was given a minor government job, and leased a farm.

This period, however, represented only a truce in his battle with poverty. The farm failed, and for the last five years of his life he struggled to support his family on his small government salary. He got deeply into debt—so much so that on his deathbed he was nearly besieged by people to whom he owed money.

Nevertheless, out of the kind of life which reduced others to pettiness and despair, Burns managed to sing. The song quality in his lyrics was immediately recognized, and many of his poems were set to music—usually gentle music with a hint of melancholy, like the poems themselves. These lyrics and songs occupy a unique place in English poetry. Never before or after Burns has there been a poet who sang of common things and common people in such an uncommonly loving and lovely way.

Sweet Afton *

One of Burns's sweethearts, Mary Campbell, died while they were engaged. Three years after her death, he wrote this poem, which was subsequently set to music.

Flow gently, sweet Afton, among thy green braes!°
Flow gently, I'll sing thee a song in thy praise!
My Mary's asleep by thy murmuring stream—
Flow gently, sweet Afton, disturb not her dream!

Thou stock dove whose echo resounds through the glen,   5
Ye wild whistling blackbirds in yon thorny den,
Thou green-crested lapwing, thy screaming forbear°—
I charge you, disturb not my slumbering fair!

How lofty, sweet Afton, thy neighboring hills,
Far marked with the courses of clear, winding rills!°   10
There daily I wander as noon rises high,
My flocks and my Mary's sweet cot° in my eye.

How pleasant thy banks and green vallies below,
Where wild in the woodlands the primroses blow;
There oft, as mild Ev'ning weeps over the lea,   15
The sweet-scented birk° shades my Mary and me.

Thy crystal stream, Afton, how lovely it glides,
And winds by the cot where my Mary resides!
How wanton° thy waters her snowy feet lave,
As, gathering sweet flowerets, she stems thy clear wave!   20

* **Afton:** a small river in Scotland. **1. braes** (brāz): hillsides. **7. forbear:** give up. **10. rills:** small streams. **12. cot:** cottage. **16. birk:** birch. **19. wanton** (won'tən): *here*, playfully.

> Flow gently, sweet Afton, among thy green braes!
> Flow gently, sweet river, the theme of my lays!°
> My Mary's asleep by thy murmuring stream—
> Flow gently, sweet Afton, disturb not her dream!

22. lays: songs.

Meaning and Method

1. Like the conductor of an orchestra, the speaker attempts to direct the "music" of nature. What methods does he use in lines 2 and 8 to persuade nature to let Mary sleep undisturbed?
2. What mood is the speaker trying to create? What words or phrases particularly contribute to the mood? Does the rhythm also contribute to it? In your answer, explain whether the meter is strictly patterned and even, or is varied and uneven.
3. What actual event is described by the personification "as mild Ev'ning weeps over the lea" (line 15)?
4. When a speaker addresses a deceased or absent person as if he were present, or addresses an animal or thing or an abstract idea or quality as if it could understand him, he is said to be using *apostrophe*. Find several examples of the use of this technique in the poem, and explain what it shows about the speaker's attitude toward nature.

Walter de la Mare

[1873–1956]

Things just outside the limits of reality—dreams, magic, ghosts—fascinated de la Mare. Surprisingly, he held onto his belief in the mystery and beauty of life despite eighteen years of working at a humdrum job in a London oil company.

His distinctive talent, evident in many poems published during this time, eventually freed him from his job. At the age of thirty-six, he was granted a British government pension to enable him to write full time. The results of this freedom to write are more than fifty volumes of poetry, fiction, and essays, most of which are marked by his special brand of fantasy.

Silver

Slowly, silently, now the moon
Walks the night in her silver shoon;°
This way, and that, she peers, and sees
Silver fruit upon silver trees;
One by one the casements° catch   5
Her beams beneath the silvery thatch;°
Couched in his kennel, like a log,
With paws of silver sleeps the dog;
From their shadowy cote° the white breasts peep
Of doves in a silver-feathered sleep;   10
A harvest mouse goes scampering by,
With silver claws and a silver eye;
And moveless fish in the water gleam,
By silver reeds in a silver stream.

2. **shoon:** shoes. 5. **casements:** windows. 6. **thatch:** straw used for roofs. 9. **cote:** (kōt): a shed or coop.

Meaning and Method

1. Why are the mouse, the doves, and the dog not presented as being totally silver? Why are the fruit, trees, reeds, and stream simply "silver"?

2. Why, in your opinion, does the poet personify the moon? Why does he not say instead that the moon shines?
3. Notice the frequent use of /s/, /sh/, and /l/ sounds. How do they help to create an atmosphere of peacefulness? Read the poem aloud before you answer.
4. Why do you think de la Mare called his poem "Silver" rather than "Moonlight"? In your answer, discuss the connotations of each word.
5. Why is this a lyric poem? What personal feeling is the poet trying to convey?

Composition

Write a descriptive paragraph about an object which you consider beautiful or ugly. By means of specific details which appeal to the senses of sight and touch, try to make the reader see and feel the beauty or ugliness of the object or scene you describe.

Six Haiku *

If prizes were given to those writers who used the least number of words to communicate the greatest number of thoughts and impressions, poets would be richer than prose writers, and haiku poets would be the richest of all.

The haiku (also called hokku), which was developed in Japan in the thirteenth century, is a short poem with a rigid form. According to Japanese rules, all haiku *must* have three lines with a total of seventeen syllables—five syllables in the first line, seven syllables in the second line, and five syllables in the third line. The haiku poet must therefore rely on the power of suggestion to an even stronger extent than other poets do. Each word must help suggest a mood, a scene, or an idea. For this reason, haiku poets usually include words which denote the time of day or time of year, times which carry many associations for all readers.

Writing haiku is difficult; translating haiku into a foreign language —and keeping the correct number of syllables in each line—is at least equally difficult. Harry Behn, the translator of the following six haiku, is one of the few people who has managed to communicate the subtlety and depth of some of these poems to the English reader.

Behn, who was born in Arizona and was graduated from Harvard College, is primarily a poet and short-story writer for children. His interest in children is apparent in his book of haiku, *Cricket Songs: Japanese Haiku*, for he has chosen haiku which show "the small marvels of nature" as a child might see them.

* **Haiku** (hī'kōō).

1

It is nice to read
news that our spring rain also
visited your town.
—ONITSURA

2

How cool cut hay smells
when carried through the farm gate
as the sun comes up!
—BONCHO

3

After the bells hummed
and were silent, flowers chimed
a peal of fragrance.
—BASHO

4

Broken and broken
again on the sea, the moon
so easily mends.
—CHOSU

From *Cricket Songs: Japanese Haiku,* translated by Harry Behn, © 1964 by Harry Behn. Reprinted by permission of Harcourt, Brace & World, Inc.

5

Tonight in this town
where I was born, my only
friends are the crickets.

—ANON.

6

I must go begging
for water . . . morning glories
have captured my well.

—CHIYO

Meaning and Method

1. How do you know (1) was written to a friend? Why is the speaker happy? In your answer, discuss the connotations of *spring rain*.
2. What details in (2) help you picture the scene? Is the scene static or is it one of motion? Does the poet indicate whether the day will be hot or cold? How can hay smell cool?
3. How does (3) show that harmony exists between the world of man and the world of nature? What words connect the flowers with the bells?
4. In nature, how is the moon "broken" on the sea? How does it mend? What change of mood occurs between the first and the third lines in (4)? How does repetition in line 1 contribute to the original mood?
5. Do you think that the loneliness of the speaker in (5) would have been equally great if he had found himself alone in a foreign town rather than in the town where he was born? Why or why not?
6. Usually one thinks of a human being as stronger than a flower. What is unusual about the attitude of the speaker in (6) toward the morning glories? In your answer, comment on the speaker's use of *begging* and *captured*. How does this haiku show the poet's love of nature?
7. Give a one-word title to each of the haiku you have read. Be prepared to defend your choices.

Composition

Read or reread Gilbert Highet's essay on haiku on pages 106–111 of *A Book of Nonfiction—1*. Then write two haiku of your own.

Sarojini Naidu *

[1879–1949]

In India, for centuries a land in which women were primarily seen and not heard, Sarojini Naidu led an unusually public life. In the 1920's, she became a leader of the fight for equal rights for women and the fight for general political and social reform. As a major figure in the civil disobedience movement of Mohandas (Mahatma) Gandhi, whose aim was to free India from British rule, she was imprisoned several times. Her political activities culminated triumphantly in 1947, however, when India gained its independence and she herself became governor of the United Provinces.

Mrs. Naidu, who attended Madras University in India and the universities of London and Cambridge in England, gave up a promising career as a poet to devote herself to politics. The three volumes of poems (in English) which she wrote between 1905 and 1917 capture Indian sentiments and sights in graceful rhythms and sensual imagery. Many of her poems have been set to music, and are sung in India today.

* Sarojini Naidu (sa·rō·jē′nē nah′i·dōō).

In the Bazaars of Hyderabad *

What do you sell, O ye merchants?
Richly your wares are displayed.
Turbans of crimson and silver,
Tunics of purple brocade,
Mirrors with panels of amber,   5
Daggers with handles of jade.

What do you weigh, O ye vendors?
Saffron° and lentil° and rice.
What do you grind, O ye maidens?
Sandalwood,° henna,° and spice.   10

* **Hyderabad** (hī′dər·a·bad′): a city in southern India. 8. **saffron** (saf′rən): a spice; also used in yellow dye; **lentil:** beans. 10. **sandalwood:** a dark red wood used in dyeing clothes; **henna:** a shrub used for reddish-orange dye.

What do you call, O ye peddlers?
Chessmen and ivory dice.

What do you make, O ye goldsmiths?
Wristlet and anklet and ring,
Bells for the feet of blue pigeons,   15
Frail as a dragonfly's wing,
Girdles° of gold for the dancers,
Scabbards° of gold for the king.

What do you cry, O ye fruitmen?
Citron, pomegranate, and plum.   20
What do you play, O musicians?
Cithār, sarangi, and drum.
What do you chant, O magicians?
Spells for aeons° to come.

What do you weave, O ye flower girls   25
With tassels of azure and red?
Crowns for the brow of a bridegroom,
Chaplets° to garland his bed,
Sheets of white blossoms new-gathered
To perfume the sleep of the dead.   30

17. **girdles:** belts. 18. **scabbards:** (skab′ardz) : sheaths for swords. 24. **aeons:** (ē′onz) : ages. 28. **chaplets:** flower wreaths.

Meaning and Method

1. How does the poet convey an impression of the colorfulness, richness, and variety of the bazaar? What words or phrases particularly appeal to the senses?
2. Why does the choice of such words as *sandalwood* and *pomegranate* contribute to the exotic atmosphere?
3. How does the question-and-answer technique give the effect of a person walking through the bazaar?
4. What effect on the poem does the last line have? Does the line introduce a new element, or does it fit in naturally with the lines above it?
5. The basic meter of this poem is *dactylic*. A *dactyl* is a foot in which one accented syllable is followed by two unaccented syllables, as in VIS·i·ble. Scan the first six lines and tell how many dactyls occur in each line.

Language: Meaning of Words from Context

Often when you read you come across unfamiliar words. Sometimes you have to consult a dictionary to understand the meanings of the words; other times, you can more or less guess the meaning by noticing the words around it—that is, the *context* in which a word appears.

For example, line 20 of "In the Bazaars of Hyderabad" reads, "Citron, pomegranate, and plum." Most of you have never come into contact with a citron or a pomegranate. However, you do know that a plum is a fruit. Therefore, from the context, you could correctly guess that citron and pomegranate are also fruits.

From the context of line 22, can you guess what a cithār and a sarangi are?

Composition

Imagine that you are a foreigner visiting an American supermarket. Describe all or some of the things you see in such a way that the reader has a sense of the richness and variety of the supermarket. Give details and particulars, and try to use words which appeal to the senses of touch, sight, taste, and smell.

Langston Hughes

[1902–1967]

A combination of talent, courage, and luck gave Hughes his start as a poet. Hughes, working as a busboy at a hotel in Washington, D.C., recognized the poet Vachel Lindsay, and left some poems beside his plate. The poems so impressed the older poet that he read them at a recital of poetry and introduced Hughes to people who could publish his poems.

Hughes's career was helped by other people who liked his poems. For example, in 1925, an editor at a large publishing house who had seen one of his poems in a magazine asked to see all of his work. This contact resulted in the publication of the first of his many books of poetry, *The Weary Blues*. At about the same time, another admirer of his work gave him a scholarship to attend Lincoln University in Pennsylvania, from which he was graduated in 1929.

Despite these strokes of fortune, Hughes, who was born in Missouri but lived in Harlem for most of his adult life, did not have an easy existence. As a Negro, he suffered because of the slights given to the "darker brother" whom white Americans send "to eat in the kitchen/ When company comes," as he wrote in one of his poems. Most of his writing—he wrote poems, novels, short stories, movie scripts, plays, songs, children's books, and biographies—was concerned with the problems of Negroes in America. His work reflects his sorrow, anger, or amusement at the plight of his characters, but is rarely bitter.

Hughes wrote in simple, rhythmic language that has been understood and appreciated by a great many people, both in this country and in the more than twenty-five countries where his work has appeared in translation. A man of deep feeling as well as intelligence, he wrote primarily for readers who respond with their hearts.

Mother to Son

Well, son, I'll tell you:
Life for me ain't been no crystal stair.
It's had tacks in it,
And splinters,

And boards torn up,   5
And places with no carpet on the floor—
Bare.
But all the time
I'se been a-climbin' on,
And reachin' landin's,   10
And turnin' corners,
And sometimes goin' in the dark
Where there ain't been no light.
So boy, don't you turn back.
Don't you set down on the steps   15
'Cause you finds it's kinder hard.
Don't you fall now—
For I'se still goin', honey,
I'se still climbin',
And life for me ain't been no crystal stair.   20

Meaning

1. Does the speaker feel sorry for herself because she has had a hard life? What does her attitude show about her character?
2. What is the mother's advice to her son? Is her attitude toward her son understanding? kind? domineering? something else?
3. What hope does the mother offer her son?
4. What is the main theme of the poem? Is it one that is universally true?

Method

1. The poem is based on an extended metaphor. What is this metaphor? What words or phrases are used to extend it? Is it appropriate to the subject of this poem? Explain your answers.
2. What images indicate that the journey through life has been difficult?
3. This poem is written in *free verse*, that is, verse which is unrhymed and has no meter. Free verse is often used when the poet wants to emphasize certain words which would naturally be emphasized when spoken, or when he wants to create a picture in type. (For example, a poet writing a poem about falling leaves might put each word on a separate line to give the impression of leaves dropping.)

   Explain why the poet places *bare* (line 7) on a separate line. Then give some examples of how free verse is used in this poem to reflect the steps described by the mother.

4. The simple words of this poem often have connotations which add to the poem's meaning or richness. What are the connotations of *bare* and *climbing?* Why does the phrase *crystal stair* (line 2) sum up the kind of life the mother did not have?

I, Too

I, too, sing America.

I am the darker brother.
They send me to eat in the kitchen
When company comes,
But I laugh,   5
And eat well,
And grow strong.

Tomorrow,
I'll be at the table
When company comes.   10
Nobody'll dare
Say to me,
"Eat in the kitchen,"
Then.

Besides,   15
They'll see how beautiful I am
And be ashamed—

I, too, am America.

Meaning and Method

1. What are the connotations of *darker brother* (line 2)? Why do you think the poet chose to use this term rather than *Negro?*
2. Why is the speaker sent "to eat in the kitchen/When company comes" (lines 3–4)? Does his exclusion make him feel inferior? Explain.
3. Is this example symbolic of a larger situation? Support your answer by discussing the position of the Negro in American life.

"I, Too" from *The Dream Keeper* by Langston Hughes, copyright © 1932 by Langston Hughes. Reprinted by permission of Harold Ober Associates Incorporated.

4. What hopes does the speaker have for the future? Who are "they" and why will "they" be ashamed? Does "beautiful" (line 16) refer only to physical beauty?
5. Why does the speaker start with "I, too, sing America"? Why did he not simply say "I sing America"?
6. When you speak, your listener can tell your attitude toward what you are saying by your tone of voice and the words you choose to emphasize. For example, you might say "He's *great*" or "*He's* great?" One statement shows admiration; the other, with the same words, shows disbelief.

In a poem, the speaker's tone, or attitude toward his subject and audience, is generally shown by his selection of details and his arrangement of words.

What is the tone of the last line? Is the tone of the poem as a whole bitter? proud? gentle? optimistic? humorous? something else?

Composition and Discussion

In a panel discussion, compare and contrast the political, social, and economic situations of black Americans and white Americans. Refer to the past and present situations and indicate what you think is ahead.

Arna Bontemps*

For many years Bontemps lived alternately in the North and the South. He was born in Louisiana in 1902, went to college in California, and taught in Harlem, Alabama, and Chicago. He finally settled in Nashville, Tennessee, where he held the post of chief librarian at Fisk University from 1943 to 1965, resigning only to work in the university's public relations office.

From his early twenties on, Bontemps wrote steadily in his spare time, producing poems, short stories, novels, children's books, and biographies. Like Langston Hughes, with whom he collaborated on collections of Negro poetry and folklore, his work is primarily about Negro life. His first novel was about a Negro jockey. (The musical *St. Louis Woman* was later based on it.) His second and third novels were about slave revolts led by Negroes. In all of his work, he emphasizes the Negro's sense of his worth and dignity.

* **Bontemps:** The name is of French origin. Because Bontemps was born in Louisiana, the name is pronounced *bawn'tämp*, in the Louisiana French dialect. In Parisian French, it would be pronounced *bōn'tawn*.

The Day-Breakers

We are not come to wage a strife
　　With swords upon this hill.
It is not wise to waste the life
　　Against a stubborn will.
Yet would we die as some have done,　　　　　5
Beating a way for the rising sun.

Meaning and Method

1. What kind of strife does the speaker wish to avoid?
2. What do you think the speaker means when he says "Beating a way for the rising sun" (line 6)? Is there a contradiction between the last two lines and the first four lines of the poem? Why or why not?
3. In the context of this poem, what does the rising sun symbolize? How is it related to the poem's title?

"The Day-Breakers" by Arna Bontemps from *American Negro Poetry* edited by Arna Bontemps, 1964. Reprinted by permission of the author.

4. *Paraphrase* is the usually brief restatement, in different words, of what an author is trying to say. In your own words, state what Bontemps has tried to say in "The Day-Breakers."

Composition

Write a composition contrasting the attitudes of the speakers in "The Day-Breakers" and "Mother to Son" or "I, Too." Which speaker would be more active in the struggle for Negro rights? Why? Which poem do you think would have more effect on the outcome of the struggle? Why?

William Butler Yeats *
[1865–1939]

One of the greatest poets of the twentieth century is the Irish poet W. B. Yeats. Yeats was born in Dublin and lived through the difficult period of Irish revolt and final independence from Great Britain. His native land had a strong effect on his poetry. Many of his early poems and verse plays are based on legends about ancient Irish heroes, both historical and supernatural, or show his interest in everyday Irishmen. Others are colored by his appreciation of the Irish countryside in which he spent much of his childhood. Some of his best later poems and verse plays deal with the Irish revolution and the civil war which followed.

Yeats was determined to be a great poet from an early age, and thought continually about the type of poetry he wanted to write. In his early twenties, when he lived in London, he was one of the founders of the Rhymers' Club, a society of young poets who wished to create "pure" poetry—imaginative, "beautiful" poems which had no moral messages. His own poems at this time were melodious and rich in images and figurative language. At their best, they were extremely lovely and delicate lyrics.

Yeats, however, did not continue to write this type of poetry. Slowly, his view of life and poetry changed, and his poems reflected these changes. As he grew older, his aim in writing verse was to be "as cold and passionate as the dawn." Most of his later poems have a conciseness, concreteness, and force which was largely absent from his early poems. It was primarily for these qualities that he was awarded the Nobel prize for literature in 1923.

*Yeats (yāts).

The Fiddler of Dooney

When I play on my fiddle in Dooney,°
Folk dance like a wave of the sea;
My cousin is priest in Kilvarnet,°
My brother in Mocharabuiee.°

1, 3, 4. Dooney, Kilvarnet (kil·var′nē), Mocharabuiee (mak·rə·bwē′): villages on the west coast of Ireland.

"The Fiddler of Dooney" from *Collected Poems* by William Butler Yeats, copyright 1906 by The Macmillan Company, renewed 1934 by William Butler Yeats. Reprinted by permission of The Macmillan Company, Macmillan & Co., Ltd., London, The Macmillan Company of Canada Limited, and Mr. M. B. Yeats.

I passed my brother and cousin: 5
They read in their books of prayer;
I read in my book of songs
I bought at the Sligo° fair.

When we come at the end of time
To Peter° sitting in state,   10
He will smile on the three old spirits,
But call me first through the gate;

For the good are always the merry,
Save by° an evil chance.
And the merry love the fiddle,   15
And the merry love to dance:

And when the folk there spy me,
They will all come up to me,
With "Here is the fiddler of Dooney!"
And dance like a wave of the sea.   20

8. **Sligo** (slī′gō): a port on the west coast of Ireland where Yeats's grandparents lived, and where he spent much of his childhood. 10. **Peter:** Saint Peter, keeper of the gates of heaven. 14. **Save by:** except for.

Meaning and Method

1. What contrasts in personality are indicated by the speaker's statement that his brother and cousin "read in their books of prayer" (line 6), while he reads in his "book of songs" (line 7)?
2. Why does the speaker think that he will be given preference over his relatives on entering heaven? In your answer, comment on lines 13–14.
3. What are the fiddler's attitudes toward his music, his listeners, his cousin and brother, and his life? Read the poem aloud. Does your tone of voice reflect his attitudes? Explain your answers.
4. What does the simile in lines 2 and 20 indicate about the type of dancing to which the fiddler is referring?
5. Does the rhythm of the poem reflect the music the fiddler plays? Why or why not?

Carl Sandburg
[1878–1967]

Both of Carl Sandburg's parents were illiterate immigrants who had come from Sweden to settle in the prairie town of Galesburg, Illinois, where Sandburg was born. Despite the fact that they worked very hard, they were poor people, and Sandburg had to leave school at the age of thirteen to earn money by working at such jobs as harvesting, laying bricks, and washing dishes.

In 1898, however, after serving in the Spanish-American War, Sandburg decided to continue his education at Lombard College in Galesburg, and worked as a fireman to put himself through college. When he left the college after almost four years of study—but without a degree—he went to Milwaukee to try to earn his living as a journalist. Eventually, he became a successful reporter and columnist for a major Chicago newspaper.

Sandburg's talents as a writer, however, were not confined to journalistic prose. Not only did he win Pulitzer prizes for both biography and poetry, but he became so popular as a poet that he was often described as "a national poet."

Sandburg had a wider audience than most poets have because he wrote poems that workers, farmers, and shopkeepers—"the people"—could understand. He wrote, as he said, the "poetry of ordinary things," such as fences, telephone wires, city life, the feeling of being lost. He "put America on paper," in the words of one commentator, and he put American speech on paper, too, by using colloquial expressions and slang in his poems. In addition, he wrote in free verse which was sometimes so close to the rhythms of everyday American speech that critics argued about whether Sandburg's poems should be classified as poetry or prose. However, the images and figurative language in both his poems and prose leave no doubt that, whatever the form, he wrote at all times in the language of poetry.

Much of Sandburg's life and work can be summed up in the phrase, *The People, Yes,* which he used as the title for one of his many books of poems. He spent years writing a six-volume biography in which he sensitively portrayed a man of the people, Abraham Lincoln, whose background had much in common with his own. Sandburg believed that the people had created unrecognized poetry, and so he traveled around the country singing their folk songs, accompanying himself on a guitar or a banjo. Instead of isolating himself, he saw and understood the problems and rewards of "ordinary" people in both city and country. And he came up with a judgment about them that might be applied to some of his own poems: "The people will live on."

Jazz Fantasia

Drum on your drums, batter on your banjos, sob on the long cool winding saxophones. Go to it, O jazzmen.

Sling your knuckles on the bottoms of the happy tin pans, let your trombones ooze, and go husha-husha-hush with the slippery sandpaper.

Moan like an autumn wind high in the lonesome treetops, moan soft like you wanted somebody terrible, cry like a racing car slipping away from a motorcycle cop, bang-bang! you jazzmen, bang altogether drums, traps,° banjos, horns, tin cans—make two people fight on the top of a stairway and scratch each other's eyes in a clinch tumbling down the stairs.

Can the rough stuff. . . . Now a Mississippi steamboat pushes up the night river with a hoo-hoo-hoo-oo . . . and the green lanterns calling to the high soft stars. . . . a red moon rides on the humps of the low river hills. . . . Go to it, O jazzmen.

3. **traps:** percussion instruments, such as drums and cymbals, which are sounded by striking.

Meaning and Method

1. In the first two stanzas, Sandburg not only gives his impression of the sounds made by various instruments in a Dixieland jazz band, but in some cases indicates the way they look as well. What types of sound, and what sights, are indicated by the phrases "sob on the long cool winding saxophones" and "let your trombones ooze"?
2. In the third and fourth stanzas, the poet indicates the various stages through which the music passes. For example, the phrase *bang-bang!*

indicates that the music at that point is fast and loud. At what other points is it fast and loud? When is it slow and soft? sad? gay?

3. The speaker talks to the jazzmen throughout the poem. Does his manner of talking to them make him seem involved in, or detached from, the music they create? Why?

4. What phrases containing verbs in the third stanza indicate that the jazz music reflects intense moments in human life?

5. A fantasia (fan·tä′zhə) is a musical composition that does not follow a strict form. Why is the type of verse Sandburg uses appropriate for a poem with this title? for the music it describes? What are the connotations of the word *fantasia*, and why are they appropriate for this poem?

Composition

Sandburg associated certain emotions or sensations with a specific type of music and the instruments used to create it. For example, the tin pans seemed "happy" to him, and the saxophone "cool" and sad. The music also called up visual images for him, such as "a red moon rides on the humps of the low river hills."

Listen to some instrumental music—jazz, classical, or modern—and write down the emotions, colors, images, or scenes which the music brings to mind. (The images do not have to be based on reality. A piece of music may make you think of blue camels or of a green sky.) Then attempt to organize these emotions and images into a stanza or two of free verse.

Alfred, Lord Tennyson

[1809–1892]

As a child growing up in a country parsonage in England, Alfred Tennyson showed two characteristics which remained with him throughout his life: a love of nature and a devotion to poetry. His talent for writing verse was evident at a young age. Before he was fifteen, he had written two verse plays, a 6,000-line narrative poem, and many shorter poems.

Nevertheless, although talent came easy, success as a poet came hard. For years Tennyson had to fight the depressing effects of criticism from reviewers as well as financial problems. More important, he had to fight his own grief after the death in 1833 of his brilliant young friend, Arthur Henry Hallam, who had been his fellow student at Trinity College, Cambridge.

Hallam's death changed the course of Tennyson's life and poetry. For many years after his friend died, Tennyson devoted himself to writing poems telling of his grief and the religious doubts caused by Hallam's death, and of his final resignation and faith. When these poems were published in 1850 under the title *In Memoriam*, they immediately became extremely popular. The book's financial success allowed Tennyson to marry the woman to whom he had been engaged for twelve years. In that same year (1850), Queen Victoria appointed him Poet Laureate of England.

Tennyson had a gift for creating tender, dreamlike lyrics, and an ability to mirror the ideas of his time in characters drawn from legend or his own imagination. These qualities made him so popular in later life that he received honors usually granted to those who had performed unusual public services. He was made a baron in 1883, and took a seat in the House of Lords. When he died, he was given the rare tribute of a funeral in Westminster Abbey in London. Though some of his poetry is shallow and sentimental, both the people and the governments of his time showed good judgment: for his best work, Tennyson ranks among the greatest English poets.

Bugle Song

The following poem appears within "The Princess," a long narrative love poem in which songs are interspersed.

The splendor falls on castle walls
    And snowy summits old in story;
The long light shakes across the lakes,
    And the wild cataract° leaps in glory.
Blow, bugle, blow, set the wild echoes flying,   5
Blow, bugle; answer, echoes, dying, dying, dying.

O, hark, O, hear! how thin and clear,
    And thinner, clearer, farther going!
O, sweet and far from cliff and scar°
    The horns of Elfland faintly blowing!   10
Blow, let us hear the purple glens replying,
Blow, bugle; answer, echoes, dying, dying, dying.

O love, they die in yon rich sky,
    They faint on hill or field or river;
Our echoes roll from soul to soul,   15
    And grow forever and forever.
Blow, bugle, blow, set the wild echoes flying,
And answer, echoes, answer, dying, dying, dying.

4. cataract: a large waterfall. **9. scar:** an isolated or protruding rock or a rocky place on a mountainside.

Meaning and Method

1. What is the setting? What words or phrases in the first two stanzas make the setting seem almost like a fairytale place? What do you think the speaker means by "the splendor" (line 1)?
2. Why might the echoes of the bugle seem to be "the horns of Elfland" (line 10)? How do the "echoes" of the lovers (see lines 15–16) contrast with the echoes of the bugle (see lines 13–14 and the refrain)? Does the speaker seem to feel that love is a weak force? a powerful, magical force?
3. What verbs of action give a sense of the movement of light, water, and sound? What is the effect of the punctuation on the pace of lines 5 and 6? Which line do you read faster? Why?

4. The repetition of the /b/ sound in the refrain gives the effect of the blowing of the bugle. Find several examples of the repetition of sounds or words which give the effect of an echo.

5. Rhyme is a type of repetition which contributes to the musical effect of a poem. In "Bugle Song," not only are there two end rhymes in each stanza, but each stanza contains two lines with internal rhymes (see page 58) as well. For example, *falls* and *walls* in line 1 is an internal rhyme. What other internal rhymes can you find in the poem?

6. Is the tone of the refrain the same as the tone of the preceding lines in each stanza? If not, how does it differ?

Language: Suffixes

Several of the words in "Bugle Song" end with the letters *ing* (for example, *flying, dying, blowing*). These letters are a *suffix*—a set form added at the end of a root to create a new word—which indicate the act or art of doing the action expressed in the root verb.

Some other common suffixes are the following:

(a) *–ation* (b) *–ion* (c) *–ity* (d) *–ly* (e) *–ous*

In a dictionary, look up the meaning of these suffixes. Then give several examples of words in which each suffix is used.

Edgar Allan Poe

In this poem, Poe (see page 86) uses many of the sound-effect techniques of poetry to create an impression of the ringing of four different types of bells.

The Bells

I

Hear the sledges° with the bells—
    Silver bells!
What a world of merriment their melody foretells!
    How they tinkle, tinkle, tinkle,
        In the icy air of night!   5
    While the stars that oversprinkle
    All the heavens, seem to twinkle
        With a crystalline delight;
    Keeping time, time, time,
    In a sort of Runic° rhyme,   10
To the tintinnabulation° that so musically wells
    From the bells, bells, bells, bells
        Bells, bells, bells—
    From the jingling and the tinkling of the bells.

II

Hear the mellow wedding bells—   15
    Golden bells!
What a world of happiness their harmony foretells!
    Through the balmy air of night
    How they ring out their delight!—
        From the molten-golden notes,   20
        And all in tune,
    What a liquid ditty floats
To the turtledove° that listens, while she gloats
        On the moon!
    Oh, from out the sounding cells,   25

1. **sledges:** sleighs. 10. **Runic** (roo′nik): magical or strange; runes were letters in an ancient Germanic alphabet. 11. **tintinnabulation** (tin′ti·nab′yə·lā′shən): a tinkling sound. 23. **turtledove:** a symbol of love.

What a gush of euphony° voluminously° wells!
    How it swells!
    How it dwells
    On the Future!—how it tells
    Of the rapture that impels   30
    To the swinging and the ringing
    Of the bells, bells, bells—
  Of the bells, bells, bells, bells,
    Bells, bells, bells—
To the rhyming and the chiming of the bells!   35

III

    Hear the loud alarum° bells—
      Brazen° bells!
What a tale of terror, now, their turbulency tells!
    In the startled ear of night
    How they scream out their affright!   40
      Too much horrified to speak,
      They can only shriek, shriek,
      Out of tune,
In a clamorous appealing to the mercy of the fire,
In a mad expostulation° with the deaf and frantic fire,   45
    Leaping higher, higher, higher,
    With a desperate desire,
  And a resolute endeavor
  Now—now to sit, or never,
By the side of the pale-faced moon.   50
    Oh, the bells, bells, bells!
    What a tale their terror tells
    Of Despair!
How they clang, and clash, and roar!
    What a horror they outpour   55
On the bosom of the palpitating° air!
    Yet the ear, it fully knows,
      By the twanging,
      And the clanging,
    How the danger ebbs and flows;   60

26. **euphony** (yo͞o′fə·nē): pleasant or smooth sound; **voluminously** (və·lo͞o′mə·nəs·lē): in great quantity. 36. **alarum:** alarm. 37. **brazen:** made of brass; also, impudent. 45. **expostulation:** earnest argument; attempt to dissuade. 56. **palpitating:** trembling.

Yet the ear distinctly tells,
    In the jangling,
    And the wrangling,
How the danger sinks and swells,
By the sinking or the swelling in the anger of the bells—   65
      Of the bells—
   Of the bells, bells, bells, bells,
     Bells, bells, bells—
In the clamor and the clanging of the bells!

IV

  Hear the tolling of the bells—   70
    Iron bells!
What a world of solemn thought their monody° compels!
    In the silence of the night
    How we shiver with affright
At the melancholy menace of their tone!   75
    For every sound that floats
    From the rust within their throats
     Is a groan.
    And the people—ah, the people—
    They that dwell up in the steeple,   80
     All alone,
    And who tolling, tolling, tolling,
     In that muffled monotone,
    Feel a glory in so rolling
     On the human heart a stone—   85
They are neither man nor woman—
They are neither brute nor human—
     They are Ghouls:°
    And their king it is who tolls:
    And he rolls, rolls, rolls,   90
     Rolls
  A paean° from the bells!
And his merry bosom swells
    With the paean of the bells!

---

72. monody (mon′ə·dē): music in which only one person sings. In ancient Greek times, a monody was a funeral song and therefore suggests sorrow. 88. Ghouls: (gōōlz): imaginary creatures who were supposed to rob graves and eat corpses. 92. paean (pē′ən): a song of praise or joy.

And he dances, and he yells;   95
Keeping time, time, time,
In a sort of Runic rhyme,
    To the paean of the bells:
     Of the bells:
Keeping time, time, time,   100
In a sort of Runic rhyme,
    To the throbbing of the bells—
Of the bells, bells, bells—
    To the sobbing of the bells:
Keeping time, time, time,   105
    As he knells,° knells, knells,
In a happy Runic rhyme,
    To the tolling of the bells,
Of the bells, bells, bells, bells,
     Bells, bells, bells—   110
To the moaning and the groaning of the bells.

106. knells: tolls mournfully.

Meaning and Method

1. What connotations do the metals assigned to each bell have? Is each metal suitable for the task it must perform?
2. What words in Part II give the impression of harmony? What words in Part III give the impression of disharmony? Are these impressions suitable for the types of bells described?
3. Notice that each of the bells is heard at night. Compare and contrast the descriptions of night in each part of the poem. How do these descriptions help to create the mood of each part?
4. *Onomatopoeia* (on′ə·mat′·ə·pē·ə) is a term used to describe a word which imitates a sound. For example, *tinkling* is an onomatopoeic word because it imitates the sound made by a certain type of bell. Find two other onomatopoeic words in lines 58–59.
5. How do (a) the /m/ sounds in part I, (b) the /l/ sounds in part II, and (c) the /k/ sounds in part III contribute to the mood of each part? In your answers, comment on whether the sounds involved are harsh or soft, pleasant or unpleasant.
6. Some readers interpret this poem as a delineation of the four ages of man: childhood, youth, adulthood, and old age. What aspects of "The Bells" might support such a view? Which do not?

Sidney Lanier *

In 1860, less than a year before the Civil War began, eighteen-year-old Sidney Lanier was graduated from Oglethorpe College in Georgia with plans for a musical career. His subsequent four years of service in the Confederate Army must have made these plans seem like wild dreams. Near the end of the war, he was captured by the Union forces and sent to a Federal prison, where he contracted tuberculosis, the disease which was to cause his death in 1881 when he was thirty-nine.

Nevertheless, despite the war and the handicap of his health, Lanier lived to have careers in both music and literature. In 1873, he became first flutist with the Peabody Orchestra in Baltimore. Because he was interested in the musical qualities of words as well as of notes, he began to write verse in which he experimented with sound patterns. His first book of poems was published in 1877, and two years later, he was appointed lecturer in English at Johns Hopkins University. The lectures he prepared for his classes were the basis of his critical book, *The Science of English Verse*, in which he attempted to show the close relationship between poetry and music.

The best of Lanier's poems are rich in rhythmic effects and sound effects. These effects are used not only for their purely musical qualities, but also to convey sense impressions, usually of physical actions. For example, in one of his poems, "The Song of the Chattahoochee," Lanier tried to imitate the changes in pace of a river which flows from northern to southern Georgia. In most of his poems, his strong appreciation of nature and his sense that man's natural dignity is often warped by society also come across clearly.

* **Lanier** (lə·ni(ə)r′). The name is of French derivation, but the Southern pronunciation differs from the French lə·nyä′.

Song of the Chattahoochee

Out of the hills of Habersham,°
Down the valleys of Hall,°
I hurry amain° to reach the plain,
Run the rapid and leap the fall,

1, 2. **Habersham, Hall:** counties in Georgia. 3. **amain:** with great haste.

Split at the rock and together again,   5
Accept my bed, or° narrow or wide,
And flee from folly on every side
With a lover's pain to attain the plain
    Far from the hills of Habersham,
    Far from the valleys of Hall.   10

All down the hills of Habersham,
    All through the valleys of Hall,
The rushes cried *Abide, abide,*
The willful waterweeds held me thrall,°
The laving laurel° turned my tide,   15
The ferns and the fondling° grass said *Stay,*
The dewberry dipped for to work delay,
And the little reeds sighed *Abide, abide,*
    Here in the hills of Habersham,
    Here in the valleys of Hall.   20

High o'er the hills of Habersham,
    Veiling the valleys of Hall,
The hickory told me manifold°
Fair tales of shade, the poplar tall
Wrought me her shadowy self to hold,   25
The chestnut, the oak, the walnut, the pine,
Overleaning, with flickering meaning and sign,
Said, *Pass not, so cold, these manifold*
    Deep shades of the hills of Habersham,
    These glades in the valleys of Hall.   30

And oft in the hills of Habersham,
    And oft in the valleys of Hall,
The white quartz shone, and the smooth brook-stone
Did bar me of passage with friendly brawl,
And many a luminous jewel lone   35
—Crystals clear or a-cloud with mist,
Ruby, garnet, and amethyst—
Made lures with the lights of streaming stone

6. or: either. **14. thrall** (thrôl): enslaved. **15. laving** (lā'ving) **laurel:** mountain laurel, which often grows along the banks of rivers, and sometimes grows into stream beds. *Laving* means "washing." **16. fondling:** caressing. **23. manifold:** many and varied.

In the clefts of the hills of Habersham,
In the beds of the valleys of Hall.   40

But oh, not the hills of Habersham,
    And oh, not the valleys of Hall
Avail: I am fain for° to water the plain.
Downward the voices of Duty call—
Downward, to toil and be mixed with the main,°   45
The dry fields burn, and the mills are to turn,
And a myriad° flowers mortally yearn,
And the lordly main from beyond the plain
    Calls o'er the hills of Habersham,
    Calls through the valleys of Hall.   50

43. fain for: compelled. **45. main:** the sea. **47. a myriad** (mir′ē·əd): composed of a very large indefinite number; innumerable.

Meaning and Method

1. Reread the second, third, and fourth stanzas. How do the plants that grow near the river, the trees in the hills, and the stones try to keep the river from reaching the plain? In your answer, explain what the following phrases or clauses mean: (a) "Fair tales of shade" (line 24); (b) "the poplar tall/Wrought me her shadowy self to hold" (lines 24–25); (c) "Overleaning, with flickering meaning and sign" (line 27).

2. What is the attitude of the river toward the plain? toward the hills and valleys it must leave? Give reasons for your answers.

3. Although the poem is about a river, the poet may also be trying to communicate to people some thoughts about pleasure and duty. Which does he feel is more important? Why?

4. The poem gives the effect of a river moving both quickly and slowly. How do lines 1–8 contribute to the effect of a rushing river? How do lines 13–18 give the effect of slower movement? (Read the lines aloud before you answer.)

5. What are the variations in the refrain at the beginning and end of each stanza? When do the variations reflect the movement of the river?

Composition

Imagine that you are a tree, a house, a mountain, a flower, a cloud, a baseball, or some other inanimate object. Write a short composition from the point of view of that object in which you describe your feelings about the world and your place in it.

Alfred, Lord Tennyson

A poem written to mourn the death of a specific person is called an *elegy*. The elegy may emphasize grief at this individual death, or it may treat the death as an occasion to lament the passing of beauty and life in general. Most elegies are long, formal poems of a meditative nature. However, they can also be short lyrics, as is this poem which Tennyson (see page 119) wrote after the death of his friend, Arthur Henry Hallam.

Break, Break, Break

Break, break, break
    On thy cold grey stones, O Sea!
And I would that my tongue could utter
    The thoughts that arise in me.

O, well for the fisherman's boy,   5
    That he shouts with his sister at play!
O, well for the sailor lad,
    That he sings in his boat on the bay!

And the stately ships go on
    To their haven° under the hill;   10
But O for the touch of a vanished hand,
    And the sound of a voice that is still!

Break, break, break,
    At the foot of thy crags, O Sea!
But the tender grace of a day that is dead   15
    Will never come back to me.

10. **haven**: a port; also, a shelter or safe place.

Meaning and Method

1. Does the physical setting of the poem reflect the speaker's grief? In your answer, comment particularly on the connotations of *cold grey stones* (line 2).

2. Why are the sounds made by the fisherman's children and the sailor lad disturbing to the speaker? How does his situation differ from theirs? In your answer, discuss lines 3–4 and 11–12. Why does the speaker envy the "stately ships" (lines 9–10)?
3. Does the speaker mourn a specific person only, or does he mourn the loss of his youth as well? Is "a day that is dead" (line 15) one day only or is it an era or period of his life that has passed?
4. In lines 1–2 and 13–14, the speaker points out that the sea continually breaks against the rocks. How is the "breaking" of the sea different from the "breaking" of a human life—that is, dying? Do you think that the speaker envies the sea for being eternal? Why or why not?
5. Would the line *Break on thy cold grey stones, O Sea* have had the same effect as the repetition of *break, break, break* in lines 1–2? In your answer, note whether one version would be read faster or slower than the other, and if so, why.

Birago Diop

Diop, an African poet and story teller, was born in Dakar in Senegal, Africa. After studying in France, he eventually became chief veterinary surgeon for the Upper Volta.

The following poem was translated from the French.

Forefathers

Listen more often to things rather than beings.
Hear the fire's voice,
Hear the voice of water.
In the wind hear the sobbing of the trees,
It is our forefathers breathing.   5

The dead are not gone forever.
They are in the paling shadows
And in the darkening shadows.
The dead are not beneath the ground,
They are in the rustling tree,   10
In the murmuring wood,
In the still water,
In the flowing water,
In the lonely place, in the crowd;
The dead are not dead.   15

Listen more often to things rather than beings.
Hear the fire's voice.
Hear the voice of water.
In the wind hear the sobbing of the trees.
It is the breathing of our forefathers   20
Who are not gone, not beneath the ground,
Not dead.

The dead are not gone forever.
They are in a woman's breast,

"Forefathers" by Birago Diop from *An African Treasury*, edited by Langston Hughes, copyright © 1960 by Langston Hughes. Reprinted by permission of Harold Ober Associates Incorporated.

A child's crying, a glowing ember.   25
The dead are not beneath the earth,
They are in the flickering fire,
In the weeping plant, the groaning rock,
The wooded place, the home.
The dead are not dead.   30

Listen more often to things rather than beings.
Hear the fire's voice,
Hear the voice of water.
In the wind hear the sobbing of the trees.
It is the breath of our forefathers.   35

Meaning and Method

1. What is the difference between *things* and *beings* (lines 1 and 16)?
   Why does the speaker want us to listen to *things?*
2. What is the main theme of this poem? Find several examples in which
   the poet uses repetition and personification to emphasize this theme.
   Does the speaker seem sure of his beliefs? Explain.

Robert Burns

A biographical sketch of Robert Burns appears on page 98.

My Heart's in the Highlands

My heart's in the Highlands,° my heart is not here,
My heart's in the Highlands a-chasing the deer,
A-chasing the wild deer and following the roe°—
My heart's in the Highlands, wherever I go!

Farewell to the Highlands, farewell to the North,   5
The birthplace of valor, the country of worth!
Wherever I wander, wherever I rove,
The hills of the Highlands forever I love.

Farewell to the mountains high covered with snow,
Farewell to the straths° and green valleys below,   10
Farewell to the forests and wild-hanging woods,
Farewell to the torrents and loud-pouring floods!

My heart's in the Highlands, my heart is not here,
My heart's in the Highlands a-chasing the deer,
A-chasing the wild deer and following the roe—   15
My heart's in the Highlands, wherever I go!

1. **Highlands:** a mountainous area of Scotland. **3. roe:** a small, graceful deer.
10. **straths:** river courses.

Meaning and Method

1. What are the qualities or characteristics of the life to which the speaker is saying farewell? Why does he love the Highlands?
2. In every line of this poem, there are two types of metric feet: iambic and anapestic. An *anapest* contains two unaccented syllables followed by one accented syllable (as in a·na·PEST).

   In the second stanza, scan each line and point out the iambic and anapestic feet. You will see that there are three anapests to every iamb in each line. Considering the fact that anapests are often used to give an impression of lightness and swiftness—they were once described as "swift anapests"—try to explain why their use is appropriate in this poem.

William Butler Yeats

A biographical sketch of William Butler Yeats appears on page 114.

The Lake Isle of Innisfree *

I will arise and go now, and go to Innisfree,
And a small cabin build there, of clay and wattles° made:
Nine bean-rows will I have there, a hive for the honeybee,
    And live alone in the bee-loud glade.

And I shall have some peace there, for peace comes dropping slow,   5
Dropping from the veils of the morning to where the cricket sings;
There midnight's all a glimmer, and noon a purple glow,
    And evening full of the linnet's° wings.

I will arise and go now, for always night and day
I hear lake water lapping with low sounds by the shore;   10
While I stand on the roadway, or on the pavements gray,
    I hear it in the deep heart's core.

---

* **Innisfree:** an island near Sligo, which Yeats visited as a child. **2. wattles:** twigs and flexible rods woven together. **8. linnet:** a songbird.

Meaning and Method

1. Where is the speaker at the time he is thinking about Innisfree? How do you know?
2. What does the speaker hope to find at Innisfree? Why can he not find this quality in his present surroundings? Why is it appropriate that Innisfree is an island?
3. Is life in Innisfree fast-moving? slow? businesslike? dreamlike? How do the long lines emphasize the atmosphere of Innisfree? (Read the poem aloud before you answer.)
4. What sounds of Innisfree does the speaker remember? Are they soothing or irritating? What effect does the poet's constant repetition of /l/ and /s/ sounds create or emphasize?

5. In lines 7 and 8, the speaker describes midnight, noon, and evening. What words in his descriptions differ from ones you might expect? What impression or atmosphere do these descriptions emphasize?
6. In this poem, would you say the speaker's tone is nostalgic? melancholy? full of anticipation? Explain.

Composition

Describe a place which you once enjoyed and to which you would like to return. Try, like Yeats, to use specific details which show why you are attracted to this place.

John Masefield
[1878–1967]

From the ages of thirteen through seventeen, John Masefield served in the British merchant marine. Although he then left the sea to spend two years in New York City doing odd jobs and went on to become a professional writer, his days at sea left an enduring mark on his memory, as many of his poems show.

Masefield's vivid recollection of life at sea won much praise when his first collection of poems, *Saltwater Ballads*, was published in 1902. Encouraged by the response to the book, he began to try a variety of other types of writing. During his long life, he wrote newspaper articles, novels, short stories, verse plays, essays, and autobiographical sketches as well as verse. Yet he continued to be most admired for his poems—particularly his long narrative poems—and, in 1930, he was appointed Poet Laureate of England.

Sea Fever

I must go down to the seas again, to the lonely sea and the sky,
And all I ask is a tall ship and a star to steer her by,
And the wheel's kick and the wind's song and the white sail's shaking,
And a gray mist on the sea's face and a gray dawn breaking.

I must go down to the seas again, for the call of the running tide   5
Is a wild call and a clear call that may not be denied;
And all I ask is a windy day with the white clouds flying,
And the flung spray and the blown spume,° and the sea gulls crying.

I must go down to the seas again to the vagrant° gypsy life.
To the gull's way and the whale's way where the wind's like a whetted
      knife;   10
And all I ask is a merry yarn from a laughing fellow-rover,
And quiet sleep and a sweet dream when the long trick's° over.

8. **spume** (spyo͞om): foam. 9. **vagrant** (vā'grənt): wandering. 12. **trick:** a turn of duty at the helm.

Meaning and Method

1. Is sea fever in this poem similar to spring fever—that is, a feeling of listlessness and restlessness? Why or why not?
2. What is it about life at sea that attracts the speaker? How powerful is the attraction?
3. The "long trick" in line 12 may be interpreted not only as a ship's watch, but as life itself. Keeping this second, symbolic meaning in mind, do you think that the speaker indicates in line 12 that he expects to feel satisfied when his life is over? something else? Explain.
4. Which images in the first stanza convey the effect of the "lonely sea" (line 1)? Which images in the second stanza convey the effect of a "wild" sea?
5. Masefield uses sound patterns to give the effect of rough and wind-blown waters. For example, in lines 3, 7, and 10, he repeats the /w/ sound to create the impression of windiness. Where in the first stanza does he repeat the /k/ sound? What effect do you think he was trying to achieve by this repetition?
6. Masefield uses rhythm to convey the rising and falling motion of the waves. He achieves this effect by grouping stressed and unstressed syllables together, as in line 3: And the WHEEL'S KICK and the WIND'S SONG and the WHITE SAIL'S SHAKing. Does he use the same method in line 4? line 7? line 10? Explain.

Composition and Discussion

In a discussion, compare and contrast the ideal life of the speaker in "Sea Fever" with that of the speaker in "My Heart's in the Highlands." How do their desired lives differ? How do the poems differ in tone? Support your points by citing specific quotations from the text.

Karl Shapiro

Karl Shapiro was so interested in becoming a poet that he left the University of Virginia in 1933, after one year of study, to devote his time to reading and writing poetry. Two years later, his first book of verse was printed at his own expense. The book aroused no interest; it was not even reviewed.

In 1937, the twenty-four-year-old Shapiro decided to return to college. This time, he chose Johns Hopkins University in Baltimore, his birthplace. However, financial difficulties and then the outbreak of the Second World War interrupted his college career permanently.

From 1942 until the end of the war, when Shapiro was stationed with the army in the Pacific, he concentrated again on his poems. His fiancée in the United States, to whom he sent his finished work, edited and collected the poems. By the end of the war, three more books of his verse had been published in the United States. These books met a very different fate from that of his first. Each was reprinted several times, and the second one, V-*Letter*, was awarded the Pulitzer prize for poetry in 1945.

Shapiro's first two wartime volumes made vivid reading because of what one critic called his "interest in his immediate surroundings," and because of his ironic but deeply concerned approach to modern life. The poems in those volumes, and some of his later poems, were admired for "the accuracy and sensitivity of his observation," and for what the poet Babette Deutsch called the "prominence of feeling."

In his third wartime book, *Essay On Rime*, Shapiro used a very different approach. This book severely criticized modern poetry, which Shapiro felt was "in decline" because it did not deal with the problems which confront individuals in the modern world. In several critical volumes, and in his subsequent books of verse, he has continued to discuss what he feels are the problems and failures of poets and poetry in the modern age.

Travelogue for Exiles

Many times in the course of history people have been forced to leave their native countries because of conquest or persecution. Often they have been refused permission by other countries to settle.

In the year this poem was written—1942—and for several years previously, the Jews of Europe, who faced extermination by Hitler and the German Nazis if they stayed in their own countries, were the people who found that they were unwanted.

Look and remember. Look upon this sky;
Look deep and deep into the sea-clean air,
The unconfined, the terminus° of prayer.
Speak now and speak into the hallowed dome.
What do you hear? What does the sky reply?   5
The heavens are taken: this is not your home.

Look and remember. Look upon this sea;
Look down and down into the tireless tide.
What of a life below, a life inside,
A tomb, a cradle in the curly foam?   10
The waves arise; sea-wind and sea agree
The waters are taken: this is not your home.

Look and remember. Look upon this land,
Far, far across the factories and the grass.
Surely, there, surely, they will let you pass.   15
Speak then and ask the forest and the loam.°
What do you hear? What does the land command?
The earth is taken: this is not your home.

3. **terminus:** end, goal, final destination. 16. **loam:** a type of soil.

Meaning and Method

1. To whom is the speaker talking? With what words or phrases—and for what reason—does the speaker make sky, sea, and land attractive to his listeners? Why might a "tomb" (line 10) be considered desirable by these people?
2. A travelogue is a lecture or film usually describing the beauties of a specific country or countries—often with the hope of attracting tourists. Considering this, explain why the title is ironic.
3. How does the poet show the cruelty of the world's attitude toward the exiles? Are only human beings cruel, or is the cruelty far more extensive? Explain.
4. What is the main theme of the poem? How does the refrain emphasize the theme?

Richard Wilbur

The poems of Richard Wilbur are primarily about what he calls the "things of this world"—fire trucks, a hole in the floor, grasshoppers, snow, laundry hanging on a line, the constant changes of light and shadow.

Wilbur precisely observes the details which make up these things, and expresses his observations in forceful, vivid metaphors. Perhaps the poet, who was born in 1921, inherited his gift for observation from his father, an artist. Perhaps his boyhood in rural New Jersey, where he grew up, in his words, "among woods, orchards, corn-fields, horses, hogs, cows, and haywagons," gave him an opportunity to develop his powers of observation. Probably his study of literature at Amherst College, from which he received a B.A. in 1942, also played a part in his development as a poet.

However, it was not until after he had served in the Second World War that Wilbur seriously began to study literature and to write poetry. His first book of verse was published in 1947, the same year in which he received an M.A. in English literature from Harvard University. These two almost simultaneous events established the direction his life would take, for since 1947, he has pursued the complementary careers of writer and teacher of literature at Harvard, Wellesley College, and Wesleyan University.

Wilbur is a careful craftsman who works on his poems until he feels that every word is right. The resulting verse has been awarded numerous honors, including the Pulitzer prize for poetry in 1962. One critic called his poems "brilliant, strong in structure, and elegant." And a fellow poet, Richard Eberhart, has said of him: "One of the best poets of his generation, Richard Wilbur has imagined excellence, and he has created it."

Boy at the Window

Seeing the snowman standing all alone
In dusk and cold is more than he can bear.
The small boy weeps to hear the wind prepare
A night of gnashings and enormous moan.

His tearful sight can hardly reach to where   5
The pale-faced figure with bitumen° eyes
Returns him such a god-forsaken stare
As outcast Adam gave to Paradise.

The man of snow is, nonetheless, content,
Having no wish to go inside and die.   10
Still, he is moved to see the youngster cry.
Though frozen water is his element,
He melts enough to drop from one soft eye
A trickle of the purest rain, a tear
For the child at the bright pane surrounded by   15
Such warmth, such light, such love, and so much fear.

6. **bitumen** (bi·too′mən) : soft coal.

Meaning and Method

1. Why does the small boy weep? How does "his tearful sight" affect his ability to see the snowman clearly—literrally and figuratively—in lines 5–8?
2. Is the stare in line 6–8 described from the point of view of the snowman or the boy? Considering the allusion in line 8, explain why the phrase *god-forsaken* in line 7 is particularly appropriate.
3. Why is the snowman content? Why does he shed a tear watching the child?
4. Why, despite the warmth, light, and love of his home, does fear surround the child? Is fear usually a part of childhood? Explain.
5. Does the poet pity or sympathize with the boy? Does he think that childhood is a wonderful period of life? a terrible one? both?

Archibald MacLeish

Although many American poets in recent times have voiced strong political views, only one—Archibald MacLeish—has actually achieved a measure of political power. MacLeish's first step to power occurred in an unlikely way when, in 1939, he was appointed Librarian of Congress by President Franklin D. Roosevelt. In that position, the many-faceted MacLeish—a man well known for his strong liberal views—quickly became a member of Roosevelt's "inner cabinet" of advisors. While still Librarian of Congress, he was appointed to two important propaganda posts: (1) Director of the Office of Facts and Figures; and (2) at the start of World War II, Assistant Director of the Office of War Information. From 1944 until Roosevelt's death in 1945, he was an Assistant Secretary of State. After the war ended, he helped in the establishment of UNESCO (United Nations Educational, Scientific, and Cultural Organization).

MacLeish was born in Illinois in 1892, and was graduated from Yale College and Harvard Law School. Although he practiced law for a time, poetry was his major interest, and in 1923, he sailed with his family to France in order to devote himself to writing poetry. "I date the beginning of my life from 1923," he later said about this decision. By the time he returned to the United States at the end of the Twenties, he had had published approximately one volume of verse a year, most of which was highly praised. In 1933, he won a Pulitzer Prize for his long verse narrative, *Conquistador*.

In 1948, after nine years of public service, he decided once again to devote most of his time to poetry. He therefore accepted an appointment as Boylston Professor of Rhetoric and Oratory at Harvard University which gave him a good deal of free time to write. The time was well spent. By 1958, he had received two more Pulitzer Prizes—one for his *Collected Poems: 1919–1952*, and one for his verse play, *J.B.*, which was produced on Broadway in 1958.

Eleven

And summer mornings the mute child, rebellious,
Stupid, hating the words, the meanings, hating
The Think now, Think, the O but Think! would leave
On tiptoe the three chairs on the verandah
And crossing tree by tree the empty lawn   5
Push back the shed door and upon the sill
Stand pressing out the sunlight from his eyes
And enter and with outstretched fingers feel
The grindstone and behind it the bare wall
And turn and in the corner on the cool   10
Hard earth sit listening. And one by one,
Out of the dazzled shadow in the room,
The shapes would gather, the brown plowshare, spades,
Mattocks,° the polished helves° of picks, a scythe
Hung from the rafters, shovels, slender tines°   15
Glinting across the curve of sickles—shapes
Older than men were, the wise tools, the iron
Friendly with earth. And sit there, quiet, breathing
The harsh dry smell of withered bulbs, the faint
Odor of dung, the silence. And outside   20
Beyond the half-shut door the blind leaves
And the corn moving. And at noon would come,
Up from the garden, his hard crooked hands
Gentle with earth, his knees still earth-stained, smelling
Of sun, of summer, the old gardener, like   25
A priest, like an interpreter, and bend
Over his baskets.
                        And they would not speak:
They would say nothing. And the child would sit there
Happy as though he had no name, as though
He had been no one: like a leaf, a stem,   30
Like a root growing—

14. mattocks: tools resembling pickaxes; **helves:** handles. **15. tines:** spikes or prongs, as of a fork.

Meaning and Method

1. Considering the capitalization in line 3, define the tone of voice in which the boy is spoken to. Why does he leave the house "on tiptoe" (line 4)? Why might he want to be "mute" (line 1) by choice?

2. Why does the boy prefer the shed to the house? What does he feel, see, and smell in the shed? How does the description in lines 6–22 indicate that the boy responds in other ways than with words?

3. In what sense might tools be "wise" (see lines 17–18)? Does "men" (line 17) refer to mankind or to the adults the boy knows?

4. What is the old gardener like? Why, in your opinion, is he compared to an "interpreter" (line 26)? How does the gardener's attitude toward the boy differ from that of the people in the house? Why is it appropriate that the boy's only visible friend should be a cultivator who nurtures mute, tender, growing things?

5. The people in the house expect the boy to think and to speak as other children normally do. Do you think that the similes in lines 30–31 suggest that the boy is developing, but in a way that the people in the house do not understand? that he is not really "stupid" (line 2), but simply different? Explain.

6. Why is the dash at the end of the last line more appropriate to the meaning than a period would have been? In your answer, comment on the connotations of *growing* and on whether the dash is generally used to indicate a stop or a continuation.

7. What is the attitude of the poet toward the boy? Is he sympathetic? unsympathetic? How do you know?

Gwendolyn Brooks

Most people like "tidy answers," Miss Brooks once wrote. She, however, is interested in "all the little ravelings" which others prefer to snip off or ignore. In her poems, she gently but precisely probes the often complex and knotty reactions of people to life.

Miss Brooks, who was born in Topeka, Kansas, in 1917, was taken to Chicago shortly after her birth and has lived in that city ever since. She was educated at Wilson Junior College in Chicago, and then, after working for several years, settled down to be a wife, a mother, and a writer.

Her poetic talents, craftsmanship, and special brand of insight have been widely recognized—most notably by the Pulitzer Prize she received for her book of verse, *Annie Allen* (1949), one of several volumes of poetry. Miss Brooks is also the author of a novel, *Maud Martha*, a partly autobiographical account of a sensitive Negro girl growing up in Chicago.

One Wants a Teller in a Time Like This

One wants a Teller in a time like this.

One's not a man, one's not a woman grown,
To bear enormous business all alone.

One cannot walk this winding street with pride,
Straight-shouldered, tranquil-eyed,   5
Knowing one knows for sure the way back home.
One wonders if one has a home.

One is not certain if or why or how.
One wants a Teller now:—

Put on your rubbers and you won't catch cold.   10
Here's hell, there's heaven. Go to Sunday School.
Be patient, time brings all good things—(and cool

Strong balm to calm the burning at the brain?) —
Behold,
Love's true, and triumphs; and God's actual.   15

Meaning and Method

1. How do you know from the poem that the speaker is a teen-ager? Why does she or he want to be given orders and advice by a Teller—an adult? Do most teen-agers you know share this attitude?
2. What problems or uncertainties does the speaker mention in lines 2–3 and 7–8? How do these contrast with what she or he imagines is the approach to life of adults? Do you think this view is realistic?
3. What is the "burning at the brain" (line 13)? Why are the italicized statements in lines 10–15 calming to the speaker?
4. The basic meter of this poem is iambic pentameter (see page 62). Count or scan the number and arrangement of stressed and unstressed syllables in lines 1–2 to prove this statement. How do lines 5, 7, 9, and 14 depart from the basic meter? Do you think these departures are used for emphasis? to reflect the meanings of the words? for some other reason?

Composition and Discussion

1. Are Tellers desirable in some situations and not in others? Is a combination of freedom and authority desirable? If so, which do you want more of—freedom or authority? Discuss.
2. Write a composition in which you explore a situation in which you would—or would not—like a Teller. Use concrete illustrations so that your reading audience will clearly understand why you feel, or do not feel, that a Teller would be desirable.

Countee Cullen
[1903–1946]

By the time he was twenty-six, Countee Cullen, who was raised in a Harlem parsonage, was one of the most admired Negro poets in America. He first attracted public attention with *Color*, a book of verse which was published in 1925, the year he was graduated from New York University. Two years later—after he had received a master's degree from Harvard University—two more collections of his poems, *Copper Sun* and *The Ballad of the Brown Girl*, were published. In 1929, his fourth book of verse, *The Black Christ*, appeared. After this volume, however, Cullen turned to nonpoetic projects, and, except for two volumes of verse for children, had few poems published in the remaining years of his life.

Cullen's poems are generally lyric poems which reveal a sensitive temperament, a romantic outlook, and a devotion to traditional verse forms. Because of this latter quality, some critics complain that his poems are too "academic." Others, such as the poet James Weldon Johnson, feel that "the old forms come from his hands filled with fresh beauty."

Tableau *

Locked arm in arm they cross the way,
   The black boy and the white,
The golden splendor of the day,
   The sable pride of night.

From lowered blinds the dark folk stare,   5
   And here the fair folk talk,
Indignant that these two should dare
   In unison to walk.

Oblivious to look and word
   They pass, and see no wonder   10
That lightning brilliant as a sword
   Should blaze the path of thunder.

* **Tableau** (tab'lō) : *here*, a striking scene.

"Tableau" from *On These I Stand* by Countee Cullen, copyright 1925 by Harper & Brothers, renewed 1953 by Ida M. Cullen. Reprinted by permission of Harper & Row, Publishers.

Meaning and Method

1. Why are both the "dark folk" and the "fair folk" indignant at the sight of the two boys? Do the boys feel their friendship is strange? What words or phrases indicate the harmony of their relationship?
2. Which metaphors in lines 3–4 and 11–12 refer to the black boy? to the white boy? Are the color contrasts between the boys carried through in the metaphors? Do the connotations of the metaphors suggest that the black and white boy each have admirable qualities? that they complement each other? Explain.

Composition

In a short composition, explain either why you think it is (a) desirable to have friends from the same background as your own, (b) from different backgrounds, or (c) from a mixture of both.

Ralph Hodgson
[1871–1962]

Hodgson, who has written what one critic called "a few of the truest poems of our time," believed that knowledge of a poet's personality was not necessary for understanding a good poem. During his lifetime he was a literary "mystery man," noted for his reticence about his private life and for a small number of published poems full of verbal and rhythmic magic.

Some facts, however, are known about him. He was born in Yorkshire, England, and as a young man worked on newspapers and magazines. Later, he was a breeder of bull terriers, an occupation that reflected his strong love of animals. Between 1907 and 1917, six thin volumes of his poems were published. He then lapsed into what seemed to be a permanent poetic silence. In 1925, he went to Japan and spent fourteen years there as a lecturer on English literature.

In 1939, just before the outbreak of the Second World War, he came to the United States with his American wife. For more than two decades, he lived on a farm near Minerva, Ohio, where part of his land was set aside as a bird sanctuary. The atmosphere must have been pleasing, for in the early 1940's, the poems of Hodgson again appeared in print.

Time, You Old Gypsy Man

Time, you old gypsy man,
  Will you not stay,
Put up your caravan°
  Just for one day?

All things I'll give you   5
  Will you be my guest,
Bells for your jennet°

3. caravan: cart used by gypsies; also, a procession of wagons. In this context, it suggests that time is being followed by a procession of days. **7. jennet** (jen'it): a horse or a female donkey.

Of silver the best,
Goldsmiths shall beat you
A great golden ring,   10
Peacocks shall bow to you,
Little boys sing,
Oh, and sweet girls will
Festoon° you with may.°
Time, you old gypsy,   15
Why hasten away?

Last week in Babylon,°
Last night in Rome,°
Morning, and in the crush
Under Paul's° dome;   20
Under Paul's dial
You tighten your rein—
Only a moment,
And off once again;
Off to some city   25
Now blind in the womb,
Off to another
Ere that's in the tomb.

Time, you old gypsy man,
Will you not stay,   30
Put up your caravan
Just for one day?

14. **festoon** (fes·to͞on′): decorate; **may:** hawthorn blossoms. 17. **Babylon:** (bab′ə·lən): the capital city of the once powerful, ancient Near Eastern empire of Babylonia. 18. **Rome:** a reference to Rome when it was the center of the Roman Empire. 20. **Paul's:** St. Paul's Cathedral, London.

Meaning and Method

1. Hodgson personifies Time as an old gypsy man. What are the connotations of *old gypsy man?* Do you think the comparison of Time to a gypsy driving a caravan is appropriate? Why or why not?
2. How and why does the speaker try to slow Time down?
3. What is the attitude of Time toward great civilizations? How is this attitude emphasized by lines 25–28?
4. Considering the examples given in the third stanza, do you think that the speaker seriously hopes to stop Time? Do you think the bribes of the second stanza would appeal to a gypsy? to Time?

5. Is the speaker's attitude toward Time admiring? envious? playful? cajoling? familiar? sad? two or more of these? something else?
6. Apostrophe (see *Glossary*) is sometimes used with personification, as in this poem, where the combination establishes a personal relationship between the speaker and Time. Do you think that this personal relationship between man and time actually exists? Why or why not?
7. Most of the lines start with stressed syllables. The result is a rhythm which gives the effect of a horse being urged on and moving fast. How does this rhythm indicate Time's answer? How does the repetition of the original question at the end of the poem also indicate Time's answer?

Language: Abstract and Concrete Words

Time is an abstraction. That is, it is a word that denotes an idea rather than something concrete, something you can see or touch. Because abstract ideas are hard to grasp and understand, concrete illustrations are often used to make them meaningful. In literature, concrete illustrations usually take the form of metaphors, similes, or personification.

Examples of concrete illustrations of Time by other writers are the following:

> "Time is but the stream I go a-fishing in"—Henry David Thoreau
> "Time is a sandpile we run our fingers in"—Carl Sandburg
> "Time, that aged nurse"—John Keats
> "Time is the rider that breaks youth"—George Herbert
> "Time, you old thief"—Leigh Hunt
> "Noiseless foot of Time"—William Shakespeare

In a simile or metaphor, or an apostrophe or personification, express what time is for you. Try to use concrete comparisons that your classmates would understand.

Carl Sandburg

The experiences which lead to poetry are often fairly commonplace ones, as Sandburg (see page 116) shows in this poem.

Limited

I am riding on a limited express, one of the crack trains of the nation.
Hurtling across the prairie into blue haze and dark air go fifteen
    all-steel coaches holding a thousand people.
(All the coaches shall be scrap and rust and all the men and women
    laughing in the diners and sleepers shall pass to ashes.)
I ask a man in the smoker where he is going and he answers: "Omaha."

Meaning and Method

1. In lines 1–2, the speaker describes a powerful train with "fifteen all-steel coaches." What phrases or clauses in line 3 indicate that he feels that the power of the train and the happiness of the people on it are illusions?
2. Do you think that the title and the phrase *limited express* in the first line have more than one meaning?
3. What is the final destination of all the people on the train, according to the speaker? Considering this, why is the answer of the man in the smoker ironic?

"Limited" from *Chicago Poems* by Carl Sandburg, copyright 1916 by Holt, Rinehart and Winston, Inc., copyright 1944 by Carl Sandburg. Reprinted by permission of the publisher.

Arna Bontemps

A biographical sketch of Arna Bontemps appears on page 112.

Blight

I have seen a lovely thing
Stark before a whip of weather:
The tree that was so wistful after spring
Beating barren twigs together.

The birds that came there one by one,   5
The sensuous leaves that used to sway
And whisper there at night, all are gone,
Each has vanished in its way.

And this whip is on my heart;
There is no sound that it allows,   10
No little song that I may start
But I hear the beating of dead boughs.

Meaning and Method

1. What is the emotional state or mood of the speaker? What season described in the poem best reflects this state? How do the effects of this season contrast with those of spring, described in lines 3, 5, 6, and 7?
2. From the images in lines 5–8, what do you think the speaker feels he has lost?
3. What is the meaning of the word *blight?* Do you think the title refers only to the blight of a tree, or to the speaker's situation as well? In your opinion, might "Blight" be a poem about growing old? losing a love? an insult? all of these? something else? Give reasons for your answers. Can you think of any reason why the cause of the speaker's mood was not directly mentioned?
4. Bontemps uses sounds which emphasize the meanings of his words. For example, in line 2, the repetition of the /w/ sound in "whip of weather" helps create the effect of whipping or lashing. How do the /b/ and /t/ sounds in line 4 and the /s/ sounds in lines 6–8 emphasize the meanings of these lines? Which of these sounds are harsh? which soft or gentle?

"Blight" by Arna Bontemps. Reprinted by permission of Harold Ober Associates Incorporated.

Rolfe Humphries

[1894–1969]

Humphries, who was born in Philadelphia in 1894 and raised in northern Pennsylvania, had the unusual experience of learning to read Latin before he learned to read English. His instructor was his father, a high school Latin teacher. Eventually, the son also became a Latin teacher, as well as a fine verse translator of great Latin classics, including Vergil's *Aeneid* and Ovid's *Metamorphoses*.

Another major interest of Humphries—sports—was also influenced by his father. The elder Humphries had been a professional baseball player for a few years, and he communicated his love for that game and others to his son. Baseball, football, hiking, and fishing were particularly enjoyed by young Humphries, and some of these have been subjects for poems he later wrote.

Polo Grounds *

Time is of the essence. This is a highly skilled
And beautiful mystery. Three or four seconds only
From the time that Riggs connects till he reaches first,
And in those seconds Jurges goes to his right,
Comes up with the ball, tosses to Witek at second   5
For the force on Reese, Witek to Mize at first,
In time for the out—a double play.

(Red Barber° crescendo.° Crowd noises, obbligato;°
Scattered staccatos° from the peanut boys,

---

* **Polo Grounds:** once the home stadium of the New York Giants (now the San Francisco Giants). It has been torn down since the game Humphries describes was played. The Brooklyn Dodgers, the opposing team, are now the Los Angeles Dodgers. Dodger players mentioned are Riggs, Reese, and Camilli. Giant players mentioned are Jurges, Witek, Mize, Hubbell, Ott, Danning, Werber, and Adams. **8. Red Barber:** a sportscaster. **8–9. crescendo** (krə·shen′dō); **obbligato; staccatos:** musical terms, meaning respectively: a gradual increase in loudness; an accompaniment necessary to the performance of a musical composition; sounds marked by abrupt, short emphasis.

"Polo Grounds" by Rolfe Humphries first appeared in *The New Yorker*, copyright 1942 by Rolfe Humphries. It was also published by Charles Scribner's Sons in *Poems Collected and New* and by Indiana University Press in *Collected Poems of Rolfe Humphries*. Reprinted by permission of Charles Scribner's Sons and Indiana University Press.

Loud in the lull, as the teams are changing sides) . . .   10
Hubbell takes the sign, nods, pumps, delivers—
A foul into the stands. Dunn° takes a new ball out,
Hands it to Danning, who throws it down to Werber;
Werber takes off his glove, rubs the ball briefly,
Tosses it over to Hub, who goes to the rosin bag,   15
Takes the sign from Danning, pumps, delivers—
Low, outside, ball three. Danning goes to the mound,
Says something to Hub, Dunn brushes off the plate,
Adams starts throwing in the Giant bullpen,
Hub takes the sign from Danning, pumps, delivers,   20
Camilli gets hold of it, a *long* fly to the outfield,
Ott goes back, back, back, against the wall, gets under it,
Pounds his glove, and takes it for the out.
That's all for the Dodgers. . . .

Time is of the essence. The rhythms break,   25
More varied and subtle than any kind of dance;
Movement speeds up or lags. The ball goes out
In sharp and angular drives, or long, slow arcs,
Comes in again controlled and under aim;
The players wheel or spurt, race, stoop, slide, halt,   30
Shift imperceptibly to new positions,
Watching the signs, according to the batter,
The score, the inning. Time is of the essence.

Time is of the essence. Remember Terry?
Remember Stonewall Jackson, Lindstrom, Frisch,   35
When they were good? Remember Long George Kelly?
Remember John McGraw and Benny Kauff?
Remember Bridwell, Tenney, Merkel, Youngs,
Chief Meyers, Big Jeff Tesreau, Shufflin' Phil?
Remember Matthewson, and Ames, and Donlin,   40
Buck Ewing, Rusie, Smiling Mickey Welch?
Remember a left-handed catcher named Jack Humphries,
Who sometimes played the outfield, in '83?

Time is of the essence. The shadow moves
From the plate to the box, from the box to second base,   45

12. **Dunn:** the home-plate umpire.

From second to the outfield, to the bleachers.
Time is of the essence. The crowd and players
Are the same age always, but the man in the crowd
Is older every season. Come on, play ball!

Meaning and Method

1. In lines 1 and 2, the speaker says, "This is a highly skilled/And beautiful mystery." What does the word *this* refer to? Is *mystery* a word commonly used about this subject?
2. The speaker uses several musical terms in lines 8–9, and compares the game to a dance in lines 25–31. What do these lines indicate about his attitude toward the spectators? toward the players? What does the speaker's comparison of music and dance to a baseball game indicate about him? Do you think the comparisons are reasonable or farfetched?
3. When *Time is of the essence* is used in lines 1 and 25, it means that timing is important. Does it have the same meaning in lines 33, 34, 44, and 47? Why or why not?
4. Why does the poet mention the names of former Giant stars in the fourth stanza? Why, in your opinion, does he include the name of his father, a minor baseball player, in the list?
5. Is the speaker enthusiastic, appreciative, or disturbed about time and life? How does the last line sum up, change, or clarify the speaker's thoughts? How are baseball, time, and life alike according to the poem?
6. In the first and second stanzas, the speaker imitates the manner of speech of a baseball broadcaster. What purpose might the poet have had for this imitation?
7. With what images appealing to the sense of sight does the poet create the impression of the movement of the game?

Language: Jargon

In "Polo Grounds," Humphries uses some expressions whose meanings when applied to baseball are quite different than their meanings in another context. These expressions are examples of baseball jargon—the specialized vocabulary used by people who are connected with a certain profession. Among the examples of baseball jargon in the poem are:

1. Hubbell *takes the sign*, nods, *pumps, delivers* (line 11)
2. *Low, outside, ball three* (line 17)
3. *takes it for the out* (line 23)

Keeping the game of baseball in mind, try to explain how you think these terms developed. Then give several examples of other types of jargon—jargon used by sailors, lawyers, policemen, disk jockeys, etc.

Composition

1. After breaking down the procedure into sequence, write a step-by-step explanation of baseball, football, skiing, basketball, volleyball, or some other sport for someone who does not know the game. Explain any "special" terms.

2. Go to a baseball game, ice-skating rink, bowyling alley, etc., and then write a description of the game or sport you watched or participated in. Be sure to use specific details to describe the setting, the type of people present, and the mood. If you wish, you may concentrate on describing one particular incident.

William Shakespeare

In 1598, Frances Meres, a contemporary of Shakespeare, referred to him as the "mellifluous and honey-tongued Shakespeare" and said that among his notable poems were the "sugared sonnets" which he passed "among his private friends."

It was not until eleven years later, in 1609, that a collection of 154 of these sonnets—fourteen-line rhymed poems usually written in iambic pentameter—were finally published. Most of the sonnets were addressed to a male friend, and others were addressed to a dark-haired woman, who has come to be called the "dark lady of the sonnets."

For biographical information on Shakespeare, see page 94.

Sonnet 18—Shall I Compare Thee to a Summer's Day?

Shall I compare thee to a summer's day?
Thou art more lovely and more temperate:
Rough winds do shake the darling buds of May,
And summer's lease hath all too short a date;
Sometimes too hot the eye of heaven shines,   5
And often is his gold complexion dimmed;
And every fair from fair sometime declines,
By chance or nature's changing course untrimmed:°
But thy eternal summer shall not fade
Nor lose possession of that fair thou ow'st;°   10
Nor shall Death brag thou wander'st in his shade,
When in eternal lines to time thou grow'st:
So long as men can breathe, or eyes can see,
So long lives this, and this gives life to thee.

8. untrimmed: shorn of its beauty. **10. ow'st:** abbreviation of ownest; that is, own or possess.

Meaning and Method

1. In the first eight lines, the speaker compares his love to summer. What faults does summer have that the speaker's love, by implication, does not have? In your answer, explain what "the eye of heaven" (line 5) is, and how the first use of *fair* in line 7 differs from the second use.

2. What does the speaker mean when he talks of his love's "eternal summer" (line 9)? Why is this type of summer superior to that of nature? Can his love achieve this state on her own, or only because of the poet? In your answer, explain the phrase *eternal lines* (line 12), and the meaning of lines 11–12 in general.

3. A *paradox* is a statement that appears self-contradictory, but actually contains some truth or insight. For example, "the pen is mightier than the sword" is a paradox. What is the paradox in lines 13–14? Why might it contain some truth?

4. Is this poem about love? time? death? the immortality of poetry? all of these? Explain.

5. This sonnet, like most others, is written in iambic pentameter (see page 62). In order to keep the meter, Shakespeare used several abbreviations. For example, line 10 is a perfect iambic pentameter line, scanned (see *Glossary*) as follows: Nor LOSE/posSES/sion OF/that FAIR/thou OW'ST. If *ow'st* had been written out as *ownest*, however, there would have been an extra syllable in the line (Nor LOSE/posSES/sion OF/that FAIR/thou OWN/est). Scan line 11 and show that the abbreviation of *wanderest* (*wander'st*) was used for the sake of the meter.

John Crowe Ransom

When Ransom was a young man, most people judged poetry simply. If a poem awakened a pleasurable emotion, it was good; if not, it was bad. Ransom, who became a critic and a teacher, did much to change our way of reading poetry. He insisted that a reader should make an effort to understand the poem before judging it. The way to understanding, in Ransom's opinion, is to concentrate on the words of a poem and the technical devices used to communicate meaning. Ransom was largely responsible for teaching modern readers that the first question after reading a poem should not be, "Do I like or dislike this poem?" but, "What is the poet trying to say?"

Ransom, who was born in Pulaski, Tennessee in 1888, was graduated with a B.A. from Vanderbilt University in 1909. The next year, he went as a Rhodes Scholar to Christ College, Oxford, from which he received a second B.A. in 1913. From 1914 to 1937, except for two years in the Army, he taught in the English department at Vanderbilt. In 1937, he became professor of English at Kenyon College in Ohio, and there founded and edited *The Kenyon Review*, a quarterly publication which is generally considered to be one of the finest literary magazines in America.

Although Ransom's activities as critic, teacher, and editor have sometimes overshadowed his contributions as a poet, he is nevertheless recognized as one of the most distinctive and distinguished of modern poets. His style is witty and ironic, and his poems often reveal strong emotions by indirect means.

Blue Girls

Twirling your blue skirts, travelling the sward°
Under the towers of your seminary,°
Go listen to your teachers old and contrary
Without believing a word.

Tie the white fillets° then about your lustrous hair   5
And think no more of what will come to pass

1. **sward** (swôrd): thick lawn. 2. **seminary:** *here,* a girls' academy. 5. **fillets:** hair ribbons.

Than bluebirds that go walking on the grass
And chattering on the air.

Practice your beauty, blue girls, before it fail;
And I will cry with my loud lips and publish   10
Beauty which all our power shall never establish,
It is so frail.

For I could tell you a story which is true;
I know a lady with a terrible tongue,
Blear eyes fallen from blue,   15
All her perfections tarnished—and yet it is not long
Since she was lovelier than any of you.

Meaning and Method

1. What lines or phrases indicate that the speaker is probably a visitor to the school, and is much older than the girls to whom he speaks? What characteristics of the girls does he notice? Are these characteristics associated with youth?
2. Why are the girls described as "blue"? What are the similarities in appearance and action between the girls and the bluebirds with which they are compared in lines 6–8?
3. What do you think is meant by the phrase "practice your beauty" (line 9)? How will beauty eventually "fail" (line 9)? Why does the speaker feel that beauty is "frail" (line 12)? What is his advice to the young girls?
4. How does the example of the "lady with a terrible tongue" in lines 14–17 emphasize the speaker's advice to the young girls? In your answer, explain the phrase "blear eyes fallen from blue" (line 15).
5. There are two dominant tones in the poem. One is a tone of admiration and pleasure. What is the other tone? Which lines are characterized by each of these tones?

Ecclesiastes (3:1–8)

from *THE KING JAMES BIBLE*

Countless generations of writers in many countries have been inspired and influenced by the Bible. Many great works of literature are elaborations or reinterpretations of biblical stories. Moreover, the style and rhythm of biblical writing have left a strong imprint on language. The rolling cadences of the English translation of the Bible known as the King James Version (first published in 1611) were constantly echoed in English prose, and are still heard today in speeches—particularly sermons. The biblical use of balanced sentences, rhetorical repetition, and metaphorical language has also been widely imitated.

The following selection from the King James Version was taken from the Book of Ecclesiastes (3:1–8). Like other poems in the Bible, it is unrhymed and nonmetrical, but strongly rhythmic.

For every thing there is a season, and a time to every purpose under heaven:
    A time to be born, and a time to die;
        A time to plant, and a time to pluck up that which is planted;

    A time to kill, and a time to heal;
        A time to break down, and a time to build up;   5

    A time to weep, and a time to laugh;
        A time to mourn, and a time to dance;

    A time to cast away stones, and a time to gather stones together;
        A time to embrace, and a time to refrain from embracing;

    A time to get, and a time to lose;   10
        A time to keep, and a time to cast away;

    A time to rend,° and a time to sew;
        A time to keep silence, and a time to speak;

    A time to love, and a time to hate;
        A time of war, and a time of peace.   15

12. **rend:** tear.

Meaning and Method

1. In each line a phrase about a positive quality, such as love, is followed by a phrase about a negative quality, such as hate, or vice-versa. What does this balanced structure reveal about the speaker's view of life? Do you think he is pessimistic?

2. A rhythmic effect is created in this poem by the repetition of sounds and words and by similarly structured sentences. Find several examples in the poem in which these techniques are used.

Language: Words and Expressions from the Bible

A number of frequently used words and expressions are derived from names in the Bible. Among these are the following:

1. philistine
2. wisdom of Solomon
3. a Jezebel
4. as strong as Samson
5. the patience of Job
6. good Samaritan

Use an unabridged dictionary to learn the meaning and origin of each of these words or expressions. Then give a sentence for each one.

Composition

One of the most famous biblical quotations is engraved both on a statue in a park near the United Nations headquarters and on the stairs across from the U.N. Secretariat building. It is:

> They shall beat their swords into plowshares,
> and their spears into pruning hooks;
> nation shall not lift up sword against nation,
> neither shall they learn war any more.
> (Isaiah 2:4)

Write a composition in which you explain (a) the meaning of this passage and (b) why it is an appropriate motto for the United Nations.

Henry Timrod

Henry Timrod, whose Civil War poems earned for him the title "laureate of the Confederacy," was born in 1828 in Charleston, South Carolina. He was deeply devoted to the Southern way of life and, when war came, to the Southern cause. In 1861, he enlisted in the Confederate Army, but was soon discharged because of ill health. For the rest of the war, he worked first as a newspaper correspondent and then as an editor in Columbia, South Carolina. During this time, he also tried to contribute to the Confederacy by writing poems which appealed to Southern patriotism.

When Columbia was captured and burned early in 1865, Timrod suffered psychologically and physically. Two years after that event, he died of malnutrition and tuberculosis. Despite his troubles, however, he had never lost his loyalty to the Confederacy. To the end, he was a man emotionally attached to a lost cause but able to write about it in verse which exhibits classical restraint. After his death, the poems he wrote during and after the Civil War were collected and published in *Poems* (1873).

Ode on the Confederate Dead

Sung at the occasion of decorating the graves of the Confederate dead at Magnolia Cemetery in Charleston, South Carolina, 1867

> Sleep sweetly in your humble graves,
>   Sleep, martyrs of a fallen cause;
> Though yet no marble column craves
>   The pilgrim here to pause.
>
> In seeds of laurel in the earth   5
>   The blossom of your fame is blown,°
> And somewhere, waiting for its birth,
>   The shaft° is in the stone!
>
> Meanwhile, behalf° the tardy years
>   Which keep in trust your storied° tombs,   10

6. **blown:** *here*, blooming. 8. **shaft:** column (for the memorial). 9. **behalf:** in behalf of. 10. **storied:** recorded in legend.

Behold! your sisters bring their tears,
   And these memorial blooms.

Small tributes! but your shades° will smile
   More proudly on these wreaths today,
Than when some cannon-molded pile°   15
   Shall overlook this bay.

Stoop, angels, hither from the skies!
   There is no holier spot of ground
Than where defeated valor lies,
   By mourning beauty crowned!   20

13. shades: *here,* spirits. The word is used to describe figures in Hades, the world of the dead in Greek mythology. **15. cannon-molded pile:** monuments made of melted cannons.

Meaning

1. Why are the graves "humble" (line 1)? Is there a monument over the graves? Will there be one? In your answer, comment on lines 3–4 and 7–8.
2. Why does the speaker use the word *tardy* in line 9? What is meant by lines 9–10?
3. What words or phrases suggest that the dedication of the graves was a ceremony with religious overtones? Why does the speaker think that "no holier spot" than this cemetery exists?
4. In ancient Greek times, laurel was a symbol of victory. Is it an appropriate symbol of this event? Why or why not? What does the use of this symbol in line 5 show about the speaker's attitude toward the Confederate dead?
5. Why, in your opinion, does the speaker think the spirits of the soldiers will prefer the wreaths to a "cannon-molded pile" (see lines 13–16)?

Method

1. An *ode* is a lyric poem usually characterized by loftiness of tone, feeling, and style. Is the title appropriate for this poem? Why or why not?
2. Give several examples of the use of apostrophe (see *Glossary*) in this poem. What does the use of this technique show about the speaker's attitude toward the dead?
3. Read this poem aloud. Can you read it either quickly or slowly? Why or why not? In your answer, point out how punctuation and line breaks

contribute to the pace at which you read the poem. Is the pace appropriate to the subject? Explain.

4. The poet attempts to create an atmosphere of peace and calm. One method he uses to do this is the repetition of certain sounds. Where does the /s/ sound occur in the first two stanzas, and how does it contribute to this atmosphere? What other sound in the first two stanzas contributes to this effect? Explain.

Walt Whitman

[1819–1892]

In "Song of Myself," one of the poems that changed the course of American poetry, Whitman identified himself as "Walt Whitman, an American, one of the roughs."

This "rough," the son of a carpenter, was born in New York on Long Island, and grew up in Brooklyn. After a formal education consisting of five years in grammar school, he was apprenticed to a printer. In his twenties, he successively became a printer, a political reporter, and a newspaper editor who passionately editorialized against slavery.

Whitman at this time occasionally wrote verse in conventional meters and on conventional themes. It was not until 1848, when he left New York for the first time in his life and went to New Orleans, that he began to discover his true poetic voice and vision. On his trip to and from New Orleans, he traveled on the Mississippi River and the Great Lakes and saw the richness, variety, and expanse of America. After he returned to Brooklyn, he began to write poems celebrating America and his own life—poems written in a free verse as unfettered as his own spirit and the country he wrote about. When the first edition of his book of poems, *Leaves of Grass* (for which he set the type), was published in 1855, it was clear that a new voice had arrived in American poetry.

Many people who read the book disliked the new voice. Whittier, for example, threw the book into the fire. Some important literary figures, however, saw its value. Among these was the poet-essayist Ralph Waldo Emerson, who wrote to Whitman that his book was "the most extraordinary piece of wit and wisdom that America has yet contributed."

Leaves of Grass represented a major contribution to American poetry for two reasons. The first is in style: Whitman showed that free verse, which had been used infrequently before his time, was uniquely suited to the natural rhythms of American speech. The second is in subject: Instead of imitating English literary subjects, Whitman wrote about his country and himself. In addition, he introduced strong emotional tones into American poetry. *Leaves of Grass* began with the enthusiastic "I celebrate myself. . . ." Whitman's poems are filled with joyful appreciation of the wonders of the world, and sorrow and horror at the ravages of war.

167

Beat! Beat! Drums!

Beat! beat! drums!—blow! bugles! blow!
Through the windows—through doors—burst like a ruthless force,
Into the solemn church, and scatter the congregation,
Into the school where the scholar is studying;
Leave not the bridegroom quiet—no happiness must he have now
    with his bride,   5
Nor the peaceful farmer any peace, ploughing his field or gathering
    his grain,
So fierce you whirr and pound you drums—so shrill you bugles blow.

Beat! beat! drums!—blow! bugles! blow!
Over the traffic of cities—over the rumble of wheels in the streets;
Are beds prepared for sleepers at night in the houses? no sleepers
    must sleep in those beds,   10
No bargainers' bargains by day—no brokers or speculators—would
    they continue?
Would the talkers be talking? would the singer attempt to sing?
Would the lawyer rise in the court to state his case before the judge?
Then rattle quicker, heavier drums—you bugles wilder blow.

Beat! beat! drums!—blow! bugles! blow!   15
Make no parley—stop for no expostulation,°
Mind not the timid—mind not the weeper or prayer,
Mind not the old man beseeching the young man,
Let not the child's voice be heard, nor the mother's entreaties,
Make even the trestles° to shake the dead where they lie awaiting the
    hearses,   20
So strong you thump O terrible drums—so loud you bugles blow.

16. **expostulation:** earnest argument, usually for protest. 20. **trestles:** beams or
bars supported by four legs, for bearing a platform.

Meaning and Method

1. What words or sounds in the first stanza help convey an impression
   of the disruption the bugles and drums—that is, war—will cause? How
   does the punctuation add to this impression of disruption?
2. What words describing the bugles and drums convey an impression of
   their harshness or disharmony? Which words are onomatopoeic?

3. Apostrophe is used in this poem to create the impression that the speaker is giving orders to the bugles and drums. Give several examples of this technique, and explain whether the harsh effect of the poem would have been the same if, for example, *Make no parley* had been changed to *You should not make a parley*.
4. Does the speaker really want the bugles and drums to do what he is telling them to do? What is his attitude toward war?
5. Is the tone of the poem one of resentment? anger? sorrow? horror? exultation? Consider the tempo or pace of the poem before you answer. (For example, a sorrowful poem would probably be read slowly, a happy poem rapidly.)

Composition

Whitman's approach to human life is shown in his statement, "For my enemy is dead, a man divine as myself is dead." Explain what Whitman means by this statement. Then tell why you think one's attitude toward the enemy should be like or unlike Whitman's. Give a specific example of an "enemy"—real or imaginary—to support your points.

Wallace Stevens
[1879–1955]

Many who read the subtle, imaginative poems of Wallace Stevens are surprised when they learn that their author worked for almost forty years as a successful insurance company executive in Hartford, Connecticut. Stevens himself professed not to understand people's surprise. "I prefer to think I'm just a man," he said, "not a poet part time, businessman the rest."

Nevertheless, although the poet and businessman were one man, the poet decidedly did not write poems in the style of business letters. In his poems, the reader is told very little information directly. Instead, he is confronted by a series of impressions and seemingly unrelated statements or images. The reader can only understand the connections if he reacts to the poems, if he contributes his own interest and imagination.

The poems of Stevens, who was born in Reading, Pennsylvania, and educated at Harvard College and New York Law School, are also quite remote from the everyday world of a businessman in subject matter. His early poems were notable for their exotic, sensuous atmosphere and for their fantasy quality. Although his later poems often commented indirectly on life in the modern world, the fantasy quality remained prominent in his work.

Disillusionment of Ten O'Clock

> The houses are haunted
> By white nightgowns.
> None are green,
> Or purple with green rings,
> Or green with yellow rings,   5
> Or yellow with blue rings.
> None of them are strange,
> With socks of lace
> And beaded ceintures.°

9. **ceintures** (san·torz′): belts.

People are not going   10
To dream of baboons and periwinkles.°
Only, here and there, an old sailor,
Drunk and asleep in his boots,
Catches tigers
In red weather.   15

11. periwinkles: either a cone-shaped salt-water snail marked by spiral bands, or a plant with blue or white flowers (also called myrtle).

Meaning and Method

1. How does the speaker give the impression in the first two lines that people without distinctive personalities live in the houses? How does he expand this impression in lines 3–9? In your answers, comment particularly on the use of the word *haunted* (line 1) and on line 7.
2. What type of dreams do "baboons and periwinkles" (line 11) symbolize? Why can the sailor dream the type of dream that the people in white nightgowns are "not going / To dream" (lines 10–11)? How did his past life probably differ from theirs? How does his present life differ?
3. Why is the speaker disillusioned at the thought of many people going to bed at ten o'clock in white nightgowns? How does the use of such words as *ceintures* and *periwinkles* show how the speaker differs from the people he describes?
4. Notice the poet's use of colors throughout the poem. If white in this context suggests emptiness and lack of imagination, what does *green* or *purple with yellow rings* suggest? What are the connotations of the phrase *red weather* (line 15)?
5. Describe the kind of life led by the people in this poem. How does the poet's use of free verse—rather than metered verse—reflect his attitude toward this type of life?

Rudyard Kipling

The following poem was written in 1897 to celebrate the Diamond Jubilee, or sixtieth anniversary, of Queen Victoria's reign. See page 43 for a biography of Kipling.

Recessional *

God of our fathers, known of old,
    Lord of our far-flung battle line,
Beneath whose awful° Hand we hold
    Dominion over palm and pine—
Lord God of Hosts,° be with us yet,   5
Lest we forget—lest we forget!

The tumult and the shouting dies;
    The captains and the kings depart:
Still stands Thine ancient sacrifice,
    An humble and a contrite heart.   10
Lord God of Hosts, be with us yet,
Lest we forget—lest we forget!

Far-called, our navies melt away;
    On dune and headland° sinks the fire:
Lo, all our pomp of yesterday   15
    Is one with Nineveh and Tyre:°
Judge of the Nations, spare us yet,
Lest we forget—lest we forget!

---

* **Recessional:** a hymn sung at the end of a service, as the choir and clergy leave the church. **3. awful:** *here,* full of awe. **5. Lord God of Hosts:** In the Old Testament, *host* is used to mean a multitude or an army. The phrase *Lord God of Hosts* occurs in the psalms (see Psalm 80, for example), and emphasizes God's power. **14. headland:** a cliff which projects from the water. **16. Nineveh** (nin′ə·və) **and Tyre** (tīr): ancient cities in the Middle East which were once centers of powerful civilizations. Old Testament prophets predicted their doom for not heeding God's commandments. Nineveh no longer exists; Tyre is now a small town in Lebanon.

"Recessional" from *Rudyard Kipling's Verse: Definitive Edition.* Reprinted by permission of Doubleday & Company, Inc., Mrs. George Bambridge, and The Macmillan Company of Canada Limited.

If, drunk with sight of power, we loose
    Wild tongues that have not Thee in awe,   20
Such boastings as the Gentiles° use,
    Or lesser breeds without the Law°—
Lord God of Hosts, be with us yet,
Lest we forget—lest we forget!

For heathen heart that puts her trust   25
    In reeking tube and iron shard,°
All valiant dust that builds on dust,
    And guarding, calls not Thee to guard,
For frantic boast and foolish word—
Thy Mercy on Thy People,° Lord!   30

21. Gentiles: used here in the Biblical sense to mean "outsiders"—those not of the "chosen people." **22. the Law:** usually a reference to the law of Moses; that is, the Hebrew law of the Old Testament. Here, however, it is also used to mean the Law of the British, who ruled much of the world. **26. reeking . . . shard:** *here*, a gun which has just fired a bullet. A shard is a fragment. The term is usually used to describe broken pieces of pottery dug up when uncovering ancient towns and cities which were buried by sand and other natural forces after they were destroyed or abandoned. **30. Thy People:** in the Bible, the Jews; *here*, the British who, says Kipling, identified themselves with the "chosen people."

Meaning and Method

1. Why does the phrase *palm and pine* (line 4) indicate the extent of the British Empire?

2. The poem was written when the power of the British Empire was at its height. Why then does the speaker make the statements in lines 13–16? Is he making a prophecy about the future? If so, on what does he base it? Why do you think he uses the title "Recessional"?

3. According to lines 25–26, what should people not trust in? What should they trust instead? Considering the theme of the poem, why are the connotations of the word *shard* (line 26) appropriate?

4. What is the speaker afraid the British people will "forget" (see the last two lines of the first four stanzas)? What is he asking of God in lines 29–30? Do you think the poem is primarily addressed to God or to the British people? Why?

Language: Multiple Meanings of Words

If you look in a dictionary, you will see that most words have more than one meaning. Among these words with multiple meanings is the word *awful*. Most of us use the word *awful* to mean "exceedingly bad and unpleasant," or "ugly." The word *awful*, however, may also mean "inspiring awe" or "causing fear or dread." It is these last two meanings that are used in line 3 of "Recessional."

The word *wild* (line 20) has more than ten meanings. Look in a dictionary and explain which definition of *wild* is used in each of the following sentences.

1. She was *wild* with anxiety.
2. The crowd went *wild* when he hit the home run.
3. You're behaving like a *wild* man.
4. That fuchsia and chartreuse dress is *wild*.
5. That was a *wild* punch.

Karl Shapiro

A biographical sketch of Karl Shapiro appears on page 138.

Manhole Covers

The beauty of manhole covers—what of that?
Like medals struck by a great savage khan,
Like Mayan calendar stones,° unliftable, indecipherable,
Not like old electrum,° chased and scored,°
Mottoed and sculptured to a turn,   5
But notched and whelked and pocked and smashed
With the great company names:
Gentle Bethlehem, smiling United States.
This rustproof artifact° of my street,
Long after roads are melted away, will lie   10
Sidewise in the grave of the iron-old world,
Bitten at the edges,
Strong with its cryptic American,
Its dated beauty.

3. **Mayan calendar stones:** The Mayans, a Central American Indian tribe, had an advanced civilization before the white man arrived. Among the signs of civilization was the development of a calendar which was carved on enormous stones. 4. **electrum:** a gold-silver alloy used in making coins; **chased and scored:** When coins are chased, they are stamped and embossed; when they are scored, they are given a grooved edge around the rim. 9. **artifact:** anything made by human labor; usually refers to something found after a civilization has vanished.

Meaning and Method

1. Which of the following characteristics of manhole covers contribute to their "beauty": (a) their weight; (b) the depth and roughness of the indentations in the metal; (c) the power of the companies which produced them? Support your answers with quotations from the text.
2. Does the comparison of manhole covers to "medals struck by a great savage khan" (line 2) and to "Mayan calendar stones" (line 3) indicate that the poet thinks that American civilization, of which the manhole covers are a symbol, is extremely powerful? that it, like these other civilizations, will inevitably pass away? both? something else? What words or phrases in lines 13–14 might be used to equate American civilization with Mayan civilization?

3. In lines 4–7, the poet compares the way coins are made to the way manhole covers are made. Which method requires more power? In your answer, comment on the meanings and connotations of the verbs used in the descriptions.

4. Bethlehem and U.S. Steel are two of the largest steel producers in the United States. Considering this, explain why you think line 8 is meant seriously or is humorously ironic. In your answer, comment on the connotations of the name *Bethlehem*.

Composition

Begin your composition with Shapiro's first line, but substitute for "manhole covers" an object which most people would think of as useful but not beautiful. For example, you can choose to describe a screwdriver, a wrench, a shopping cart, a toothbrush, a refrigerator, or a can-opener. Use words which will indicate the way the object looks and feels to you.

Emily Dickinson
[1830–1886]

Although biographers know many facts about Emily Dickinson, they understand very little about her. They know that she led an outwardly simple life—that she never married, and, except for two trips with her father, spent all her life in Amherst, Massachusetts. They know that she studied for a year at Mount Holyoke Seminary (now College), a few miles from her home. Despite many guesses, however, no biographer understands exactly why she began to withdraw from the world in her early twenties or why she eventually became a recluse who was never seen outside her house.

Even in her self-imposed isolation, however, she did have friends. She communicated with them by writing letters in which she sometimes enclosed poems. While she was alive, no one knew how much poetry she had written. It was only after her death that almost 1,800 poems and fragments of poems were found. Some of these were on sheets of paper tied neatly together. Others were on scraps of paper, such as the backs of invitations or brown paper bags.

The richness of the poems themselves was even more amazing than their existence. Startlingly precise, imaginative metaphors reflected Emily Dickinson's unique way of looking at the world. Most people watching a bee, for example, would see an insect with yellow and black stripes. Emily Dickinson, however, saw that, "Bees are black, with gilt surcingles,/Buccaneers of buzz. . . ." * Her use of the word *surcingles*, which means "belts" or "bands," shows how conscious she was of the sound qualities of words. *Surcingles*, unlike *belts*, repeats the /i/ sound of *gilt* and suggests something which glitters. *Buccaneers of buzz* reflects the sound a bee makes and gives an imaginative but accurate description. (Bees, like buccaneers or pirates, do "board" flowers and "steal" pollen.)

Emily Dickinson generally used connotative words to compress a large or complex idea into a small space. As a result, her poems, like her life, often seem simple on the surface but are sometimes difficult to understand.

---

* From "Bees are Black, with gilt Surcingles" by Emily Dickinson from *The Poems of Emily Dickinson*, edited by Thomas H. Johnson, Cambridge, Mass.: The Belknap Press of Harvard University Press, copyright 1951, 1955 by The President and Fellows of Harvard College. Reprinted by permission of the publishers and the Trustees of Amherst College.

I Never Saw a Moor

I never saw a moor,
   I never saw the sea;
Yet know I how the heather looks,
   And what a wave must be.

I never spoke with God,   5
   Nor visited in heaven;
Yet certain am I of the spot
   As if the chart were given.

1. **moor** (mo͞or): *chiefly British*; a wasteland covered with low shrubs, such as heather. Usually a deserted, lonely place.

Meaning and Method

1. Why might the speaker know what a moor and the sea looked like though she had never seen either one? Is she certain about the existence of Heaven for the same reasons?
2. What characteristics of the speaker's faith are emphasized by (a) the shortness of the poem and of the lines, and (b) the use of simple one- and two-syllable words?
3. How would you characterize the speaker from these eight lines?

Language: Inverted Word Order

In normal word order, the subject is generally followed by the verb and then by the object of the sentence. In poetry, however, the normal word order is occasionally reversed, or inverted, to produce a desired effect. For example, in line 3, the normal order would have been: "Yet I know how the heather looks." The poet, however, inverted the subject and verb ("know I") in order to emphasize the word *know* and indicate the certainty she felt about her knowledge.

What would the normal word order of line 7 have been? What word is emphasized by the poetic inversion?

From *Poems by Emily Dickinson*, edited by Martha Dickinson Bianchi and Alfred Leete Hampson, published by Little, Brown and Company.

The Wind Tapped Like a Tired Man

The wind tapped like a tired man,
And like a host, "Come in,"
I boldly answered; entered then
My residence within

A rapid, footless guest,   5
To offer whom a chair
Were as impossible as hand
A sofa to the air.

No bone had he to bind him,
His speech was like the push   10
Of numerous humming-birds at once
From a superior bush.

His countenance a billow,
His fingers, as he passed,
Let go a music, as of tunes   15
Blown tremulous° in glass.

He visited, still flitting,
Then, like a timid man,
Again he tapped—'twas flurriedly°—
And I became alone.   20

16. **tremulous** (trem′yə·ləs): trembling. 19. **flurriedly**: excitedly, or nervously.

Meaning and Method

1. Does the fact that the speaker personifies the wind—and specifically sees him as a guest—indicate that she is isolated? lonely? sensitive? something else? What other details in the poem help characterize her?
2. Describe in your own words the character of the wind. Support your description by reference to specific details in the poem.
3. What words or phrases make you see or feel the movement of the wind? What sounds in lines 10–12 give you the impression of the sound of the wind? In your answer, tell why the effect of lines 10–12 would change if you substituted *many* for *numerous* (line 11).

From *Poems by Emily Dickinson*, edited by Martha Dickinson Bianchi and Alfred Leete Hampson, published by Little, Brown and Company.

4. The speaker first thinks that the wind taps "like a tired man," but at the end, when he taps again, she comments, "like a timid man." Do you think she changed the word *tired* to *timid* to indicate her disappointment with him? Why or why not?

Composition

Rewrite this poem, opening with the following line: "The wind knocked like an angry man." Make other changes in the poem accordingly. Note how the first verb gives focus to the entire poem.

I'm Nobody!

I'm nobody! Who are you?
Are you nobody, too?
Then there's a pair of us—don't tell!
They'll banish us, you know.

How dreary to be somebody!   5
How public, like a frog
To tell your name the livelong day
To an admiring bog!

Meaning and Method

1. Is the speaker satisfied or dissatisfied at being "nobody?" Does she expect that her readers are like her? unlike her? In your answers, comment on lines 2 and 3.
2. Why should being nobody be kept a secret? Why would telling people about it lead to banishment? In your answers, explain to whom *they* in line 4 refers.
3. What is a "somebody?" What is the speaker's attitude toward somebodies? How do the connotations of *frog* (line 6) and *bog* (line 8) emphasize her attitude?
4. What word or phrase is emphasized by the comma in line 6? Do you pause only because of the comma in your reading of this line, or is the pause necessary to the meaning? Explain.
5. One of the ways in which the poet creates a conversational effect is by addressing the reader directly, as in line 1. Where else in the poem does she use this method? What phrases particularly give the impression of an intimate conversation?
6. What comment on social values does the poem make?

From *Poems by Emily Dickinson*, edited by Martha Dickinson Bianchi and Alfred Leete Hampson, published by Little, Brown and Company.

Edna St. Vincent Millay
[1892–1950]

A passionate desire for new experiences characterized Edna St. Vincent Millay through three phases of her life: as a young girl growing up in Maine, as a student at Vassar College, and as a writer and actress in Greenwich Village. She was proud of her intense approach to life, and defiant about the dangers, as the following poem from her Village days shows:

> My candle burns at both ends;
> It will not last the night;
> But ah, my foes, and oh, my friends—
> It gives a lovely light!

One of the ways in which her "candle" burned fast and bright was in her writing. Her poetic talents matured early. At nineteen, she wrote "Renascence," the long poem with which she first won fame; by the time she was thirty-one, she had won a Pulitzer Prize for poetry. She was, moreover, the most popular poet of her time, because she expressed in her personal lyrics the feelings of a generation of romantic young rebels.

Shortly after the age of thirty, however, both her life and her poetry underwent a striking change. In 1923, she married Eugen Boissevain and moved to the farm in Austerlitz, New York, which was to be her home until her death. Increasingly, her poems became more somber, less devoted to explorations of her own feelings and more to social problems.

Critical response to the change varied. Some critics preferred the romantic lyrics which had made her so popular. Others saw a deepening of her talents in many of her newer poems. Most critics, however, felt that in her best lyrics, old and new, she exhibited both rare talent and rare accomplishment.

Second Fig

Safe upon the solid rock the ugly houses stand:
Come and see my shining palace built upon the sand!

Meaning and Method

1. What are the main contrasts between the sand castle and the houses?
2. Is being safe a positive quality in the speaker's view? Why or why not?
3. Which house represents reality? Which represents imagination? Which does the speaker prefer? Why?
4. Does this poem simply reject something, or does it make a positive assertion about life? neither? Explain.

On Hearing a Symphony of Beethoven *

Sweet sounds, oh, beautiful music, do not cease!
Reject me not into the world again.
With you alone is excellence and peace,
Mankind made plausible, his purpose plain.
Enchanted in your air benign and shrewd,°   5
With limbs a-sprawl and empty faces pale,
The spiteful and the stingy and the rude
Sleep like the scullions in the fairy-tale.°
This moment is the best the world can give;
The tranquil blossom on the tortured stem.   10
Reject me not, sweet sounds! oh, let me live,
Till Doom espy° my towers and scatter them,
A city spell-bound under the aging sun,
Music my rampart,° and my only one.

* **Beethoven** (bā'tō·vən): Ludwig van Beethoven (1770–1827), a German composer. **5. shrewd:** *here,* difficult to surpass. **8. scullions . . . tale:** scullions once denoted kitchen servants, or base, contemptible people in general. In the fairy tale "The Sleeping Beauty," the scullions were enchanted by the same spell which made the princess sleep until the arrival of Prince Charming. **12. espy:** catch sight of. **14. rampart:** a bulwark or defense.

Meaning and Method

1. Explain the speaker's statement in line 2. What reasons for her attitude toward the world are indirectly suggested by lines 3–4? In your answer, explain how mankind's purpose can be made "plain" (line 4) by music.
2. What qualities in people does music figuratively put to sleep according to lines 5–8? Why are the faces of people who are dominated by these qualities "empty" (line 6)? What does the comparison of these people to "scullions" indicate about about the speaker's attitude toward them? What is the meaning of *enchanted* (line 5) in the context of the poem?
3. Considering line 9, explain the meaning of *tortured stem* and *tranquil blossom* (line 10). What paradox (see page 159) is the speaker pointing out?
4. In lines 12–14 of this sonnet, the speaker uses an extended metaphor in which the world created by music is compared to an enchanted city. What words or phrases extend this metaphor?
5. While the music plays, the speaker feels enchanted, as if time had stopped. What word in line 13 indicates that time has not stopped? What does the speaker fear will happen when the music ceases?
6. Throughout the poem, the speaker uses the technique of apostrophe, and talks to the music as if it were human. What words or phrases indicate that she regards the music as a lover?
7. Does the speaker regard listening to music as an escape? relaxation? a deep spiritual experience? something else? Explain.

The Buck in the Snow

White sky, over the hemlocks bowed with snow,
Saw you not at the beginning of evening the antlered buck and his
    doe
Standing in the apple-orchard? I saw them. I saw them suddenly go,
Tails up, with long leaps lovely and slow,
Over the stone-wall into the wood of hemlocks bowed with snow.   5

Now lies he here, his wild blood scalding the snow.

How strange a thing is death, bringing to his knees, bringing to his
    antlers

The buck in the snow.
How strange a thing,—a mile away by now, it may be,
Under the heavy hemlocks that as the moments pass   10
Shift their loads a little, letting fall a feather of snow—
Life, looking out attentive from the eyes of the doe.

Meaning and Method

1. What are the connotations of *white?* Why does the speaker begin by addressing the "white sky"? What else besides the sky is white? Do you think that the emphasis on whiteness increases the shock or horror of the buck's death? Why or why not?
2. Is the speaker's attitude toward the buck and the doe in the first five lines one of indifference? admiration? something else? What words or phrases convey this attitude? Does the repetition of the phrase *I saw them* (line 3) indicate her personal involvement in the scene? her disbelief at what happens? both? something else?
3. What is the speaker's attitude toward the death of the buck? toward death in general? Explain.
4. What contrast does the speaker draw between the hemlocks and the deer in lines 3–5 and 10–12? Can you think of a type of person that the deer might represent? the hemlocks represent? In presenting the contrast, what comment about life may the speaker be making?
5. In your opinion, is the main theme of the poem (a) life and death are unjust, (b) the will to live overcomes the knowledge of death, (c) both, (d) something else? Explain.
6. The poem is divided into three sections. What mood characterizes each? Why does line 6 stand alone?
7. Is there a metric pattern to the poem? If so, how strict is it? How is line length used to complement the thought in lines 4, 5, 7 and 8? (For example, a long line—one with many syllables—may be used to give an impression of heaviness; a short line may be used to give an impression of lightness.)

E. E. Cummings

An innovator, experimenter, and questioner, Edward Estlin Cummings did not take the English language or its grammatical rules for granted. In his poems, he tried to shock his readers into realizing the vitality of our language by breaking rules and making his readers look at words as if they were seeing them for the first time.

For example, he changed nouns and adjectives into adverbs ("green*ly*"), adverbs into adjectives ("never*ish*"), and adjectives into nouns ("much*ness*"). To emphasize meaning, he also changed the normal arrangement of words and separated parts of words. He left out punctuation marks where they were expected, and scattered them, sometimes haphazardly, in unexpected places. Often he arranged words on a page in such a way as to create a picture of what he was describing, and occasionally he used punctuation marks as illustrations.

His best-known typographical innovation was his use of small letters where capital letters were usually used. Instead of beginning a sentence with *When*, Cummings would begin with *when*. Instead of *I*, he would write *i*. When he did use capital letters in his poems, he always used them for a specific purpose. (The same general approach holds for the often strange titles of his books. *CIOPW*, for example, contains *c*harcoal, *i*nk, *o*il, *p*encil, and *w*atercolor illustrations by Cummings, who was an artist as well as a poet.)

Cummings was born in Cambridge, Massachusetts, in 1894. He attended Harvard University—where his father had taught English literature before becoming a Unitarian minister—and earned both a bachelor's and a master's degree there. His later career was foreshadowed by the poems he wrote at Harvard: although their subject matter was traditional and romantic, these poems show the typographical experimentation which was to become his trademark.

When his first volume of poems was published in 1923, Cummings was recognized by some as an important and original talent, and dismissed by others as a novelty. By the time of his death in 1962, however, he was not only accepted as a major figure in modern American poetry, but also was widely considered "the most truly delightful lyric poet in America."

i thank You God

i thank You God for most this amazing
day:for the leaping greenly spirits of trees
and a blue true dream of sky;and for everything
which is natural which is infinite which is yes

(i who have died am alive again today,   5
and this is the sun's birthday;this is the birth
day of life and of love and wings:and of the gay
great happening illimitably earth)

how should tasting touching hearing seeing
breathing any—lifted from the no   10
of all nothing—human merely being
doubt unimaginable You?

(now the ears of my ears awake and
now the eyes of my eyes are opened)

Meaning and Method

1. How does capitalization in line 1 indicate the relative importance of man to God in the speaker's opinion? In your answer, comment on the speaker's statements in lines 11–12.
2. During what season does "this amazing day" occur? Does line 6 indicate that the day is a specific one? Explain.
3. What type of things does the speaker think of as "yes" things (line 4)? Why might the season lead him to think of positive things?
4. What state of mind—and what season—might make someone feel he was dead (see line 5)? How does "this amazing / day" (lines 1–2) change the speaker's attitude toward life? What words or phrases in the first two stanzas particularly express his new feeling?
5. Does the speaker believe in God's existence because he has reasoned the matter out? because of his sensual enjoyment of nature? something else? Explain.
6. What qualities in the speaker does the season bring out, according to the last two lines?

D-re-A-mi-N-gl-Y

D-re-A-mi-N-gl-Y

leaves
(sEe)
locked

in   5

gOLd
after-
gLOw

are

t   10
ReMbLiN
g

, ; : . : ; ,

Meaning and Method

1. Which line tells you that the speaker is talking to someone?
2. What time of day and what time of year are being described? How do you know?
3. Does the capitalization of some letters in D-re-A-mi-N-gl-Y—and the frequent use of hyphens to divide the word—slow you down in reading the word? emphasize the meaning of the word? both? neither? Explain.
4. How does the division of *trembling* and the alternation of capital letters with small letters reflect the meaning of the word?
5. How might the line of punctuation at the end of the poem reflect the movement of the leaves?

maggie and milly and molly and may

maggie and milly and molly and may
went down to the beach(to play one day)

and maggie discovered a shell that sang
so sweetly she couldn't remember her troubles,and

milly befriended a stranded star°   5
whose rays five languid° fingers were;

and molly was chased by a horrible thing
which raced sideways while blowing bubbles:and

may came home with a smooth round stone
as small as a world and as large as alone.   10

For whatever we lose(like a you or a me)
it's always ourselves we find in the sea

5. **star:** starfish. 6. **languid:** lacking in energy or vigor.

Meaning and Method

1. According to the speaker in the last line of the poem, "it's always ourselves we find in the sea." With this in mind, explain what the things they find show about each of the girls.
2. Explain what you think the poet meant in line 10 when he described "a world" as "small," and "alone" as "large."
3. Although each line contains four stressed syllables, the number of unstressed syllables in each line varies, and some lines are longer or shorter than others. Can you see how this variation in meter and line length reflects the sea's movement? Explain.
4. What characteristics does this poem have in common with nursery rhymes? In your answer, comment on the names of the girls as well as on rhythm and rhyme.

Robert Frost

A biographical sketch of Robert Frost appears on page 63.

The Tuft of Flowers

I went to turn the grass once after one
Who mowed it in the dew before the sun.

The dew was gone that made his blade so keen
Before I came to view the leveled scene.

I looked for him behind an isle of trees;   5
I listened for his whetstone° on the breeze.

But he had gone his way, the grass all mown,
And I must be, as he had been,—alone,

'As all must be,' I said within my heart,
'Whether they work together or apart.'   10

But as I said it, swift there passed me by
On noiseless wing a bewildered butterfly,

Seeking with memories grown dim o'er night
Some resting flower of yesterday's delight.

And once I marked° his flight go round and round,   15
As where some flower lay withering on the ground.

And then he flew as far as eye could see,
And then on tremulous wing came back to me.

I thought of questions that have no reply,
And would have turned to toss the grass to dry;   20

6. **whetstone:** a stone to sharpen metal instruments or tools. **15. marked:** noticed.

But he turned first, and led my eye to look
At a tall tuft of flowers beside a brook,

A leaping tongue of bloom the scythe had spared
Beside a reedy brook the scythe had bared.

I left my place to know them by their name,   25
Finding them butterfly weed when I came.

The mower in the dew had loved them thus,
By leaving them to flourish, not for us,

Nor yet to draw one thought of ours to him,
But from sheer morning gladness at the brim.   30

The butterfly and I had lit upon,
Nevertheless, a message from the dawn,

That made me hear the wakening birds around,
And hear his long scythe whispering to the ground,

And feel a spirit kindred to my own;   35
So that henceforth I worked no more alone;

But glad with him, I worked as with his aid,
And weary, sought at noon with him the shade;

And dreaming, as it were, held brotherly speech
With one whose thought I had not hoped to reach.   40

'Men work together,' I told him from the heart,
'Whether they work together or apart.'

Meaning and Method

1. In order for hay to be made, the tall grass must first be mowed down and then turned over to dry in the sun. Is the speaker's mood when he comes to turn the grass one of enthusiasm? desolation? something else? In your answer, comment on the connotations of *leveled* (line 4), and on lines 8–10.
2. Why is the butterfly "bewildered" (line 12)? Why does he fly around a "withering" flower (line 16)?

3. Why did the mower leave the tuft of flowers? What change occurs in the speaker's mood when he sees them? Why does he no longer feel alone?
4. Explain the meaning of the last two lines. Does the poet show throughout the poem that there may be subtle bonds not only between men but all of nature—in this case, men, butterflies, and weeds? Support your answer.
5. Considering the setting of the poem, explain why the type of language used by the speaker is or is not appropriate.
6. One of the themes of this poem is that communication may take place without speech. How do the metaphors in lines 23 and 34 reflect this theme? What are some other themes?

Dust of Snow

The way a crow
Shook down on me
The dust of snow
From a hemlock tree

Has given my heart   5
A change of mood
And saved some part
Of a day I had rued.°

8. **rued** (rōōd): regretted.

Meaning and Method

1. What was the mood of the speaker before the incident he describes? How does it change?
2. Why is it ironic that a crow caused the day to be saved (line 7)? In your answer, comment on the connotations of *crow*. What word or phrase indicates that the bird's act might have been deliberate? humorous?
3. What contrast of colors is implied in the poem? Do you think that the speaker would have reacted in the same way if the bird had been a blue jay? if a large amount of snow had fallen?

Acquainted with the Night

I have been one acquainted with the night.
I have walked out in rain—and back in rain.
I have outwalked the furthest city light.

I have looked down the saddest city lane.
I have passed by the watchman on his beat   5
And dropped my eyes, unwilling to explain.

I have stood still and stopped the sound of feet
When far away an interrupted cry
Came over houses from another street,

But not to call me back or say good-bye;   10
And further still at an unearthly height,
One luminary clock against the sky

Proclaimed the time was neither wrong nor right.
I have been one acquainted with the night.

Meaning and Method

1. What do you think of when you hear the word *night?* when you hear the word *rain?* Do you think that someone who frequently takes long walks on rainy nights is a nature lover? a lonely person? something else? Explain.
2. Why do you think the speaker looked down when he passed by the watchman? What does this action show about his character? What might he have been "unwilling to explain"?
3. Why is the time "neither wrong nor right"? Is the passage of time meaningful in the life of the speaker? Is the night in question one specific night, or does the poem refer to many nights?
4. What is your impression of the speaker in this poem? Is he young or old, rich or poor, popular or friendless, satisfied or dissatisfied? What is his mood? How does the weather and time of day affect or reflect it?
5. What details in the poem indicate the isolation of the speaker from the life around him? In your answer, comment on the connotations of *acquainted* (lines 1 and 14).
6. Explain why the city at night is an appropriate setting for this poem.
7. How does the punctuation at the end of lines 1, 2, and 3 indicate whether the poem is meant to be read rapidly or slowly? How does

"Acquainted with the Night" from *Complete Poems of Robert Frost,* copyright 1928 by Holt, Rinehart and Winston, Inc., copyright © 1956 by Robert Frost. Reprinted by permission of the publisher.

repetition contribute to the poem's pace and its overall effect? Is the pace suitable for the subject? Why or why not?

8. Read the poem aloud. Why is your tone of voice different when you read lines 1 and 14, both of which contain the same words? Is your tone as you read the last line bitter, ironic, or sad?

Tree at My Window

Tree at my window, window tree,
My sash° is lowered when night comes on;
But let there never be curtain drawn
Between you and me.

Vague dream-head lifted out of the ground,   5
And thing next most diffuse° to cloud,
Not all your light tongues talking aloud
Could be profound.

But tree, I have seen you taken and tossed,
And if you have seen me when I slept,   10
You have seen me when I was taken and swept
And all but lost.

That day she put our heads together,
Fate had her imagination about her,
Your head so much concerned with outer,   15
Mine with inner, weather.

2. **sash**: window frame. 6. **diffuse**: spread out, scattered.

"Tree at My Window" from *Complete Poems of Robert Frost*, copyright 1928 by Holt, Rinehart and Winston, Inc., copyright © 1956 by Robert Frost. Reprinted by permission of the publisher.

Meaning and Method

1. From what point of view is the speaker looking at the tree? Why might it seem to have a head—especially one which is "vague," a "thing next most diffuse to cloud" (line 6)? Do you think that the phrase *vague dream-head* (line 5) has anything to do with the time at which the speaker is looking at the tree? Why or why not?
2. What are the tree's "light tongues" (line 7)? What major difference between a tree and a human being is implied in lines 7–8?

3. What experiences does the speaker feel he and the tree share?
4. What is "outer" weather? What is "inner" weather? How are they alike? different?
5. Is the speaker's attitude toward the tree one of affection? admiration? something else? Explain. What is the predominating figure of speech in the poem, and how does its use help indicate the speaker's attitude?

Once by the Pacific

The shattered water made a misty din.
Great waves looked over others coming in,
And thought of doing something to the shore
That water never did to land before.
The clouds were low and hairy in the skies,   5
Like locks° blown forward in the gleam of eyes.
You could not tell, and yet it looked as if
The shore was lucky in being backed by cliff,
The cliff in being backed by continent;
It looked as if a night of dark intent   10
Was coming, and not only a night, an age.
Someone had better be prepared for rage.
There would be more than ocean-water broken
Before God's last *Put out the Light* was spoken.

6. locks: clusters or curls of hair.

Meaning and Method

1. Describe in your own words the scene the speaker witnessed. Where do you think he was watching from? How can waves make "a misty din"? What words or images make the clouds seem threatening?
2. What words or phrases in lines 1–9 indicate the violence of the waves? suggest that they had malicious intentions?
3. The sea's attempt to destroy or violently dominate the land seems to symbolize to the speaker man's vicious attempts to destroy or dominate others. Therefore, the speaker prophesies "a night of dark intent" (line 10)—a time when evil forces of violence will dominate the worlds of both nature and man. How long will this "night" last? What effects will it have on the world?

4. What words or phrases personify nature in this poem? Considering the speaker's attitudes toward man and nature, explain why personification is an appropriate device to use.

Language: Colloquial Expressions

Colloquial expressions are words or phrases used in informal, everyday speech. Frost, for example, is using a colloquial expression when he writes that the shore was *lucky*, rather than the more literary or formal expression, *fortunate*.

What are the colloquial terms for the following "formal" expressions:

1. coiffure
2. automobile

3. motion pictures
4. stationery

Dramatic
· Poetry

A S THE NAME SUGGESTS, *dramatic poetry* uses many of the techniques of drama. A dramatic poem always has a speaker who talks to someone else. The other person or persons may or may not answer, but his or their presence is always mentioned in the poem.

Dramatic poetry deals with a moment of conflict or stress which causes characters to reveal their "true" selves as they react to it. This process is particularly evident in the *dramatic monologue*, in which only one person talks (*mono* is the Greek word for "one"). In a dramatic monologue, the speaker often reveals his character by seeming to think aloud about his problems. He usually answers questions or objections that he has thought up, or that he imagines his listener to be asking silently.

Rudyard Kipling

In this poem, Kipling (see page 43) presents a dialogue between two soldiers in the British Army. Both soldiers speak in the cockney dialect of East London.

Danny Deever

"What are the bugles blowin' for?" said Files-on-Parade.°
"To turn you out, to turn you out," the Color-Sergeant° said.
"What makes you look so white, so white?" said Files-on-Parade.
"I'm dreadin' what I've got to watch," the Color-Sergeant said.
   For they're hangin' Danny Deever, you can 'ear the Dead March
     play,   5
   The regiment's in 'ollow square°—they're hangin' him today;
   They've taken of his buttons off an' cut his stripes away,
   An' they're hangin' Danny Deever in the mornin'.

"What makes the rear-rank breathe so 'ard?" said Files-on-Parade.
"It's bitter cold, it's bitter cold," the Color-Sergeant said.   10
"What makes that front-rank man fall down?" said Files-on-Parade.
"A touch of sun, a touch of sun," the Color-Sergeant said.
   They are hangin' Danny Deever, they are marchin' of 'im round.
   They 'ave 'alted Danny Deever by 'is coffin on the ground:
   An' 'e'll swing in 'arf a minute for a sneakin', shootin' hound—   15
   O they're hangin' Danny Deever in the mornin'!

"'Is cot was right-' and cot to mine," said Files-on-Parade.
"'E's sleepin' out an' far tonight," the Color-Sergeant said.
"I've drunk 'is beer a score o' times," said Files-on-Parade.
"'E's drinkin' bitter beer alone," the Color-Sergeant said.   20
   They are hangin' Danny Deever, you must mark 'im to 'is place,
   For 'e shot a comrade sleepin'—you must look 'im in the face;
   Nine 'undred of 'is county an' the regiment's disgrace,
   While they're hangin' Danny Deever in the mornin'.

1. **Files-on-Parade:** the soldier who directs marching formation. (A file is a line of soldiers.) 2. **Color-Sergeant:** the flag-bearer. 6. **'ollow square:** At a hanging, the ranks of soldiers form three sides of a square; the fourth side is the gallows.

"Danny Deever" from *Departmental Ditties and Ballads and Barrack Room Ballads* by Rudyard Kipling. Reprinted by permission of Mrs. George Bambridge, Doubleday & Company, Inc., and The Macmillan Company of Canada Limited.

"What's that so black agin the sun?" said Files-on-Parade.   25
"It's Danny fightin' 'ard for life," the Color-Sergeant said.
"What's that that whimpers over'ead?" said Files-on-Parade.
"It's Danny's soul that's passin' now," the Color-Sergeant said.
    For they're done with Danny Deever, you can 'ear the quickstep
        play,
    The regiment's in column, an' they're marchin' us away;   30
    Ho! the young recruits are shakin', an' they'll want their beer today,
    After hangin' Danny Deever in the mornin'.

Meaning

1. Is the Color-Sergeant distressed by the hanging? If so, is he distressed because he feels that Danny did not deserve to be hanged? because he has to witness the hanging? something else?
2. How do the soldiers react to the hanging before and after? Do the explanations for the soldiers' reactions given by the Color-Sergeant to Files-on-Parade in lines 9–12 make sense? Why or why not? If not, why did he use these explanations?
3. Why is Files-on-Parade sympathetic to Danny Deever?
4. What information in the poem indicates that the murder was pre-meditated? Can you tell from the poem whether Kipling approves or disapproves of (a) the death penalty as a punishment for this crime, (b) the public spectacle the hanging becomes? Does he seem to have any sympathy for Danny?

Method

1. Kipling never tells the reader *why* Danny committed the murder. Why do you think he has withheld this information? Does its absence detract from the poem? Why or why not?
2. The dialogue is presented in single sentences with an alternation of *said Files-on-Parade* and *the Color-Sergeant said* after each comment. This creates a somewhat mechanical effect. How does this reflect the movement of the speakers? Why is a dialogue a more effective way of relating the incident than an impersonal narrative would have been?
3. If you read the poem aloud, you will hear a strong marching rhythm as well as an echo of the type of music played during marches. Why do you think Kipling used the rhythm and musical echoes of a march?

Composition

Write a composition in which you defend or attack the type of justice meted out by the army to Danny Deever. Or write a composition in which you explain whether you think capital punishment—the death penalty for a crime—is ever justified. Give reasons for your opinions.

Alfred, Lord Tennyson

Tennyson (see page 119) said that he wrote this poem after the death of his friend, Arthur Hallam, to describe his "feeling about the need of going forward. . . ." He drew his subject from two ancient Greek epics, the *Iliad* and the *Odyssey*.

The *Iliad* begins near the end of a ten-year war in Troy, in Asia Minor, between the Greeks and the Trojans, and describes the gods and the heroic figures on both sides who took part in this war. The *Odyssey* is devoted to the fantastic adventures and misadventures of the Greek hero Odysseus—called Ulysses by the Romans—in his ten-year attempt to reach home after the Trojan War had ended. It ends with his return to Ithaca, the island off the Greek mainland over which he ruled, and his reunion with his faithful wife, Penelope.

Tennyson began his poem where the *Odyssey* left off, imagining Ulysses three years after his return to Ithaca.

Ulysses

It little profits that an idle king,
By this still hearth, among these barren crags,
Matched with an aged wife, I mete and dole°
Unequal laws unto a savage race,
That hoard, and sleep, and feed, and know not me.   5
I cannot rest from travel: I will drink
Life to the lees.° All times I have enjoyed
Greatly, have suffered greatly, both with those
That loved me, and alone; on shore, and when
Through scudding° drifts the rainy Hyades°   10
Vexed the dim sea. I am become a name;
For always roaming with a hungry heart
Much have I seen and known—cities of men
And manners, climates, councils, governments,
Myself not least, but honored of them all—   15

---

3. mete and dole: measure and give out. **7. lees:** dregs, usually of wine, which settle to the bottom of a cup. **10. scudding:** rushing or moving swiftly; **Hyades** (hī′ə·dēz): "rainy ones" in Greek; stars in the constellation Taurus, whose appearance signaled the rainy season.

And drunk delight of battle with my peers,
Far on the ringing plains of windy Troy.
I am a part of all that I have met;
Yet all experience is an arch wherethrough
Gleams that untraveled world whose margin fades   20
Forever and forever when I move.
How dull it is to pause, to make an end,
To rust unburnished,° not to shine in use!
As though to breathe were life. Life piled on life
Were all too little, and of one to me   25
Little remains: but every hour is saved
From that eternal silence, something more,
A bringer of new things; and vile it were
For some three suns to store and hoard myself,
And this gray spirit yearning in desire   30
To follow knowledge, like a sinking star,
Beyond the utmost bound of human thought.
     This is my son, mine own Telemachus,°
To whom I leave the scepter and the isle—
Well-loved of me, discerning to fulfill   35
This labor, by slow prudence to make mild
A rugged people, and through soft degrees
Subdue them to the useful and the good.
Most blameless is he, centered in the sphere
Of common duties, decent not to fail   40
In offices of tenderness, and pay
Meet° adoration to my household gods,°
When I am gone. He works his work, I mine.
     There lies the port; the vessel puffs her sail:
There gloom the dark broad seas. My mariners,   45
Souls that have toiled, and wrought, and thought with me—
That ever with a frolic welcome took
The thunder and the sunshine, and opposed°
Free hearts, free foreheads—you and I are old;
Old age hath yet his honor and his toil.   50
Death closes all; but something ere the end,

---

23. unburnished: unpolished; to burnish is to polish by means of friction. **33. Telemachus** (tə·lem′ə·kəs): Ulysses' son, who by this time is old enough to rule. **42. meet:** proper; **household gods:** special gods, generally the souls of ancestors, who were supposed to watch over each house. **48. opposed:** *here,* fought with.

Some work of noble note, may yet be done,
Not unbecoming men that strove with gods.
The lights begin to twinkle from the rocks:
The long day wanes; the slow moon climbs; the deep   55
Moans round with many voices. Come, my friends,
'Tis not too late to seek a newer world.
Push off, and sitting well in order smite
The sounding furrows; for my purpose holds
To sail beyond the sunset, and the baths   60
Of all the western stars, until I die.
It may be that the gulfs will wash us down:
It may be we shall touch the Happy Isles,°
And see the great Achilles,° whom we knew.
Though much is taken, much abides; and though   65
We are not now that strength which in old days
Moved earth and heaven, that which we are, we are,—
One equal temper of heroic hearts,
Made weak by time and fate, but strong in will
To strive, to seek, to find, and not to yield.   70

63. **Happy Isles:** in Greek mythology, the home of heroes after death (also called the Elysian Fields). 64. **Achilles** (ə·kil′ēz): a Greek hero of the Trojan War who was killed before the war ended.

Meaning and Method

1. To whom is Ulysses speaking? What does he want his listeners to do?
2. Why is he dissatisfied with his present life? How do memories of his past life contribute to his dissatisfaction?
3. What is "that untraveled world" (line 20)? Why does its margin or edge fade when he moves? Why does "experience" (line 19) not satisfy Ulysses?
4. What kind of existence is *not* life according to Ulysses in lines 22–24? Why does he want more than one life (see lines 24–25)? What great goal in life does he describe in lines 30–32?
5. In lines 33–43, what differences does Ulysses note between himself and his son Telemachus? How is he different from the people over whom he rules, described in lines 4–5 and 37–38? Does he feel he is superior to Telemachus? to his people? Why or why not?
6. How does Ulysses want to spend his old age (see lines 50–61)? Is he determined to carry out his plans or merely wishing?
7. Tennyson said that he had written "Ulysses" with a sense that despite

all losses, "life must be fought out to the end." What other theme of the poem is indicated in lines 19–21 and 70?

8. Reread the definition of dramatic monologue on page 197. Is "Ulysses" a dramatic monologue? Why or why not?

Composition and Discussion

Do you think that Ulysses is noble, or is he selfish and deliberately avoiding responsibilities? In a composition or a class discussion, give reasons for your point of view.

Thomas Hardy
[1840–1928]

Few writers were as strongly influenced by the area in which they lived as Thomas Hardy. Hardy's home county of Dorset in southern England is characterized by heaths—desolate tracts of open land covered with low shrubs. This heath country (called "Wessex" in his novels and poems) is much more than a setting for most of his works. In Hardy's works, an oppressive atmosphere of bleakness and of impending tragedy emanates from the heaths and affects people and their actions. The human products of heath country whom he characterizes are primarily men and women of thwarted hopes and wasted lives. Unable to communicate honestly with one another, they head toward destruction. The few who are innocent or good are indifferently crushed by others or by nature itself.

Hardy won fame with such novels as *Far from the Madding Crowd, The Return of the Native, The Mayor of Casterbridge,* and *Tess of the d'Urbervilles.* However, after more than a quarter of a century as a successful novelist, he abruptly ended this career because of the furor which arose after *Jude the Obscure* was published in 1896. This novel points out harshly and bitterly the differences between the Christian ideals of nineteenth-century English society and the self-righteous and destructive actions of that same society. Clergymen regarded the book as blasphemous; Victorian ladies were shocked. Hardy, who refused to modify the truth as he saw it, decided to return to his first literary love, poetry, a branch of literature which attracted less public attention.

For three decades, until his death, Hardy wrote poems which ranged from short lyrics to a large verse epic, *The Dynasts.* In most of his poems, the same dark, ironic view which characterized his novels continued to prevail.

At the Draper's *

"I stood at the back of the shop, my dear,
But you did not perceive me.

* **Draper's:** clothier's.

Well, when they deliver what you were shown
   I shall know nothing of it, believe me!"

And he coughed and coughed as she paled and said,   5
   "O, I didn't see you come in there—
Why couldn't you speak?"—"Well, I didn't. I left
   That you should not notice I'd been there.

"You were viewing some lovely things. *'Soon required*
   For a widow, of latest fashion';   10
And I knew 'twould upset you to meet the man
   Who had to be cold and ashen

"And screwed in a box before they could dress you
   'In the last new note in mourning,'
As they defined it. So, not to distress you,   15
   I left you to your adorning."

Meaning and Method

1. What is the relationship of the two speakers to each other? How can you tell? How do you know that the man is very sick—and probably dying?
2. What was the woman doing at the draper's? What does her presence there reveal about her character? about her attitude toward the man?
3. Is the woman upset about the man's discovery? What is his attitude toward it? toward the woman? Why did he not confront her at the draper's?
4. Who originally said the italicized statements in lines 9–10 and line 14? In what tone do you think they were originally said? In what tone are they repeated? Explain.
5. The man and the woman in this poem are, respectively, gentlemanly and ladylike. What elements in the poem indicate this? Considering the situation, explain why their politeness toward each other is ironic.
6. How do lines 9–16 contribute to the ironic tone of the poem? For example, was the man really concerned that he would "distress" the woman if he let her see him? Why is the use of the word *adorning* (line 16) particularly ironic in the circumstances?

Humorous
and Satirical
Poetry

HUMOROUS POETRY is designed to make the reader laugh or smile. In order to do this, the poet uses many of the comedian's techniques, particularly those of exaggeration and surprise. And like a comedian, who often says the most outrageous things with a straight face, the poet often sounds serious but is not. As a result, many humorous poems have an ironic effect.

Writers of humorous or light verse play with the elements of poetry —words, rhyme, and rhythm—continually delighting the reader with the unexpected. Even the subjects they choose are unlikely material for poetry. For example, one poet writes about sand in a house, and another about a roach. These and other poets achieve humor by exaggerating the importance of the subject.

Another type of humor, satirical humor, uses the opposite technique. Serious themes are presented in a superficially light manner, so that the reader often does not realize the writer's true purpose until the very end, where the realization has the greatest impact. *Satires*, which may be in verse or prose, are aimed at making individuals and society better by ridiculing vice or folly. Although many satires are simply bitter, and heap ridicule directly on the idea or person to be scorned, humorous satires are indirect, and tease the reader as they teach.

Phyllis McGinley

In situations where other people see only irritation, Phyllis Mc-Ginley points out humor. Her special province is Suburbia—the home of housewives, commuting husbands, assorted children, and domestic problems. Instead of bemoaning the fate of the suburban woman or complaining about boredom, Miss McGinley, with controlled irony and an easy mastery of poetic technique, makes the reader laugh. As a result, she has become one of the most popular poets in the United States, and is the particular favorite of tens of thousands of housewives who ordinarily feel forgotten and misunderstood.

Miss McGinley, who was born in Oregon in 1905, is herself a suburban wife and the mother of two grown daughters. However, the Pulitzer Prize winner does not like to be thought of as a housewife who is also a poet. In support of her contention, she could point to the fact that her first book of poems was published in 1934, three years before she married Charles Hayden and settled in Larchmont, New York. She could also point out that many of her poems and essays are concerned with the general foibles of twentieth-century man. Nevertheless, her experiences as a wife and mother have given her most of her material for her poetry. In her most characteristic poems, her heroine is a housewife attempting to battle the enemies of order and sanity with a sense of humor.

Season at the Shore

Oh, not by sun and not by cloud
And not by whippoorwill, crying loud,
And not by the pricking of my thumbs,
Do I know the way that the summer comes.
Yet here on this seagull-haunted strand,   5
Hers is an omen I understand—
Sand:

Sand on the beaches,
  Sand at the door,

Sand that screeches   10
    On the new-swept floor;
In the shower, sand for the foot to crunch on;
Sand in the sandwiches spread for luncheon;
Sand adhesive to son and sibling,°
From wallet sifting, from pockets dribbling;   15
Sand by the beaker°
    Nightly shed
From odious sneaker;
    Sand in bed;
Sahara always in my seaside shanty   20
Like the sand in the voice
Of J. Durante.°

Winter is mittens, winter is gaiters°
Steaming on various radiators.
Autumn is leaves that bog the broom.   25
Spring is mud in the living room
Or skates in places one scarcely planned.
But what is summer, her seal and hand?
Sand:

Sand in the closets,   30
    Sand on the stair,
Desert deposits
    In the parlor chair;
Sand in the halls like the halls of ocean;
Sand in the soap and the sun-tan lotion;   35
Stirred in the porridge, tossed in the greens,
Poured from the bottoms of rolled-up jeans;
    In the elmy street
        On the lawny acre;
    Glued to the seat   40
        Of the Studebaker;°
Wrapped in the folds of the *Wall Street Journal*;
Damp sand, dry sand,
Sand eternal.

14. sibling: a sister or brother. **16. beaker:** a large, wide-mouthed goblet. **22. J. Durante:** Jimmy Durante; a singer-comedian famous for his large nose and gravelly voice. **23. gaiters:** *here,* leggings. **41. Studebaker:** an automobile which is no longer made in the United States.

When I shake my garments at the Lord's command,   45
What will I scatter in the Promised Land?
Sand.

Meaning and Method

1. How does the speaker's way of defining the seasons in lines 23–29 show that she is a housewife and a mother?
2. One humorous technique used in this poem is that of leading up to a point and then giving a totally unexpected answer or example. Where has Phyllis McGinley used this technique? Explain your answers with examples from the poem.
3. Why does the poet use the /s/ alliteration throughout the poem? Find several examples of this technique.
4. Many rhymes seem connected to each other by meaning as well as sound. For example, *moon* and *June* both have romantic connotations. Phyllis McGinley, however, deliberately uses rhymes which seem incongruous or out of place. For example, she rhymes the word *sibling*— a word more often seen in textbooks than heard in informal speech— with *dribbling*. In what other rhymes has she mixed levels of vocabulary, or used surprising combinations?

Composition

1. Write a humorous composition about homework in which you exaggerate the amount and type your teachers give you. However, write the composition as if you were complaining seriously.
2. Characterize one of the seasons humorously in prose (or in poetry), much as Phyllis McGinley has done in lines 23–27. Use details which give your impression of the season.

John Bennett

A parody is a humorous imitation of a serious literary work. The following parody of "The Raven" was written by John Bennett (1865–1956), an American editor, poet, and nonfiction writer from Chillicothe, Ohio. ("The Raven" appears on page 87.)

What Troubled Poe's Raven

Could Poe walk again to-morrow, heavy with dyspeptic° sorrow,
While the darkness seemed to borrow darkness from the night before,
From the hollow gloom abysmal,° floating downward, grimly dismal,
Like a pagan curse baptismal from the bust above the door,
He would hear the Raven croaking from the dusk above the door.   5
        "Never, never, nevermore!"

And, too angry to be civil, "Raven," Poe would cry, "or devil,
Tell me why you will persist in haunting Death's Plutonian shore?"
Then would croak the Raven gladly, "I will tell you why so sadly,
I so mournfully and madly, haunt you, taunt you, o'er and o'er,   10
Why eternally I haunt you, daunt you, taunt you, o'er and o'er—
        Only this, and nothing more.

"Forty-eight long years I've pondered, forty-eight long years I've
    wondered,
How a poet ever blundered into a mistake so sore.
How could lamp-light from your table ever in the world be able,   15
From *below*, to throw my sable shadow 'streaming on the floor,'
When I perched up here on Pallas, high above your chamber-door?
        Tell me that—if nothing more!"

Then, like some wan, weeping willow, Poe would bend above his
    pillow,
Seeking surcease in the billow where mad recollections drown,   20
And in tearful tones replying, he would groan "There's no denying
Either I was blindly lying, or the world was upside down—
Say, by Joe!—it was just midnight—so the world *was* upside down—
        Aye, the world was upside down!"

1. **dyspeptic** (dis·pep′tik): gloomy, irritable. Dyspepsia is a digestive ailment.
3. **abysmal** (ə·biz′məl): bottomless.

Meaning and Method

1. Which of Poe's techniques does Bennett parody?
2. Which words or phrases does Bennett use to capture the melancholy mood of Poe's poem?
3. What phrases in Bennett's poem are contradictory or senseless? Do you think he used these deliberately?
4. What is Bennett's main objection to Poe's poem?
5. Do you think that this parody is fair? Why or why not?

Composition

Write one stanza in which you parody one of the poems you have read.

Christopher Morley
[1890–1957]

For Christopher Morley, the words of the English language were like a variety of tools, fascinating for their own sake and for the many things that could be made with them. Morley used these tools to write more than fifty volumes of essays, short stories, novels, plays, and poems. In one of his books, *The Trojan Horse*, he even combined verse, prose, and drama.

Morley, who was born in Haverford, Pennsylvania, was graduated from Haverford College and went on to become a Rhodes Scholar at Oxford University. From the time his first book was published, when he was twenty-two, he won critical praise for his wit and skill with words. However, although his style remained witty, as he grew older he became increasingly concerned with the serious problems of living in the modern world.

Particularly in the last three decades of his life, the bright surface of his work covered a deep pessimism in his outlook on the future. In *The Trojan Horse*, which was written two years before the outbreak of the Second World War, he pictured the world he knew as facing destruction, "perhaps on account of its luxury, lethargy, frivolity, and complacence." His autobiography, *John Mistletoe*, was written in 1930, when he was forty, because he felt that "life had grown so uncertain that anyone who desires an autobiography had better compile it promptly."

Nursery Rhyme for the Tender-Hearted

Scuttle, scuttle, little roach—
How you run when I approach:
Up above the pantry shelf,
Hastening to secrete yourself.

Most adventurous of vermin,   5
How I wish I could determine
How you spend your hours of ease,
Perhaps reclining on the cheese.

Cook has gone, and all is dark—
Then the kitchen is your park: 10
In the garbage heap that she leaves
Do you browse among the tea leaves?

How delightful to suspect
All the places you have trekked:
Does your long antenna whisk its   15
Gentle tip across the biscuits?

Do you linger, little soul,
Drowsing in our sugar bowl?
Or, abandonment most utter,
Shake a shimmy° on the butter?   20

Do you chant your simple tunes
Swimming in the baby's prunes?
Then, when dawn comes, do you slink
Homeward to the kitchen sink?

Timid roach, why be so shy?   25
We are brothers, thou and I.
In the midnight, like yourself,
I explore the pantry shelf!

20. **shimmy**: a dance in which you shake your hips.

Meaning and Method

1. What do you think of when you hear the word *roach?* What is unusual about the speaker's approach to the insect?
2. Considering most people's reaction to roaches, explain why you think
   that the speaker did *not* mean the following: "How *delightful* to
   suspect/All the places you have trekked." Why is the word *trekked*
   appropriate to describe the roach's activities? What connotations does
   this word have that the word *walked*, for example, does not have?
3. Why does the speaker use *thou* when addressing the roach in line 26?
   Is its use natural? out of place? Explain. Do you think that the
   speaker is serious when he suggests that he and the roach are
   "brothers" (line 26)? Why or why not?
4. Do you think that the speaker is one of the tender-hearted to whom
   he dedicated this poem? Why or why not? After reading the poem,
   explain why you think the title is or is not ironic.

5. The poet uses apostrophe when he addresses the "little roach" in line 1. Where else does he use it? Does his use of apostrophe ever seem ironic? Why or why not?
6. The meter of this poem is the same as that of the nursery rhyme, "Twinkle, Twinkle, Little Star." By comparing first lines, explain how Morley's parody of the nursery rhyme increases the ironic effect of the poem.

Composition

The war between the Greeks and the Trojans, described in Homer's *Iliad*, was won because of the Greeks' use of the Trojan horse. Look up the story of the Trojan horse in a dictionary or book of mythology, and then write a stanza or two which you start with the line: "Welcome, welcome, Trojan horse." Or write a poem starting with: "Welcome, welcome, hurricane," or "Welcome, welcome, midterm test."

David Daiches *

A well-known university professor of English literature in both Great Britain and the United States, David Daiches is that rare creature in the academic world—a creative scholar and critic. In his many books, he offers insights into the whole range of English literature, and most of American literature as well. From the time his first book, *New Literary Values* (1936), was published, he has shown a constant interest in contemporary writers. In addition, he has written critical studies of such varied writers of the past as the seventeenth-century English poet John Milton and the Scottish writers Robert Burns and Robert Louis Stevenson.

Daiches was born in 1912 in Sunderland, England, but grew up in Edinburgh, Scotland, where his father was a rabbi and leader of the Scottish Jewish community. He showed himself to be an exceptional student from an early age, and won first-class honors when he was graduated from Edinburgh University. At the age of twenty-four, he received a doctorate from Balliol College, Oxford.

Daiches' scholarly successes, then and later, did not turn him into a pompous academic. He always had a lively interest in both the world around him and the world of words. His interest in the latter is shown not only in his prose but also in his light verse.

* **Daiches** (dā′tchəz).

Thoughts on Progress

In days of old when knights caught cold,
They were not quickly cured;
No aspirin pill would check the ill,
Which had to be endured.
You sat it out if toothache hurt you;   5
Patience was esteemed a virtue.

The dentist's way in Hogarth's° day
Was pretty rough and ready;
His foot he'd rest on patient's breast

7. **Hogarth:** a seventeenth-century English illustrator who caricatured the social and political life of his time.

To keep his pincers° steady,   10
And if the dentist's patient screamed,
The dentist was the more esteemed.

De Quincey's° age could well assuage°
Some kinds of pain and grief;
To bard° in bed with aching head   15
Laudanum° gave relief,
And sometimes in the process brought
A quickening of poetic thought.

When chloroform became the norm
For those who faced the surgeon,   20
A man or wife would meet the knife
Without excessive urgin',
And dentists learned to stop the pain
With useful things like novocain.

The anesthetic's with us yet,   25
And so's the analgesic,°
And dramamine° relieves the keen
Afflictions of the seasick.
And we've new blessings for the ill in
Sulfa drugs and penicillin.   30

When modern wight° retires at night
With streptomycin handy,
He finds repose at once; he knows
That everything is dandy.
No fear of sudden plague will keep   35
The trustful modern from his sleep.

Yet pharmacists have got long lists
Of pills that hasten slumber,

---

10. **pincers** (pin′sərz): an instrument used for gripping things; for example, pliers.
13. **De Quincey:** nineteenth-century English writer, author of *Confessions of an English Opium Eater;* **assuage** (ə·swāj′): to lessen or diminish. 15. **bard:** poet, particularly one who writes about historic and legendary events. 16. **Laudanum:** an opium drug. 26. **analgesic** (an′əl·jē′zik): a pain-killing drug. 27. **dramamine** (dram′ə·mēn). 31. **wight:** an archaic word for person.

And they report that of that sort
They sell a shocking number,   40
For somehow still we cannot find,
It seems, a settled peace of mind.

Try, try again, you medicine men!
The riddle's tough and bitter;
We've got the drugs that kill the bugs   45
But still we tense and jitter.
Ancestral terrors haunt us still—
Anxiety, where is thy pill?

Meaning and Method

1. The speaker describes "progress" in terms of changes in medical and dental practice, noting particularly the invention of drugs which reduce pain. What specific changes does he mention? According to the speaker, what have new inventions not been able to do? In your answer, explain the meaning of *ancestral terrors* (line 47).
2. *Satire* is a method of criticism in which vice or folly is made to seem ridiculous. Is this poem a satire on medicine? on the idea of progress? something else? In your answer, comment on the connotations of such expressions as *trustful modern* (line 36), and *medicine men* (line 43).
3. One way in which Daiches creates a humorous tone is through his use of unexpected rhymes, as in "hurt you/virtue" (lines 5 and 6). What other rhymes do you consider humorous? Note that several of the humorous rhymes appear as *rhymed couplets* at the end of each stanza —that is, as two successive lines of verse with the same rhyming sound. Besides his use of rhyme, how does Daiches achieve a humorous tone?
4. Why do you think Daiches has written this satirical poem? Does he merely want to expose certain fallacies in attitude, to hurt someone or attack some idea, or to correct a malpractice or folly?
5. Why is the allusion to De Quincey (line 13) particularly appropriate?

Language: How Scientific and Medical Terms Are Formed

If you had invented a new product, one of the first things you would do would be to try to think of a name for it. You might make up the name out of random sounds or from a random combination of words. However, if you were seriously thinking of a name for your product, you would be more likely to describe it by combining existing words, or Latin and Greek roots of words.

The latter method is the one most often used in forming new scientific and medical words. For example, when its discoverer wanted to describe the fungus (a low form of plant life) which eventually produced penicillin, he called it Penicillium from the Latin *penicillus*, or paintbrush, because the tufts of the fungus resembled a paintbrush. When its discoverer wanted to describe the moldlike organism from which we get the drug streptomycin, he took the Greek roots *streptos*, which means "twisted," and *mykus*, which means "fungus," to describe the way the organism looked and to denote its place in the plant kingdom.

Many other scientific and medical terms were formed from Latin and Greek roots. Among these are the following:

1. radium	**5.** Terramycin
2. telescope	**6.** asthma
3. seismograph	**7.** poliomyelitis
4. antihistamine	**8.** tuberculosis

Look up the origins of these words in a dictionary and be prepared to explain why the roots of these words give some indication of the meanings of the words.

Composition and Discussion

1. Since Daiches wrote this poem, tranquilizers, which are drugs to relieve feelings of anxiety, have become popular. Write one stanza containing three rhymed couplets beginning with the line: "Anxiety, you have your pill."

2. In his final stanza, Daiches stresses the presence of anxiety in modern life. Another poet, W. H. Auden, has written a long dramatic poem on this subject, entitled *The Age of Anxiety*. Do you think ours is an "age of anxiety"? Is the phrase a more appropriate description of our era than of past eras? In a panel discussion, explain your viewpoint.

Ralph Waldo Emerson
[1803–1882]

"My life is for itself and not for a spectacle," Emerson once said. Perhaps the most striking example of his acting on this principle occurred in 1832 when he resigned his position as the minister of a Unitarian church in Boston because he disagreed with some Unitarian concepts. With this act, Emerson, who had gone through great financial struggles in order to attend Harvard College and Harvard Divinity School, discarded not only certain prestige but also financial security. Moreover, he broke a long-standing family tradition—his father and six other ancestors had been ministers.

Emerson did not discard the preacher in him when he left the ministry. He thought of himself as a "preacher to the world" and felt that his task was to help people understand their own capabilities. In 1833, he settled in Concord, Massachusetts, and spent the rest of his life "preaching" in his essays and in the lectures which took him all over the United States.

In his works, particularly in the essay "Self-Reliance," he reiterated his basic belief that men must have the courage to be themselves and to trust their inner forces. Those who trust in themselves, according to Emerson, can change their minds publicly. "Foolish consistency," he said, "is the hobgoblin of little minds. . . . Speak what you think now in hard words and tomorrow speak what tomorrow thinks in hard words again, though it contradict everything you said today." It is, indirectly, a comment on his own resignation from the ministry.

Emerson the preacher and the thinker is clearly present in his poetry as well as his prose works. Such things as a snowstorm, a flower, or the birth of his son were occasions for meditative poems on nature, art, and man. More than most poets, he was interested in teaching people by means of poetry. Yet because he had the ability to create sharp, precise images and clear, forceful pictures, many of his poems are admired even by those readers who think a poem should not contain a message.

Fable

The mountain and the squirrel
Had a quarrel,
And the former called the latter "Little Prig";°
Bun° replied,
"You are doubtless very big;   5
But all sorts of things and weather
Must be taken in together,
To make up a year
And a sphere.

And I think it no disgrace   10
To occupy my place.
If I'm not so large as you,
You are not so small as I,
And not half so spry.
I'll not deny you make   15
A very pretty squirrel track;
Talents differ; all is well and wisely put;
If I cannot carry forests on my back,
Neither can you crack a nut."

3. **prig**: a contemptuous term for someone who is overly rigid in insisting on certain formalities or details, especially in social behavior. 4. **Bun**: the squirrel.

Meaning and Method

1. Why does the mountain look down on the squirrel? What is the squirrel's attitude toward his smallness? toward the mountain? toward the variety of the world? What specific words and images indicate these attitudes?
2. A fable is a brief tale in which animals or inanimate things are the characters. Usually, fables have a *moral*—that is, the story is told to teach a lesson. What is the moral of this fable?
3. Can this fable be considered a satire? If so, what type of people are the objects of the satire?

Composition

Emerson is noted more for his essays than for his poems. One of the reasons for this is that many of the individual sentences in his essays are memorable, and, when quoted out of context, have become "familiar quotations." Among such sentences are "Hitch your wagon to a star." "Keep cool: it will all be one a hundred years from now." "The civilized man has built a coach, but he has lost the use of his feet."

Write a two- or three-paragraph composition in which you (1) use one of Emerson's sentences as your topic sentence, and illustrate or develop it by means of real or imaginary examples; or (2) explain what Emerson means by one of these sentences and then explain why you agree or disagree with him.

The
Epic

Epics, which were originally long narrative poems about the exploits of a national hero or heroes, are found in many lands and in many languages. For example, the English have the epic *Beowulf* (written in Old English, or Anglo-Saxon), and the French have *The Song of Roland*. The oldest existing western epics are the Greek epics, the *Iliad* and the *Odyssey*.

Folk epics, like folk ballads, were composed in the days before printing. Although the ones which survived were eventually written down, they were first spread by wandering bards who sang or recited them. Some of these epics are so long that it is hard to believe that anyone could have sung them from memory. Most likely, they were not memorized word for word. The singer had to know the basic stories, but could add or delete details. He could also interpret the stories as he chose, emphasizing certain parts and de-emphasizing others to bring out the points he wished to make.

Epics were usually based on actual events, but these events and the people who took part in them became interwoven with the supernatural as the deeds were told and retold. In the Greek epics, for example, the gods helped or hindered the heroes, and constantly appeared on earth in various disguises. The gods were themselves like super-mortals: they played favorites, fell in and out of love, and quarreled with one another, often producing enormous catastrophes for human beings as a result.

The epic poets, like the people to whom they sung, saw human qualities in gods, magic in ordinary things, and godlike qualities in human beings. The world of the epics is a world which existed before science had been conceived, before things had been diagnosed and classified. It is a world not unlike the world of a child, where the dark hides unknown terrors, the woods may conceal monsters, and everything is both more beautiful and terrible than adults can imagine.

Homer

No facts are known about Homer, the Greek poet who is traditionally credited with having written both the *Iliad* and the *Odyssey*. It is believed that he lived in Asia Minor in the eighth or ninth century B.C. According to legend, he was a blind poet who wandered from place to place reciting his epics. In his own day, and for generations afterward, he was considered by the Greeks to be divinely inspired.

Many scholars think that the stories in the Homeric epics had been sung about separately for centuries before Homer was born, but that Homer wove these legends together, rejecting some parts, unifying the whole, and presenting the characters and events from his own point of view.

The real war on which Homer's epic, the *Iliad*, is based took place at the end of the twelfth century B.C. and is believed to have been a trade war between the Greeks and their Asia Minor rivals, the Trojans. Homer, probably following previous legends, ignored the economic motive for the devastating ten-year-long war. Instead, he presented the war as the direct result of the abduction of Helen, the beautiful wife of the Greek king Menelaus, by the Trojan prince Paris. He also presented the war as being ultimately caused by a rivalry among the gods, rather than a human event. The *Iliad* is a moving illustration of the theme that even the greatest heroes are prey not only to their human weaknesses but also to powers over which they have no control. Betrayal and tragedy are the rewards for the heroes in the *Iliad*.

The *Odyssey*, a very different type of epic, is about the trials and adventures of Odysseus, one of the Greek kings who plays a prominent part in the *Iliad*. The *Odyssey* relates the wanderings of Odysseus after the Trojan War had ended with a Greek triumph. According to Homer, Odysseus was prevented by the angry gods from returning home for ten years because the Greeks, on their last day in Troy, had pillaged and burned the temples of the gods.

The *Odyssey* is a fantastic story. Odysseus and his men meet giants, enchantresses, sea monsters, and ghosts who materialize after drinking blood. However, many of the details in the story are realistic and show much about the life of the Homeric and pre-Homeric Greeks. For example, we see the primitive rural life of one of the giants, a man-eater who milks goats and makes cheese. Throughout the *Odys-*

sey, we get a feeling of the terror of seamen who were at the mercy of wind and waves in boats powered by oars and sails, and who were forced to land on unknown islands in order to get food for their survival. In this realistic fantasy, unlike the *Iliad*, the strong human being triumphs, though with the aid of the gods. Odysseus returns home in time to save his faithful wife, Penelope, from the suitors she had warded off for twenty years and regains his kingdom.

Since Homer wrote in Greek, much of the impact—or lack of impact—of his work on the English-speaking reader is due to the translator. The translator of the following selection is Robert Fitzgerald, a poet as well as a classical scholar, who has turned Homer's Greek into vivid and vibrant English poetry.

The Odyssey

The Odyssey, *which is composed of twenty-four parts, begins near the end of Odysseus' voyage. However, because Odysseus tells of his past adventures, we find out about all the strange sights he has seen and the perils he has endured during his long voyage. The selection presented here, which includes parts of books nine and twelve, opens when Odysseus begins relating his experiences to a friendly king.*

The following is a list of characters encountered in this excerpt:

CHARACTERS (in alphabetical order)

Aeolus (*ē′ə·ləs*): *king of the winds.*

Calypso (*kə·lip′sō*): *a nymph on whose island Odysseus and his men were shipwrecked. She kept him from leaving her for seven years but finally allowed him to go.*

Charybdis (*kə·rib′dis*): *a monster who lived in a whirlpool. See* **Scylla.**

Cicones (*si·kōn′ēz*): *a people in whose country Odysseus and his men landed.*

Circe of Aiaia (*sûr′sē; ē′ē·ə*): *an enchantress who changed Odysseus' sailors into swine.*

Cyclopes (*sī·klō′pēz*): *a mythical race of giants who had only one eye each in the middle of their foreheads. They were supposedly descended from Poseidon, god of the sea.*

Cyclops (*sī'klops*): *one of the Cyclopes. See* **Polyphemos.**
Laestrygones (*les·trig'on·ēz*): *a tribe of man-eaters.*
Lotus Eaters: *a people who lived an indolent, drugged life.*
Odysseus (*ō·dis'yōōs*): *Greek king of Ithaca, and hero of the Odyssey.*
Polyphemos (*pol'i·fē'məs*): *the one Cyclops whom Odysseus and his men encountered; he is usually referred to simply as Cyclops.*
Scylla (*sil'ə*): *a six-headed sea monster. Odysseus and his men had to pass between Scylla and Charybdis, two great horrors.*
Sirens: *three sea nymphs who were part women, part bird. They lured sailors to their deaths on rocky coasts by their singing.*

> "I am Laertes'° son, Odysseus.
>   Men hold me
> formidable for guile in peace and war:
> this fame has gone abroad to the sky's rim.
> My home is on the peaked sea-mark° of Ithaca
> under Mount Neion's° wind-blown robe of leaves,   5
> in sight of other islands—Doulikhion,°
> Same,° wooded Zakynthos°—Ithaca
> being most lofty in that coastal sea,
> and northwest, while the rest lie east and south.
> A rocky isle, but good for a boy's training;   10
> I shall not see on earth a place more dear,
> though I have been detained long by Calypso,
> loveliest among goddesses, who held me
> in her smooth caves, to be her heart's delight,
> as Circe of Aiaia, the enchantress,   15
> desired me, and detained me in her hall.
> But in my heart I never gave consent.
> Where shall a man find sweetness to surpass
> his own home and his parents? In far lands
> he shall not, though he find a house of gold.   20

[*Odysseus then describes landing in the country of the Cicones, where he and his men took plunder and enslaved the women. They stayed too long, however, and had to battle the army of the Cicones, losing a number of men in the process. Back at sea, they faced a storm that lasted for nine days.*]

1. Laertes (lā·ûr'tēz). **4. sea-mark:** an elevated object which sailors use to guide them. **5. Mount Neion's** (nē·ī'ənz). **6. Doulikhion** (dōō·lik'ē·on). **7. Same** (sā'mē); **Zakynthos** (zā·kin'thos).

The Lotus Eaters

Nine days I drifted on the teeming sea
before dangerous high winds. Upon the tenth
we came to the coastline of the Lotus Eaters,
who live upon that flower.° We landed there
to take on water. All ships' companies   25
mustered alongside for the mid-day meal.
Then I sent out two picked men and a runner
to learn what race of men that land sustained.
They fell in, soon enough, with Lotus Eaters,
who showed no will to do us harm, only   30
offering the sweet Lotus to our friends—
but those who ate this honeyed plant, the Lotus,
never cared to report, nor to return:
they longed to stay forever, browsing on
that native bloom, forgetful of their homeland.   35
I drove them, all three wailing, to the ships,
tied them down under their rowing benches,
and called the rest: 'All hands aboard;
come, clear the beach and no one taste
the Lotus, or you lose your hope of home.'   40
Filing to their places by the rowlocks
my oarsmen dipped their long oars in the surf,
and we moved out again on our seafaring.

The Cyclopes

In the next land we found were Cyclopes,
giants, louts, without a law to bless them.   45
In ignorance leaving the fruitage of the earth in mystery
to the immortal gods, they neither plow
nor sow by hand, nor till the ground, though grain—
wild wheat and barley—grows untended, and
wine-grapes, in clusters, ripen in heaven's rain.   50
Cyclopes have no muster and no meeting,°
no consultation or old tribal ways,
but each one dwells in his own mountain cave
dealing out rough justice to wife and child,
indifferent to what the others do.   55

24. that flower: the lotus, which induced forgetfulness and a mood of tranquillity.
51. no muster and no meeting: no institutions to make laws or community decisions.

[*Before crossing to the land of the Cyclopes, Ulysses and his men had spent the night on a nearby desert island. He describes the island, and tells how he prepared to enter the Cyclopes's territory, which lay across the bay.*]

When the young Dawn with finger tips of rose
came in the east, I called my men together
and made a speech to them:
                                          'Old shipmates, friends,
the rest of you stand by; I'll make the crossing
in my own ship, with my own company,   60
and find out what the mainland natives are—
for they may be wild savages, and lawless,
or hospitable and god-fearing men.'

At this I went aboard, and gave the word
to cast off by the stern. My oarsmen followed,   65
filing in to their benches by the rowlocks,
and all in line dipped oars in the grey sea.

As we rowed on, and nearer to the mainland,
at one end of the bay, we saw a cavern
yawning above the water, screened with laurel,   70
and many rams and goats about the place
inside a sheepfold—made from slabs of stone
earthfast° between tall trunks of pine and rugged
towering oak trees.
                              A prodigious° man
slept in this cave alone, and took his flocks   75
to graze afield—remote from all companions,
knowing none but savage ways, a brute
so huge, he seemed no man at all of those
who eat good wheaten bread; but he seemed rather
a shaggy mountain reared in solitude.   80
We beached there, and I told the crew
to stand by and keep watch over the ship;
as for myself I took my twelve best fighters
and went ahead. I had a goatskin full

73. **earthfast:** stuck in the earth. 74. **prodigious** (prə·dij′əs): enormous; *here,* like a monster.

of that sweet liquor that Euanthes'° son   85
Maron,° had given to me. He kept Apollo's°
holy grove at Ismaros;° for kindness
we showed him there, and showed his wife and child,
he gave me seven shining golden talents°
perfectly formed, a solid silver winebowl,   90
and then this liquor—twelve two-handled jars
of brandy, pure and fiery. Not a slave
in Maron's household knew this drink; only
he, his wife and the storeroom mistress knew;
and they would put one cupful—ruby-colored,   95
honey-smooth—in twenty more of water,
but still the sweet scent hovered like a fume
over the winebowl. No man turned away
when cups of this came round.
                            A wineskin full
I brought along, and victuals in a bag,   100
for in my bones I knew some towering brute
would be upon us soon—all outward power,
a wild man, ignorant of civility.

We climbed, then, briskly to the cave. But Cyclops
had gone afield, to pasture his fat sheep,   105
so we looked round at everything inside:
a drying rack that sagged with cheeses, pens
crowded with lambs and kids, each in its class:
firstlings apart from middlings, and the 'dewdrops,'
or newborn lambkins, penned apart from both.   110
And vessels full of whey° were brimming there—
bowls of earthenware and pails for milking.
My men came pressing round me, pleading:
                                    'Why not
take these cheeses, get them stowed, come back,
throw open all the pens, and make a run for it?   115
We'll drive the kids and lambs aboard. We say
put out again on good salt water!'

---

85. Euanthes (yōō·an'thēz). **86. Maron** (mā'rən); **Apollo** (ə·pol'ō): the Greek
god of music, poetry, medicine, prophecy, and of the sun. **87. Ismaros** (is'mā·ros).
89. talents: coins used in ancient Greece; gold talents were of great value.
111. whey (hwā): the watery part of milk. In cheese-making, whey is separated
from the *curd,* or thick part.

Ah,

how sound that was! Yet I refused. I wished
to see the caveman, what he had to offer—
no pretty sight, it turned out for my friends.   120

We lit a fire, burnt an offering,°
and took some cheese to eat; then sat in silence
around the embers, waiting. When he came
he had a load of dry boughs on his shoulder
to stoke his fire at suppertime. He dumped it   125
with a great crash into that hollow cave,
and we all scattered fast to the far wall.
Then over the broad cavern floor he ushered
the ewes he meant to milk. He left his rams
and he-goats in the yard outside, and swung   130
high overhead a slab of solid rock
to close the cave. Two dozen four-wheeled wagons,
with heaving wagon teams, could not have stirred
the tonnage of that rock from where he wedged it
over the doorsill. Next he took his seat   135
and milked his bleating ewes. A practiced job
he made of it, giving each ewe her suckling;°
thickened his milk, then, into curds and whey,
sieved out the curds to drip in withy° baskets,
and poured the whey to stand in bowls   140
cooling until he drank it for his supper.
When all these chores were done, he poked the fire,
heaping on brushwood. In the glare he saw us.

'Strangers,' he said, 'who are you? and where from?
What brings you here by sea ways—a fair traffic?°   145
Or are you wandering rogues, who cast your lives
like dice, and ravage other folk by sea?'

We felt a pressure on our hearts, in dread
of that deep rumble and that mighty man.
But all the same I spoke up in reply: 150

---

121. offering: a sacrifice to the gods or a god. 137. suckling: *here*, a baby lamb.
139. withy: flexible twigs (usually willow) woven together. 145. a fair traffic:
lawful trade.

'We are from Troy, Akhaians,° blown off course
by shifting gales on the Great South Sea;
homeward bound, but taking routes and ways
uncommon; so the will of Zeus° would have it.
We served under Agamemnon,° son of Atreus°—   155
the whole world knows what city°
he laid waste, what armies he destroyed.
It was our luck to come here; here we stand
beholden for your help, or any gifts
you give—as custom is to honor strangers.°   160
We would entreat you, great Sir, have a care
for the gods' courtesy; Zeus will avenge
the unoffending guest.'
                          He answered this
from his brute chest, unmoved:
                                'You are a ninny,
or else you come from the other end of nowhere,   165
telling me, mind the gods! We Cyclopes
care not a whistle for your thundering Zeus°
or all the gods in bliss; we have more force by far.
I would not let you go for fear of Zeus—
you or your friends—unless I had a whim to.   170
Tell me, where was it, now, you left your ship—
around the point, or down the shore, I wonder?'

He thought he'd find out, but I saw through this,
and answered with a ready lie:
                                'My ship?
Poseidon Lord, who sets the earth a-tremble,°   175
broke it up on the rocks at your land's end.
A wind from seaward served him, drove us there.
We are survivors, these good men and I.'
Neither reply nor pity came from him,

---

151. **Akhaians** (ə·kē′ənz): Greeks; also spelled Achaeans.. 154. **Zeus** (zo͞os): king
of the gods and ruler of heaven and earth. 155. **Agamemnon** (ag′ə·mem′non):
the king who led the Greek forces in the Trojan War; **Atreus** (a′trē·əs). 156.
what city: Troy. 160. **custom is to honor strangers**: The Greeks believed that it
was their duty to help peaceful strangers. They believed that the gods sent wan-
derers and beggars to test them. 167. **thundering Zeus**: The symbol of Zeus's
power was a thunderbolt. 175. **Poseidon** (pō·sī′dən) . . . **a-tremble**: Besides
being god of the sea, Poseidon was god of earthquakes; he was commonly called
the "earth-shaker."

but in one stride he clutched at my companions   180
and caught two in his hands like squirming puppies
to beat their brains out, spattering the floor.
Then he dismembered them and made his meal,
gaping and crunching like a mountain lion—
everything: innards, flesh, and marrow bones.   185
We cried aloud, lifting our hands to Zeus,
powerless, looking on at this, appalled;
but Cyclops went on filling up his belly
with manflesh and great gulps of whey,
then lay down like a mast° among his sheep.   190
My heart beat high now at the chance of action,
and drawing the sharp sword from my hip I went
along his flank to stab him where the midriff
holds the liver. I had touched° the spot
when sudden fear stayed me: if I killed him   195
we perished there as well, for we could never
move his ponderous doorway slab aside.
So we were left to groan and wait for morning.

When the young Dawn with finger tips of rose
lit up the world, the Cyclops built a fire   200
and milked his handsome ewes, all in due order,
putting the sucklings to the mothers. Then,
his chores being all dispatched, he caught
another brace° of men to make his breakfast,
and whisked away his great door slab   205
to let his sheep go through—but he, behind,
reset the stone as one would cap a quiver.°
There was a din of whistling as the Cyclops
rounded his flock to higher ground, then stillness.
And now I pondered how to hurt him worst,   210
if but Athena° granted what I prayed for.
Here are the means I thought would serve my turn:

a club, or staff, lay there along the fold—
an olive tree, felled green and left to season

190. **like a mast:** as straight and tall as a ship's mast. **194. had touched:** almost
touched. **204. brace:** a pair; the term is usually used when describing a catch of
birds or game. **207. quiver:** a case in which arrows are carried. **211. Athena**
(ə·thē′nə): Greek goddess of wisdom.

for Cyclops' hand. And it was like a mast   215
a lugger of twenty oars, broad in the beam—
a deep-sea-going craft—might carry:
so long, so big around, it seemed. Now I
chopped out a six foot section of this pole
and set it down before my men, who scraped it;   220
and when they had it smooth, I hewed again
to make a stake with pointed end. I held this
in the fire's heart and turned it, toughening it,
then hid it, well back in the cavern, under
one of the dung piles in profusion there.   225
Now came the time to toss for it: who ventured
along with me? whose hand could bear to thrust
and grind that spike in Cyclops' eye, when mild
sleep had mastered him? As luck would have it,
the men I would have chosen won the toss—   230
four strong men, and I made five as captain.

At evening came the shepherd with his flock,
his woolly flock. The rams as well, this time,
entered the cave: by some sheep-herding whim—
or a god's bidding—none were left outside.   235
He hefted his great boulder into place
and sat him down to milk the bleating ewes
in proper order, put the lambs to suck,
and swiftly ran through all his evening chores.
Then he caught two more men and feasted on them.   240
My moment was at hand, and I went forward
holding an ivy bowl of my dark drink,
looking up, saying:
                    'Cyclops, try some wine.
Here's liquor to wash down your scraps of men.
Taste it, and see the kind of drink we carried   245
under our planks. I meant it for an offering
if you would help us home. But you are mad,
unbearable, a bloody monster! After this,
will any other traveller come to see you?'

He seized and drained the bowl, and it went down   250
so fiery and smooth he called for more:

'Give me another, thank you kindly. Tell me,
how are you called? I'll make a gift will please you.
Even Cyclopes know the wine-grapes grow
out of grassland and loam° in heaven's rain,   255
but here's a bit of nectar and ambrosia!'°

Three bowls I brought him, and he poured them down.
I saw the fuddle and flush come over him,
then I sang out in cordial tones:
                                        'Cyclops,
you ask my honorable name? Remember   260
the gift you promised me, and I shall tell you.
My name is Nohbdy:° mother, father, and friends,
everyone calls me Nohbdy.'
                                        And he said:
'Nohbdy's my meat, then, after I eat his friends.
Others come first. There's a noble gift, now.'   265
Even as he spoke, he reeled and tumbled backward,
his great head lolling to one side; and sleep
took him like any creature. Drunk, hiccuping,
he dribbled streams of liquor and bits of men.

Now, by the gods, I drove my big hand spike   270
deep in the embers, charring it again,
and cheered my men along with battle talk
to keep their courage up: no quitting now.
The pike of olive, green though it had been,
reddened and glowed as if about to catch.   275
I drew it from the coals and my four fellows
gave me a hand, lugging it near the Cyclops
as more than natural force nerved them; straight
forward they sprinted, lifted it, and rammed it
deep in his crater eye,° and I leaned on it   280
turning it as a shipwright turns a drill
in planking, having men below to swing

255. **loam:** a type of soil consisting of clay, sand, and silt. 256. **nectar and ambrosia:** Nectar was the liquid the gods drank; ambrosia was the food they ate. Cyclops is saying that the wine is like food of the gods. 262. **Nohbdy:** Nobody. 280. **crater eye:** Cyclops' one eye was large and deep.

the two-handled strap that spins it in the groove.
So with our brand° we bored that great eye socket
while blood ran out around the red hot bar.   285
Eyelid and lash were seared; the pierced ball
hissed broiling, and the roots popped.
                              In a smithy
one sees a white-hot axehead or an adze°
plunged and wrung in a cold tub, screeching steam—
the way they make soft iron hale and hard—:   290
just so that eyeball hissed around the spike.
The Cyclops bellowed and the rock roared round him,
and we fell back in fear. Clawing his face
he tugged the bloody spike out of his eye,
threw it away, and his wild hands went groping;   295
then he set up a howl for Cyclopes
who lived in caves on windy peaks nearby.
Some heard him; and they came by divers° ways
to clump around outside and call:
                              'What ails you,
Polyphemos? Why do you cry so sore   300
in the starry night? You will not let us sleep.
Sure no man's driving off your flock? No man
has tricked you, ruined you?'
                              Out of the cave
the mammoth Polyphemos roared in answer:
'Nohbdy, Nohbdy's tricked me, Nohbdy's ruined me!'   305
To this rough shout they made a sage reply:

'Ah well, if nobody has played you foul
there in your lonely bed, we are no use in pain
given by great Zeus. Let it be your father,
Poseidon Lord, to whom you pray.'
                              So saying   310
they trailed away. And I was filled with laughter
to see how like a charm the name deceived them.
Now Cyclops, wheezing as the pain came on him,
fumbled to wrench away the great doorstone
and squatted in the breach with arms thrown wide   315

---

284. brand: *here,* a burning piece of wood. **288. adze** (adz): a carpenter's tool.
298. divers: various.

for any silly beast or man who bolted—
hoping somehow I might be such a fool.
But I kept thinking how to win the game:
death sat there huge; how could we slip away?
I drew on all my wits, and ran through tactics,   320
reasoning as a man will for dear life,
until a trick came—and it pleased me well.
The Cyclops' rams were handsome, fat, with heavy
fleeces, a dark violet.

               Three abreast
I tied them silently together, twining   325
cords of willow from the ogre's bed;
then slung a man under each middle one
to ride there safely, shielded left and right.
So three sheep could convey each man. I took
the woolliest ram, the choicest of the flock,   330
and hung myself under his kinky belly,
pulled up tight, with fingers twisted deep
in sheepskin ringlets for an iron grip.
So, breathing hard, we waited until morning.

When Dawn spread out her finger tips of rose   335
the rams began to stir, moving for pasture,
and peals of bleating echoed round the pens
where dams with udders full called for a milking.
Blinded, and sick with pain from his head wound,
the master stroked each ram, then let it pass,   340
but my men riding on the pectoral fleece°
the giant's blind hands blundering never found.
Last of them all my ram, the leader, came,
weighted by wool and me with my meditations.
The Cyclops patted him, and then he said: 345

'Sweet cousin ram, why lag behind the rest
in the night cave? You never linger so,
but graze before them all, and go afar
to crop sweet grass, and take your stately way
leading along the streams, until at evening   350
you run to be the first one in the fold.

---

341. pectoral fleece: wool of the chest.

Why, now, so far behind? Can you be grieving
over your Master's eye? That carrion° rogue
and his accurst companions burnt it out
when he had conquered all my wits with wine.   355
Nohbdy will not get out alive, I swear.
Oh, had you brain and voice to tell
where he may be now, dodging all my fury!
Bashed by this hand and bashed on this rock wall
his brains would strew the floor, and I should have   360
rest from the outrage Nohbdy worked upon me.'
He sent us into the open, then. Close by,
I dropped and rolled clear of the ram's belly,
going this way and that to untie the men.
With many glances back, we rounded up   365
his fat, stiff-legged sheep to take aboard,
and drove them down to where the good ship lay.
We saw, as we came near, our fellows' faces
shining; then we saw them turn to grief
tallying those who had not fled from death.   370
I hushed them, jerking head and eyebrows up,
and in a low voice told them: 'Load this herd;
move fast, and put the ship's head toward the breakers.'
They all pitched in at loading, then embarked
and struck their oars into the sea.   375

[As Odysseus is leaving, he cannot resist taunting the Cyclops, who
finally throws an enormous rock at the ship, but does not hit it.

[Odysseus' next stop is the island of Aeolus, king of the winds.
Aeolus gives Odysseus a bag containing the storm winds so that he
will not be disturbed on his trip. However, as Odysseus' ship ap-
proaches Ithaca, his sailors, thinking the bag contains treasure, open
it. The ship is blown back to the island of Aeolus, where the king tells
Odysseus that he is obviously cursed by the gods and refuses to help
him again.

[Odysseus and his crew sail next to the land of the man-eating
Laestrygones, where they lose a number of men. The survivors escape,
set sail again, and land on the island of Circe. Circe is a sorceress who
turns some of Odysseus' men into swine, but Odysseus, with the gods'
help, eventually gets her to turn the men back to human form. He

353. carrion: dead flesh in the process of decaying; here, rotten, disgusting.

and his shipmates then spend a year on the island, and are treated
royally by Circe. When they leave, they visit the land of the dead,
and then return to Circe, who gives the following prophecy.]

Circe's Warning

'Listen with care
to this, now, and a god will arm your mind.
Square in your ship's path are Sirens, crying
beauty to bewitch men coasting by;
woe to the innocent who hears that sound!   380
He will not see his lady nor his children
in joy, crowding about him, home from sea;
the Sirens will sing his mind away
on their sweet meadow lolling. There are bones
of dead men rotting in a pile beside them   385
and flayed skins shrivel around the spot.
                              Steer wide;
keep well to seaward; plug your oarsmen's ears
with beeswax kneaded soft; none of the rest
should hear that song.
                        But if you wish to listen,
let the men tie you in the lugger, hand   390
and foot, back to the mast, lashed to the mast,
so you may hear those harpies'° thrilling voices;
shout as you will, begging to be untied,
your crew must only twist more line around you
and keep their stroke up, till the singers fade.   395

[*Circe next describes two possible courses Odysseus can take. One,*
by way of the Prowling Rocks, or Drifters, is exceptionally dangerous.
Circe tells Odysseus that only one ship has ever made it safely past the
rocks, and its captain was helped by Hera, wife of Zeus. This course
is therefore effectively ruled out. She then describes the other course.]

'A second course
lies between headlands. One is a sharp mountain
piercing the sky, with stormcloud round the peak

---

392. harpies: The harpies, like the Sirens, were part women, part bird, but unlike
the Sirens, they were ugly monsters. Their victims were chosen by the gods. Circe
here uses the term to indicate that the effect of the Sirens and the harpies was the
same.

dissolving never, not in the brightest summer,
to show heaven's azure there, nor in the fall.   400
No mortal man could scale it, nor so much
as land there, not with twenty hands and feet,
so sheer the cliffs are—as of polished stone.
Midway that height, a cavern full of mist
opens toward Erebos° and evening. Skirting   405
this in the lugger, great Odysseus,
your master bowman, shooting from the deck,
would come short of the cavemouth with his shaft;
but that is the den of Scylla,° where she yaps
abominably, a newborn whelp's cry,   410
though she is huge and monstrous. God or man,
no one could look on her in joy. Her legs—
and there are twelve—are like great tentacles,
unjointed, and upon her serpent necks
are borne six heads like nightmares of ferocity,   415
with triple serried° rows of fangs and deep
gullets of black death. Half her length, she sways
her heads in air, outside her horrid cleft,
hunting the sea around that promontory
for dolphins, dogfish, or what bigger game   420
thundering Amphitrite° feeds in thousands.
And no ship's company can claim
to have passed her without loss and grief; she takes,
from every ship, one man for every gullet.

The opposite point seems more a tongue of land   425
you'd touch with a good bowshot, at the narrows.
A great wild fig, a shaggy mass of leaves,
grows on it, and Charybdis lurks below
to swallow down the dark sea tide. Three times
from dawn to dusk she spews it up   430
and sucks it down again three times, a whirling
maelstrom;° if you come upon her then

---

405. Erebos (er′ə·bəs): the entrance to Hades (hā′dēz), the land of the dead in
Greek mythology. **409. Scylla:** a once-beautiful nymph whom Poseidon had loved.
Poseidon's jealous wife Amphitrite (am′fə·trīt′ē), goddess of the sea, had changed
her to a monster. **416. serried:** ranked. **421. thundering Amphitrite:** The goddess of the sea was especially tempestuous when near Scylla. **432. maelstrom**
(māl′strəm): a whirlpool which violently sucks in objects.

the god who makes earth tremble could not save you.
No, hug the cliff of Scylla,° take your ship
through on a racing stroke. Better to mourn   435
six men than lose them all, and the ship, too.'
So her advice ran; but I faced her, saying:

'Only instruct me, goddess, if you will,
how, if possible, can I pass Charybdis,
or fight off Scylla when she raids my crew?'   440
Swiftly that loveliest goddess answered me:

'Must you have battle in your heart forever?
The bloody toil of combat? Old contender,
will you not yield to the immortal gods?
That nightmare cannot die, being eternal   445
evil itself—horror, and pain, and chaos;
there is no fighting her, no power can fight her,
all that avails is flight.
                              Lose headway there
along that rockface while you break out arms,
and she'll swoop over you, I fear, once more,   450
taking one man again for every gullet.
No, no, put all your backs into it, row on;
invoke Blind Force, that bore this scourge° of men,
to keep her from a second strike against you.

Then you will coast Thrinakia,° the island   455
where Helios'° cattle graze, fine herds, and flocks
of goodly sheep. The herds and flocks are seven,
with fifty beasts in each.
                              No lambs are dropped,°
or calves, and these fat cattle never die.
Immortal, too, their cowherds are—their shepherds—   460
Phaëthousa° and Lampetia,° sweetly braided
nymphs that divine Neaira° bore
to the overlord of high noon, Helios.

428–434. Charybdis . . . Scylla: If a man has to choose between two evils, he is often said to be between Scylla and Charybdis. **453. scourge** (skûrj): one who inflicts severe punishment. **455. Thrinakia** (thri·nā′kē·ə). **456. Helios** (hē′lē·ōs): another name for Apollo in his role as god of the sun. **458. dropped:** born. **461. Phaëthousa** (fā·thōō′sə); **Lampetia** (lam·pē′shə). **462. Neaira** (nē·ē′rə).

These nymphs their gentle mother bred and placed
upon Thrinakia, the distant land,   465
in care of flocks and cattle for their father.

Now give those kine° a wide berth, keep your thoughts
intent upon your course for home,
and hard seafaring brings you all to Ithaca.
But if you raid the beeves,° I see destruction   470
for ship and crew.
                          Rough years then lie between
you and your homecoming, alone and old,
the one survivor, all companions lost.'

[*When Odysseus leaves Circe, he tells his sailors what she had said
about the Sirens, gives them wax to put in their ears, and because he
wants to hear the Sirens, orders them to tie him to the mast in accord-
ance with Circe's instructions. As Circe predicted, when he hears the
Sirens sing, Odysseus orders the men to untie him, but they cannot
hear him. Finally they pass the Sirens. Odysseus continues.*]

Scylla and Charybdis

                          My faithful company
rested on their oars now, peeling off   475
the wax that I had laid thick on their ears;
then set me free.
                          But scarcely had that island
faded in blue air than I saw smoke
and white water, with sound of waves in tumult—
a sound the men heard, and it terrified them.   480
Oars flew from their hands; the blades went knocking
wild alongside till the ship lost way,
with no oarblades to drive her through the water.

Well, I walked up and down from bow to stern,
trying to put heart into them, standing over   485
every oarsman, saying gently,
                          'Friends,
have we never been in danger before this?
More fearsome, is it now, than when the Cyclops
penned us in his cave? What power he had!

---

467. kine (kīn) : cows. **470. beeves:** a plural of *beef.*

Did I not keep my nerve, and use my wits　　　　　490
to find a way out for us?
　　　　　　　　　Now I say
by hook or crook this peril too shall be
something that we remember.
　　　　　　　　　　　Heads up, lads!
We must obey the orders as I give them.
Get the oarshafts in your hands, and lay back　　495
hard on your benches; hit these breaking seas.
Zeus help us pull away before we founder.

You at the tiller, listen, and take in
all that I say—the rudders are your duty;
keep her out of the combers° and the smoke;　　　500
steer for that headland; watch the drift, or we
fetch up in the smother, and you drown us.'

That was all, and it brought them round to action.
But as I sent them on toward Scylla, I
told them nothing, as they could do nothing.　　　505
They would have dropped their oars again, in panic,
to roll for cover under the decking. Circe's
bidding against arms had slipped my mind,
so I tied on my cuirass° and took up
two heavy spears, then made my way along　　　510
to the foredeck—thinking to see her first from there,
the monster of the grey rock, harboring
torment for my friends. I strained my eyes
upon that cliffside veiled in cloud, but nowhere
could I catch sight of her.
　　　　　　　　　And all this time,　　　515
in travail, sobbing, gaining on the current,
we rowed into the strait—Scylla to port
and on our starboard beam Charybdis, dire
gorge of the salt sea tide. By heaven! when she
vomited, all the sea was like a cauldron　　　520
seething over intense fire, when the mixture
suddenly heaves and rises.

---

500. **combers:** long, crested waves. 509. **cuirass** (kwi·ras′): a piece of armor which covers the chest.

The shot spume
soared to the landside heights, and fell like rain.
But when she swallowed the sea water down
we saw the funnel of the maelstrom, heard   525
the rock bellowing all around, and dark
sand raged on the bottom far below.
My men all blanched° against the gloom, our eyes
were fixed upon that yawning mouth in fear
of being devoured.
                    Then Scylla made her strike,   530
Whisking six of my best men from the ship.
I happened to glance aft at ship and oarsmen
and caught sight of their arms and legs dangling
high overhead. Voices came down to me
in anguish, calling my name for the last time.   535

A man surfcasting on a point of rock
for bass or mackerel, whipping his long rod
to drop the sinker and the bait far out,
will hook a fish and rip it from the surface
to dangle wriggling through the air: 540
                    so these
were borne aloft in spasms toward the cliff.

She ate them as they shrieked there, in her den,
in the dire grapple, reaching still for me—
and deathly pity ran me through
at that sight—far the worst I ever suffered,   545
questing the passes of the strange sea.
                    We rowed on.
The Rocks were now behind; Charybdis, too,
and Scylla dropped astern.
                    Then we were coasting
the noble island of the god, where grazed
those cattle with wide brows, and bounteous flocks   550
of Helios, lord of noon, who rides high heaven.°'"

[Odysseus' men, disobeying their leader and ignoring Circe's warn-

528. **blanched:** turned white. **551. who rides high heaven:** Apollo was supposed
to drive the chariot of the sun across the sky each day. When he started his ride,
it was dawn, and when he finished, it was sunset.

ing, eat the cattle of the sun. As a result, when they leave, their ship is wrecked. Odysseus alone survives by making a makeshift raft of the ship's mast and keel. On this, he drifts to an island on which the nymph Calypso lives. Calypso detains him for seven years, until Zeus orders her to give up her hopes of marrying Odysseus and release him. She then provides Odysseus with a well-stocked raft, which, however, is wrecked by Poseidon, god of the sea.

[*After his raft is wrecked, Odysseus floats to the land of a friendly king, who entertains him and helps him finally to return to Ithaca. There he finds that his faithful wife, Penelope, is besieged by suitors who insist that she choose one of them as a husband. With the help of his son, Telemachus, Odysseus eventually kills the suitors, is reunited with Penelope, and regains his former position as ruler.*]

Meaning

1. Odysseus says in line 2 that he is "formidable for guile." Explain the phrase and point out the incidents in the story that show his guile.
2. What statements or incidents show Odysseus' qualities of leadership? adventurous spirit? feeling for his men? love of his home? Which of these qualities is most dominant? least dominant?
3. What does the Lotus symbolize? Why does Odysseus pull his men away from the land of the Lotus Eaters?
4. Before Odysseus enters the country of the Cyclopes, he feels that he will meet some brute "all outward power,/ a wild man, ignorant of civility" (lines 102–103). Does the Cyclops fit all of this description, or only part of it? Give reasons for your answer.
5. Compare and contrast the attitudes of Odysseus and the Cyclops toward civilization. Support your answers with references to lines 44–55 and 158–168.
6. Circe indicates her own—and perhaps the ancient Greek—view of human limitations in her warnings to Odysseus in lines 442–448 and 467–471. Why is she angry with Odysseus in the first of these passages? What is her attitude toward evil? toward men's capacity to destroy it? Why does she tell Odysseus not to raid the cattle of the sun in the second passage?
7. Is Odysseus' desire to listen to the Sirens—and the precautions he takes—in keeping with his character as we know it from other incidents? Explain.
8. Does Odysseus lie to his men in lines 486–493, as they approach Scylla and Charybdis? What reason does Odysseus give in lines 504–507 for not repeating Circe's prediction of destruction? Why does Odysseus go on, despite what he has been told? How is he different from his men in this respect, and in general?

Method

1. What does the description of the Cyclops' cavern in lines 69–74 and lines 107–112 tell you about its inhabitant?
2. What words or phrases in lines 74–80 and 129–136 convey a sense of the monstrous size and strength of the Cyclops? What visual images in lines 179–190 make him appear a horrifying beast?
3. In lines 276–291, which words or phrases reinforce the impression of the difficulty of blinding the Cyclops?
4. What characteristics of Odysseus make him seem human? Why does the Cyclops appear to be partially human, and Scylla completely inhuman? In your answers, comment on the physical descriptions given as well as on the actions of these characters.
5. One of the characteristics of epics is the use of *epithets*, descriptive words or phrases which are used repeatedly in a work, and which sometimes come to be used in place of the name of a person. One frequently used epithet in the *Odyssey* is *the young Dawn with finger tips of rose*. Why is this epithet appropriate? What epithet describes Helios in line 551? Why is it appropriate?
6. Among the characteristics of epics are the following:
   (a) a main character who is a great hero;
   (b) a setting of vast dimensions;
   (c) action consisting of deeds which require great—sometimes superhuman—courage;
   (d) intervention of supernatural forces.

   Which of these characteristics appear in the selection from the *Odyssey* that you have just read? Give specific examples to support your answers.

Composition

1. Think of an incident in history—recent or otherwise—which strikes you as being of epic proportions. Write a paragraph summarizing or explaining the incident, and another paragraph telling why you have chosen it.
2. Scylla, the Sirens, and the Cyclopes may be said to be present symbolically in the modern world as well as in the world of the ancient Greeks. The monster Scylla, the symbol of eternal evil, may be reflected in the prejudice and hate which still exist in our world. The Sirens, partly beautiful women who are the symbols of sensual lures, may be reflected in our desire for material possessions. The Cyclopes, symbols of brute force, may be reflected in wars and in some uses of the police.

Choosing Scylla, the Sirens, or the Cyclopes as your focus, write a composition in which you illustrate the presence and effect of these symbolic characters in our world. Use specific examples to support your points.

A Glossary
of Literary Terms

Abstract and Concrete Terms: an abstract term refers to an idea or quality, such as *truth* or *sweetness.* Its opposite, a concrete term, refers to something real—something which can be touched or seen, such as *book* or *sky.*

Alliteration: the repetition of sounds, usually consonant sounds, but sometimes vowel sounds, at the beginnings of words in the same line or in successive lines. For example:

> "O wild West Wind, thou breath of Autumn's being"
> —Percy Bysshe Shelley, "Ode to the West Wind"

Allusion: a reference to a presumably familiar person, object, place, or event, or to a literary, historical, artistic, mythological, or biblical passage or work which the writer expects will be known to his readers. For example, in John Keats's "Ode to a Nightingale," the following lines appear:

> "Perhaps the selfsame song that found a path
> Through the sad heart of Ruth, when, sick for home,
> She stood in tears amid the alien corn"

These lines allude to the biblical Book of Ruth, which tells the story of a young widow who left her own country to follow her mother-in-law, Naomi, to Naomi's homeland. Readers who know the story of Ruth will understand that alien corn refers to the fields in Naomi's country—a foreign or alien land to Ruth—in which Ruth gathered corn, or grain, for food.

Anapest: see **Meter.**

Apostrophe: the direct address to a deceased or absent person as if he were present, or to an animal or thing, or an abstract idea or quality as if it could understand you. Apostrophe is sometimes used with personification.

An example of apostrophe without personification is:

> "Little Lamb, who made thee?"
> —William Blake, "The Lamb"

An example of apostrophe with personification is:

> "With how sad steps, O Moon, thou climb'st the skies,
> How silently, and with how wan a face!"
> —Philip Sidney, "With How Sad Steps, O Moon"

Assonance: the repetition of vowel sounds followed by different consonants. These words may appear in the same line or in successive lines. For example:

> "Not marble, nor the gilded monuments
> Of princes, shall outlive this powerful rhyme."
> —William Shakespeare, "Sonnet 55"

Atmosphere: a pervasive element or influence. For example, there can be an atmosphere of melancholy, of gaiety, and so forth.

Ballad: a relatively short poem which tells a story. There are two types of ballads, *folk ballads* and *literary ballads*. Folk ballads were meant to be sung; literary ballads were meant to be printed and read. (See the discussion of the ballad on pages 7–8.)

Ballad Stanza: the most common stanza—or grouping of lines—used in ballads. It is a *quatrain*, or four-line stanza, with the second and fourth lines rhyming (see **Rhyme**). Generally each quatrain has four stressed syllables in the first and third lines, and three stressed syllables in the second and fourth lines. For example:

> "There LIVED a WIFE at USHer's WELL,
> And a WEALthy WIFE was SHE:
> She HAD three STOUT and STALwart SONS,
> And SENT them O'ER the SEA."
> —Anonymous, "The Wife of Usher's Well"

Blank Verse: unrhymed poetry, in which each line usually has ten syllables. Five of the syllables are stressed—generally the second, fourth, sixth, eighth, and tenth syllables. For example:

> "But, SOFT! What LIGHT through YONder WINdow BREAKS?
> It IS the EAST, and JULiet IS the SUN!
> ARISE, fair SUN, and KILL the ENvious MOON
> Who IS alREADy SICK and PALE with GRIEF
> That THOU her MAID art FAR more FAIR than SHE."
> —William Shakespeare, *Romeo and Juliet*

This arrangement of stressed and unstressed syllables in a ten-syllable line is called *iambic pentameter* (see **Meter**).

Character: a person in a play, story, novel, or poem.

Characterization: the creation of a literary character by such methods as description of physical appearance, presentation of thoughts and actions, and dialogue.

Colloquial Speech: a manner of speaking that is characteristic of informal conversation.

Concrete Terms: see **Abstract and Concrete Terms.**

Conflict: the clash of opposing forces—for example, people, ideas, themes, ways of life, or contradictory impulses within an individual.

Connotation: an association or suggestion which a word calls to mind in addition to its literal meaning (see **Denotation**). For example, a tree is literally "a perennial woody plant having usually a single self-supporting trunk of considerable height, with branches and foliage growing at some distance above the ground," but the word may suggest shade, a specific tree, a texture and color, etc.

Context: for a word, the other words surrounding it and having an effect on its meaning or use. The same words may have a different meaning in different contexts. For example, compare the meaning of the word *love* in "I love candy," and in the following lines by Elizabeth Barrett Browning:

> "I love thee to the depth and breadth and height
> My soul can reach. . . ."

Couplet: two successive lines, usually rhymed, which form a single unit of verse. For example:

> "I was angry with my foe.
> I told it not, my wrath did grow."
> —William Blake, "A Poison Tree"

Dactyl: see **Meter**.

Denotation: the literal or dictionary meaning or meanings of a word (see also **Connotation**).

Dialect: the characteristic or distinctive speech of a particular group or the inhabitants of a certain geographical region. Dialect differs markedly in pronunciation and colloquial expressions from the standard speech of a country.

Dramatic Monologue: a type of poem in which a speaker addresses a listener or listeners who do not speak. The speaker reveals his character by commenting on a crucial problem or conflict in his life. (See page 197.)

Dramatic Poetry: poetry in which one or more characters speak to other characters who may or may not answer. (See page 197.) The dramatic monologue is one type of dramatic poetry.

Elegy: a poem mourning the death of an individual. It is often also a melancholy meditation on the trials and griefs of life in general. It is one type of lyric poem (see **Lyric**).

End Rhyme: see **Rhyme**.

Epic: a long story-poem which relates the deeds of a heroic character, usually a national hero. (See page 223 for a discussion of the epic.)

Fable: a brief story in prose or verse aimed at illustrating a truth or moral (see **Moral**). Many fables, such as those of the Greek slave Aesop, are *beast fables* in which the characters are animals with distinctly human characteristics.

Figurative Language: language that is not meant to be interpreted on a strict literal level because it would make no sense or little sense if it were.

Figure of Speech: a word or phrase which describes something in a way that is not literally true but may be meaningful in a deeper sense. The effect of a figure of speech on the reader is generally stronger than that produced by everyday language (see **Simile, Metaphor, Personification, Irony,** and **Symbol** for discussions of some types of figures of speech).

Foot: a unit used in measuring or *scanning* lines of poetry. Each foot usually contains at least one stressed syllable. In addition, it usually has one or two unstressed syllables (see **Meter**).

Free Verse: poetry that does not have a strict or fixed rhythmic pattern or equal line lengths, and which does not rhyme. For example:

> "When Lilacs last in the dooryard bloom'd,
> And the great star early droop'd in the western sky in the night,
> I mourn'd, and yet shall mourn with ever-returning spring."
> —Walt Whitman, "When Lilacs Last in the Dooryard Bloom'd"

Iamb: see **Meter**.

Iambic Pentameter: see **Meter**.

Image: a word or phrase which brings a picture to the reader's mind or appeals to his senses of sight, hearing, touch, taste, or smell. The collective term for images is *imagery*.

Internal Rhyme: see **Rhyme**.

Irony: a figure of speech in which the writer says something in such a way that the opposite meaning is implied. For example, in Shakespeare's play, *Julius Caesar*, Mark Antony repeatedly calls Brutus, one of the murderers of Caesar, an "honorable man." However, because Mark Antony gives examples to show that Brutus' justification for the murder—that Caesar was "ambitious" and wanted to become dictator—was false, it becomes clear that he is really saying that Brutus was *not* honorable.

Irony may be present in a situation as well as in words. For example, in the ballad "Johnnie Armstrong," the outlaw Johnnie Armstrong insists that his men dress in their best clothes because the king has asked to see them. Because the king's intention is to hang him and his men, Johnnie's concern with the luxurious details of his men's clothing is part of an ironic situation.

Light Verse: verse which is primarily humorous or entertaining.

Lyric: a poem whose sole purpose is the expression of an individual's emotion or attitude. It is usually short and musical (see **Elegy, Ode,** and **Sonnet** for some specific types of lyrics).

Metaphor: a figure of speech in which one thing is compared indirectly to another dissimilar thing, without the use of *like* or *as.* (See page 3.) For example:

> "I'll tell you how the sun rose—
> A ribbon at a time."
> —Emily Dickinson, "I'll Tell You How the Sun Rose"

Although metaphors usually contain nouns (for example, "ribbon" in the above lines), they may also be expressed solely in the verb. For example:

> "Clouds and eclipses *stain* both moon and sun"
> —William Shakespeare, "No More Be Grieved"

Metaphors may appear in one line of verse only, or they may be extended through many lines. For example, the first four lines of Shakespeare's "Sonnet 73" contain an *extended metaphor* in which late middle age is compared to late autumn:

> "That time of year thou may'st in me behold
> When yellow leaves, or none, or few, do hang
> Upon those boughs which shake against the cold,
> Bare ruined choirs where late the sweet birds sang"

Meter: an organized rhythmic pattern created by the repetition of the same foot, or group of stressed and unstressed syllables, throughout a poem. Among the common metrical feet are:

anapestic—two unstressed syllables followed by one stressed syllable, as in in·ter·VENE. A single anapestic foot is called an *anapest.*

dactylic—one stressed syllable followed by two unstressed syllables, as in HIS·to·ry. A single dactylic foot is called a *dactyl.*

iambic—one unstressed syllable followed by one stressed syllable, as in de·FEND. A single iambic foot is called an *iamb.* A frequently used combination of iambic feet is called *iambic pentameter,* in which each line consists of five iambic feet. For example:

> "True EASE/in WRIT/ing COMES/from ART,/not CHANCE"
> —Alexander Pope, "Essay on Criticism"

trochaic—one stressed syllable followed by one unstressed syllable, as in ES·say. A single trochaic foot is called a *trochee.*

Mood: the overall emotional atmosphere or feeling in a literary work.

Moral: an ethical or practical lesson, usually illustrated by a story.

Narrator: one who tells or narrates a story.

Narrative Poem: a poem which tells a story, whether briefly as in the ballad or at length as in the epic. (See pages 7–8.)

Ode: a lyric poem which is lofty and dignified in subject matter and style.

Onomatopoeia (on′ə·mat·ə·pē′ə): the use of words whose sounds imitate natural sounds. For example: *buzz, whirr, moo, hiss.*

Paradox: a self-contradictory statement which nevertheless reveals some truth. For example:

"Stone walls do not a prison make,
Nor iron bars a cage."
—Richard Lovelace, "To Althea, from Prison"

Parody: the conscious exaggerated imitation of a literary style or individual work with the intention of achieving humor through distortion.

Personification: a figure of speech in which the writer attributes human qualities to animals, inanimate objects, or ideas. For example:

"Pale Ocean in unquiet slumber lay,
And the wild Winds flew round, sobbing in their dismay."
—Percy Bysshe Shelley, "Adonais"

Personification is often used with apostrophe (see **Apostrophe**).

Poetic Inversion: words arranged in such a way that they reverse in some manner the normal word order of a sentence. Often inversion is used for the sake of a rhyme. For example:

"None from his darts can fly,
I am sick, I must die."
—Thomas Nashe, "Adieu, Farewell Earth's Bliss"

Point of View: the standpoint from which a literary work is written. The point of view may change the way the writer presents a subject. For example, if he is writing from the "I" or personal point of view, he may present only details that personally affected the "I." If he is writing from the "he" or third person point of view, he may present details of which the participants in an action may not be aware. The point of view of the speaker may or may not be that of the poet.

Quatrain: a four-line stanza (see **Stanza**).

Refrain: a group of words, a line, or a group of lines repeated throughout a poem, usually at the end of each stanza.

Rhyme: the repetition of two or more words reasonably close to each other in which the last vowel sound and the last consonant sound are the same. Example: June—moon; sea—me; sleep—weep. If the rhyme occurs at the end of the line, it is called an *end rhyme*. For example:

> "He hangs in shades the orange bright,
> Like golden lamps in a green night."
> —Andrew Marvell, "Bermudas"

If a rhyme occurs within a line, it is called an *internal rhyme*. For example:

> "The ant and the mole sit both in a hole."
> —Ben Jonson, "The Masque of Queens"

Rhyme Scheme: the pattern in which end rhyme occurs throughout a stanza or an entire poem. Rhyme schemes are usually denoted by italicized letters of the alphabet. For example, if the first and third lines of a four-line stanza rhyme, we say that the rhyme scheme is *abac* (*a* represents the rhyming words, while *b* and *c* represent the words that do not rhyme). If there are two rhymes in a four-line stanza, the rhyme scheme is *abab*, and if all four lines rhyme, it is *aaaa*.

Rhythm: in poetry, the recurrence or repetition of stressed and unstressed syllables in a regular pattern or manner. When rhythm in poetry is so strictly patterned that it can be measured in feet (see **Foot**), it is called meter (see **Meter**).

Satire: the use of ridicule, sarcasm, wit, or irony in order to expose, set right, or destroy a vice or folly.

Scansion: the method of determining the meter of a poem. When one *scans* a line, one counts the number and determines the type of poetic feet in that line.

Setting: the physical background of a work.

Simile: a figure of speech in which the comparison between two unlike things is expressed directly, usually by means of *like* or *as*. Two examples are William Wordsworth's line, "I wandered lonely *as* a cloud," and Robert Burns's line, "O, my luve's *like* a red, red rose."

Sonnet: a lyric poem of fourteen lines usually written in rhymed iambic pentameter (see **Meter**). Sonnets usually follow one of two types of rhyme schemes, but the rhymes may vary.

Speaker: the person whose voice we "hear" in the poem. (Note that the use of *I* does not necessarily mean that the speaker is the poet.)

Stanza: a group of lines which constitute a division in a poem. There is space before the first line, and after the last line of each group. In most poems, each stanza contains the same number of lines.

Symbol: in a poem, generally a figure of speech in which an object, person, place, event, or quality is chosen to stand for something other than itself—something which is not directly compared in the poem. For example, the road is a symbol of movement through life in "Sixty-Eighth Birthday" by James Russell Lowell:

> "As life runs on, the road grows strange
> With faces new, and near the end
> The milestones into headstones change,
> 'Neath every one a friend."

Notice that although life is mentioned, the road is not described directly as the road of life, or compared to life by means of *like* or *as*.

Theme: the central idea or one of the main ideas underlying a literary work.

Tone: the poet's attitude toward his subject or audience. Tone in poetry corresponds to tone in speaking.

Trochee: see **Meter.**

Type: a character who embodies the characteristics of a group or class rather than a strong individual personality.

Verse: a work consisting of metrical or rhythmical lines made up of a specified number of feet (see **Meter**). Verse may also be used as a synonym for poetry.

The Language Arts Program

Throughout the text, language arts have been integrated with the presentation of literature. The majority of language arts activities appear in the end-of-selection questions and assignments under the headings *Meaning, Method, Language, Composition,* and *Discussion.* Additional material relating to language arts is introduced and discussed in the general introductions. And some information, especially that concerning word origins and derivations, appears in the text footnotes.

The following indexes are intended to serve as guidelines to specific aspects of the language arts program in *A Book of Poetry—1.*

Vocabulary Development

Speaking and Listening

Composition

Narration:

Description:

Describe what you found on "exploration" (54, 1)

Describe what you can expect to find on another planet (54, 2)

Describe object considered beautiful or ugly, using specific details which appeal to the senses of touch and sight (102)

Describe variety in supermarket, using words which appeal to the senses of touch, taste, smell, and sight (107)

Describe place where you would like to return, using specific details which show why place is attractive (135)

Describe a sports event, including setting, audience, and mood (157, 1)

Describe a useful object, indicating the way it looks and feels (176)

Exposition:

Give reasons to explain why certain parts of a newspaper story would be emphasized in a ballad (19)

Explain benefits and disadvantages of automation, using specific examples (32)

Using reasons, explain why a specific literary ballad is like and unlike folk ballads (42)

Personal essay, explaining why you want to explore some place in space (54, 2)

Research essay, explaining problems of American Indians today (66, 1)

Compare and contrast the attitudes of two colonials in two poems (66, 2)

Compare and contrast attitudes of two speakers toward struggle for Negro rights (113)

Personal essay, explaining a situation in which you would or would not want a Teller, using concrete illustrations (146, 1)

Personal essay, explaining why you think it is desirable to have friends from your own background or from a variety of backgrounds (148)

Step-by-step explanation of the way a sport is played (157, 2)

Explain meaning of a Biblical passage and why it is an appropriate motto for the U.N. (163)

Explain meaning of a specific statement which shows poet's attitude toward life and tell why you agree or disagree; use specific examples (169)

Explain why you think capital punishment is or is not ever justified (199)

Give reasons to explain why you feel a character described in a poem is noble or selfish (203)

Explain meaning of statement by Emerson, and why you agree or disagree with it (222)

Explain why a specific historical incident you have chosen is of epic proportions (245, 1)

Illustrate the symbolic presence and effect of Scylla, the Sirens, and the Cyclopes in our world, using specific examples (245, 2)

Argumentation:

Defend a theme statement by James Russell Lowell (81)

Defend or attack specific case of capital punishment described in a poem (199)

Writing Poetry:

Write several humorous ballad stanzas, given first line (28)

Write two haiku (104)

Write free verse using images after listening to music (118)

Rewrite poem, changing words to follow the initial change of two key words (180)

Write one stanza parody (212)

Write humorous stanza or two in imitation of a poem, given first line (214)

Write three rhymed couplets, given first line (219)

Miscellaneous:

Paraphrase, in rewriting a newspaper story (19)

Modernize a folk ballad, changing spelling, expressions (25)

Illustrate a given moral with an original fable (59)

Write from the point of view of a nonhuman object (128)

Humor; writing a humorous composition on homework (210, 1), about a season (210, 2)

Illustrate or develop a given topic sentence (222)

Summarize event in history (245)

F
G
H
I   7
J   8